D1395489

THE CELTIC REVOLUTION

The
CELTIC REVOLUTION

IN SEARCH OF
TWO THOUSAND FORGOTTEN YEARS
THAT CHANGED OUR WORLD

Simon Young

GIBSON SQUARE

This first edition first published by

Gibson Square

Tel: (UK)	+44 (0)20 7096 1100
Fax:	+44 (0)20 7993 2214

Tel: (US)	+1 646 216 9813
Fax:	+1 646 216 9488

| Tel: (Eire) | +353 (0)1 657 1057 |

rights@gibsonsquare.com
www.gibsonsquare.com

ISBN 978-1906142-43-8

CONTENTS

'Ac nyt oed uawr yna y weilgi: y ueis yd aeth ef.'

Branwen

THE CHALLENGE OF WRITING
THE HISTORY OF A 'NON-EXISTENT' PEOPLE

In late 1998 the present author arrived in Galicia in North-Western Spain to study a British-Celtic colony that had been founded there in the early Middle Ages. Two weeks were spent in familiarising himself with a previously unknown region and language and then, at the end of this period of frantic initiation, a new acquaintance invited him to a dinner party: his first foray into Galician social life. The evening began well enough. At 7.00 o'clock on a Friday night he knocked on his host's door, was seated with several other guests and asked, in jolly tones, to explain the nature of his project. And, haltingly, in what was, after all, a still difficult tongue, he attempted to do so. However, he only managed 'a British-Celtic settlement that…' before voices around him cut in; for the magic word 'Celt' had been uttered, a syllable that creates apoplexy in some, wonder in others, something akin to sexual excitement in a minority, and, at least, on this occasion, ruined a promising evening.

'The Celts…', said one wannabe druid in the corner, 'they were special.' The host tutted. The Celts, she stated flatly, had never existed. Consternation. Her fiancé moderated. Certainly the Celts had never been to Spain, he said, but... (Oh yes they had, said two visitors from Asturias.) No, no, the host insisted, the Celts had never existed anywhere. A radical let out a glorious Galician 'harrumph' and announced that in denying the existence of a people that had been so important to Galicia's history the host had showed herself a fascist, a particularly strong word in Spain. And what about bagpipes shouted someone off to the right? And Celtic art shouted another? No, no, the Celts had never existed, said the host. And, at this point, one world-weary academic waded in to support her, while another world-weary academic started shaking his head.

Now the word 'Celt' has long had the potential to create such scenes. It has had that potential because, whereas with 'Roman', 'Greek' or 'Persian' different people mean the same thing, with 'Celt' different people have the unfortunate habit of meaning different things. Even in the confines of the universities, an archaeologist, a linguist, a classicist and an art historian will use 'Celt' and 'Celtic' with slightly or, sometimes, radically different senses, making studies that cross academic boundaries hazardous. And, when you step outside the bounds of academia, the differences become still wider and will depend on whether you are talking to a practitioner of neo-paganism; a fan of Celtic music; a speaker of Gaelic; a Cornish nationalist; or Joe Bloggs.

Of course, if this were all, the dinner party above would never have ended in tears. But, in the last thirty years, a new way of looking at the Celts has arisen, especially among archaeologists, some of whom claim that the Celts never existed. The effect is best visualised. Imagine some of the personalities above, the neo-pagan, the linguist and Joe Bloggs, having an animated but civil discussion about a word that has, at best, overlapping

10

meanings for each. Into the room comes a severe-looking man with a trowel on his belt (a token archaeologist) and pulls out the rug on which they are all standing, screaming 'the Celts no more!' A confused situation rapidly becomes a tense one and the dinner party in Galicia was a casualty in that war. Back in 1998 you could never ruin a get-together by saying 'Roman', 'Greek', or 'Persian': whereas with a well-placed 'Celt' you might just have got lucky.

That though was 1998 and things have since changed. The long and acrimonious debate over whether the Celts existed was a frenetic affair. But it spurred on a series of scholars to dig into the early evidence for an apparently phantom people. In the last two or three years this evidence has been published with accompanying arguments and we are entering a new and exciting world in which the ancient Celts are very much alive. These scholars brought together the early proofs for language to show that a large swathe of Europe spoke Celtic tongues. This was always suspected, but the case for numerous antique Celtic-speakers is now irrefutable. Language does not always mean that people think of themselves as belonging to the same civilisation. But archaeological and artistic evidence suggests that a large part of Celtica, as this area is sometimes called, shared the same style of possessions and art. And a better understanding of the religious customs of this area hints that the inhabitants had broadly similar spiritual traditions; while the very few clues that exist concerning their social organisation point to a sense of oneness among the tribes there. The Celts, in short, did exist.

But, at the same time, it has become clear that the old view of the Celts was in some respects defective and that the man with the trowel on his belt (our sceptical archae-ologist) had at least one good point. For, if there was a

11

Celtic civilisation in ancient Europe in the early centuries BC, it certainly did not, as Celticists had long implied, survive into modern times. That civilisation was, in fact, in terminal decline (or perhaps 'terminal change') by the early centuries AD. After all, if, in the Iron Age, the Celts had covered much of Europe—they were perhaps the most populous European people—by the dawn of the Middle Ages, c. 500 AD, the only significant groups of Celtic-speakers left were to be found in Britain and Ireland and Brittany (France).

And, crucially, if Celtic-speakers continued to survive in these regions, all our evidence suggests that within this reduced space *a common sense of Celtic identity was also dying*. After 500 AD, the two remaining Celtic peoples, the British Celts and the Irish Celts (or, as they are also known, the Gaels) continued to speak Celtic languages. But these two languages were drifting apart, so much so that a British-Celtic speaker and an Irish-Celtic speaker could no longer communicate each using their own language. And, with time, the last two Celtic families ceased to think of themselves as brothers or even cousins. Remnants of a common Celtic past survived. But, by the eighth century, the memory of that common past had dimmed. And, by the twelfth century, it had been entirely lost: the British Celts and the Gaels had become mere neighbours.

It would not be until the eighteenth century that linguists would rediscover that the Celtic languages of Britain and Ireland were relations. And modern references to the 'Celtic fringe' or the present day 'Celtic peoples' follow on from that discovery, but are terms of convenience. They are a way of labelling a series of communities on the western edge of Europe that have enjoyed similar political and economic fortunes in the last two centuries. While much of what we think of as 'Celtic', be it ethereal folk music, 'Celtic' nationalism, 'Celtic' prayer weekends, or those lovely pre-Raphaelite works showing dreamy 'Celtic' priestesses walking through bluebell-laden woodlands, are also cases of 'Celtic' convenience—be that convenience political, commercial or imaginative.

Modern accruements stripped away, the story of the Celts is, and can only properly be, the story of a series of European communities—defined by common language, customs and sense of identity—that prospered in the Iron Age and then declined to vanishing point in the early Middle Ages. And then there are also the fossils of this civilisation that appear for several more centuries in the regions where the last Celts lived—Britain, Ireland and France—before falling into the abyss of time. These are the Celts and it is from what we know of this people's fortunes that we can write their history or, at least, parts of it.

If these are the outlines for Celtic history, then there is also the question of the words employed to describe that history. In the present work I have erred on the side of comprehensibility. So I call the Celtic inhabitants of ancient France the Gauls or even, risking redundancy, the Celtic Gauls. I refer to the Irish in Ireland and Northern Britain as the Irish, the Irish Celts or the Gaels, an Anglicised version of the word that this people gave themselves. With the Celts of Britain it is normal to talk of 'the British' or (as an adjective) 'British' or even 'Brittonic'. I have found this confusing especially in such phrases as 'the English fought the British at the Battle of Heavenfield'. I, therefore, use 'British Celt' and, as an adjective, 'British-Celtic'.

Two Irish saints described in the second part of this

13

book were both called Columba: to avoid confusion we—
as many writers do—call Columba of Iona 'Colum Cille'
and Columba of Bobbio, 'Columbanus'. Likewise in part
two we assume a degree of 'Celtic Christianity', an
unfashionable concept: but one that has no institutional
overtones (there was no Celtic Church) and one that is
more than justified for the sixth and seventh centuries.

To describe the period from 400-1000 we employ—
apologies to Late Antiquity and other competitors—'the
Dark Ages', a phrase that has the merit of being widely
understood, that communicates something of our
chronic lack of sources in those centuries and one that
may even be coming back into fashion among academics.

We also refer to 'barbarian' and 'civilised', 'barbarism'
and 'civilisation' throughout because, though they have
been outlawed for our own times, they were once the
essence of perception—like respectability for the
Victorians or sanctity for the Middle Ages. A historian
today could no more ignore 'civilisation' and 'barbarism'
while writing about the Celts than a historian of the
future will be able to write a history of our times while
overlooking relativism. We have used 'tribe' to describe
the kin-based groupings that were the most important
unit in Celtic society. It goes without saying that 'tribe' is
not used in a derogatory fashion in the present work—far
from it.

The Celtic Revolution covers a little less than two
millennia of history, crosses the borders of over twenty
modern countries on three continents, while drawing on a
bibliography in several languages. The inadequacies of the
present author meant that this work would have been
impossible without the help of a score of family, friends
and colleagues. Some gave expert advice, some read
passages of the book, some read passages of the book

repeatedly, some supplied references and photocopies, others were kind enough to give permission for quotations from their own work. I would like to set down here my *overwhelming* sense of gratitude to Richard Barber, Nigel Bryant, Benjamin Buchan, Salvatore Costanza, David Dumville, Paola de Fougerolles, Adrian Gallegos, Tom Green, Chris Hale, Julius Lipner, Andrew Lownie, Dave Musgrove, Giovanni Orlandi (†), Droo Ray, Lawrie Robertson, Judith Round, Martin Rynja, Maria del Sasso, Richard Sharpe, Patrick Sims-Williams, Stuart Spencer, Jonathan Wooding, Stephen Young and, above all, my darling wife Valentina. I dedicate this book to the memory of my grandmother Leonora 'Nin' Young (2001†): '¡Toma lo que quieras…'

Santa Brigida,
July 2009

INTRODUCTION

THE CELTS AND SUCCESS

hen we think of the ancient Celts—the tribal people that dominated much of Europe in antiquity—our associations are legion: Celtic art, Celtic legends, Celtic music, certainly; Celtic manuscripts, Celtic jewellery and Celtic Christianity, probably; even Celtic warriors, Celtic tattoos and Celtic spirituality. But marching bands, tickertape and bugles do not figure. It is decline rather than success that defines the Celts, for the Celts are, our text books and television programmes would have us believe, among history's great losers: condemned to a slow if romantic extinction, hunted down by more efficient if less interesting civilisations.

Celtic decline was, by any standards, dramatic. In the early centuries BC, Celtic-speakers were to be found through large parts of Europe: the Iberian Peninsula, northern Italy, Austria, Switzerland, parts of Germany, parts of the Lowlands, Gaul, Turkey (tipping over into Asia), Britain and Ireland. But this massive swathe of territory—in reality a mosaic of independent tribal federations—passed under foreign domination and was largely absorbed between 100 BC and 100 AD. And, by

17

500 AD, the Celts survived predominantly in Britain and Ireland at 'the ends of the earth'. Another five hundred years passed and Celtic-speakers had all but disappeared, reduced to the edges of the edge, where their descendants survive today in Wales, Ireland and a few other western regions.

But failure is ultimately a characteristic of all peoples be they tribal commonwealths or strong centralised states. Why then do we concentrate on Celtic decline, as opposed to Celtic success of which there were several conspicuous instances? The reason that the Celts and failure are so easily coupled has to do with the cock-eyed way our society and prior societies have viewed the Celts. For, true, ancient writers and their medieval successors saw the Celts as barbarians, standing outside the circle of European civilisation and staring in: the grubby peasant face at the manor house window. But they also characterised them as 'noble savages', a spiritually pure and hence an ineffective and doomed people.

The following pages have been written as a partial antidote to the poisonous idea of Celtic failure. They are a reminder that on at least three occasions in their history the Celts worked a revolution in their neighbours' affairs and that the world we live in today would be a different one if the Celts had never existed. Now, of course, just as all civilisations will, with time, fail, so all civilisations will make a difference. By saying then that the Celts changed the world I am not claiming that the Celts were special or blessed. I am canvassing for their right to matter as the Greeks or Romans, the Etruscans or Carthaginians matter, and to be recognized as a major influence on our history.

The three 'revolutions' are quickly described. The first were the Celtic invasions of the fifth through the second century BC when Celtic warbands, tens of thousand strong, threatened the peoples of the Mediterranean Basin. The second was at the very end of antiquity, when Celtic, and particularly Irish Celtic, monks left their homeland intent on spreading or upholding the Gospel. And the third came in the Middle Ages, after the demise of the ancient Celts, when their fossilised legends, including those of Arthur and Tristan, Merlin and Gawain, spread out over Europe.

And why did these three movements of Celtic individuals and ideas matter? Well, to take the three in reverse order, the third, the legendary one, brought about changes in how European man and woman thought, helping to create the modern mind and calling time on the Middle Ages: Celtic stories became a way of expressing subversive ideas. The second, a monkly migration, consolidated European Christianity in some very difficult centuries. And the first, the Iron Age invasions, were, as we will see in the next pages, an important force in creating the Roman Empire. And with this we invite the reader to the Alps, c. 500 BC, where the *carnyx*, the ancient Celtic battle horn, is blowing, calling the tribes to war, and western civilisation is about to be transformed by a people from its outer marches...

Map 1 The Celtic World BC to AD

From the west I saw fly
the dragons of expectation,
and open the way of the fire-powerful;
they beat their wings,
so that everywhere it appeared to me
that earth and heaven burst

Sólarljóð (trans. by Thomas Wright)

I

Making the
Roman Empire

c. 700-500 BC	*Probable date of first Celtic penetration into Italy*
c. 390 BC	*The Senones attack Chiusi*
c. 387 BC	*The Senones attack Rome*
335 BC	*Celtic ambassadors visit Alexander the Great*
298 BC	*Cambaules attacks Macedonia*
c. 283 BC	*Senones defeated by Rome*
280 BC	*Celtic attack on Macedonia*
279 BC	*Celtic attack on Greece*
278 BC	*Celtic warband passes into Asia Minor*
228 BC	*Romans bury Celts and Greeks alive*
225 BC	*The Battle of Telamon*
189 BC	*Roman campaign in Asia Minor*
146 BC	*Roman rule established in Greece*
51 BC	*Roman rule established in Gaul*
43 AD	*The Roman invasion of Britain*

1

THE IRON AGE CELTS

here has always been a line that separates southern from northern Europe, a wavering frontier that has divided, depending on the century: beer-swilling northerners from wine-guzzling southerners, Protestants from Catholics or 'the Germans' from 'the Latins'. However, there has perhaps been no time in history when that line was drawn more sharply than in the early centuries BC. On the southern littoral of the continent, city-dwelling peoples including the Macedonians, the Greeks, the Carthaginians and the Romans, were pioneering a version of urban life that would later dominate both Europe and the world. They were developing new fields of knowledge, such as mathematics, history and philosophy, in their libraries, academies and legislatures. And critically, they could write about these experiences—the first substantial records of the European past begin at this time.

In the north, meanwhile, various other peoples, above all the Celts, dwelt tribally as the southerners had long before. They had forts not towns, story-tellers rather than scribes, and, as they were for the most part

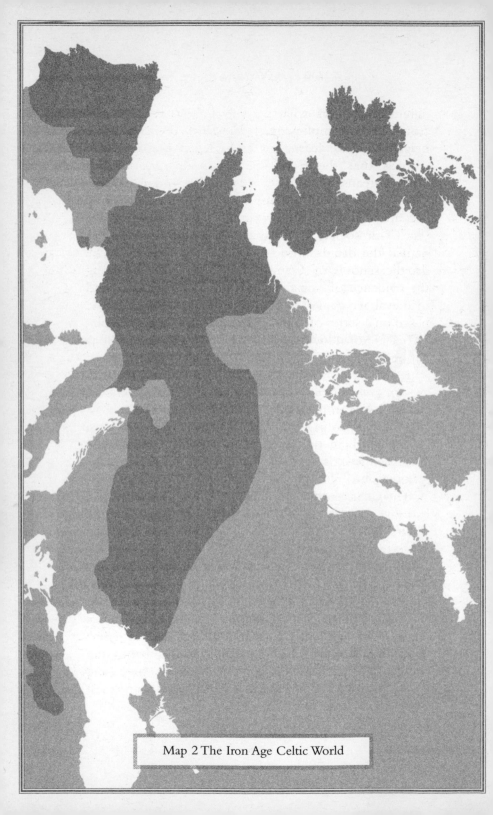

Map 2 The Iron Age Celtic World

illiterate, most of what we know about them comes from the uncomplimentary asides of their southern neighbours. We learn, for example, in these antique records that the Celts—or Gauls or Galatians or Hyperboreans as they were also called—were 'trouser wearers': normality for us, of course, but a horrific eccentricity for the toga-wearing south. We learn too that Celtic society included a caste of priests or judges named the druids, who went for their training to the druidic schools of Celtic Britain. And picking among the evidence of social organisation, both ancient and medieval, we come to understand that their society was based on a series of clans organised into tribes and that, on exceptional occasions, these tribes coalesced into nations, millions strong.

It goes without saying that north and south did not get on. Their mutual unease has often been described as a clash between barbarism and civilisation. It would be truer though to say that it was a clash of civilisations: and it is telling that even the main channel between these two worlds, war, was understood in a completely different way.

The Celts had fought each other for as long as they had dwelt in the recesses of darkest northern Europe. Theirs was a society based on war: one where a powerful chief was the man able to impose his will on neighbours through raid and invasion, a battle-leader who could bring back to the tribal fires the prizes of stolen gold and stolen cattle. In the north of Europe war was the currency of the tribe. It created balance between the different clans. Tribes not able to assert themselves in raids were coerced into joining tribes that could. Tribes that were strong or ambitious attempted to knock to the ground other raiding tribes. The result was that between the different tribes there was a constant state of readiness and hostility. War was not an extraordinary state of affairs: it was day-to-day, unremarkable.

And almost everything Celtic that was recorded in antiquity involves either the practice or the glorification of conflict. So the high point of Celtic social life was the feast where drunken warriors told tall stories about what they had done and would do in battle and sometimes duelled with members of their own tribe. Next to the family, the most important institution in Celtic society were the armed freemen that gathered around war-leaders. We know of one particularly impressive elder who persuaded several thousand warriors to swear loyalty to him. Another indispensable figure in Celtic life was the poet who sang of the martial deeds of his patron. The druids encouraged bravery in battle by reminding warriors that their souls would survive death. We learn from the ancients of the popularity of war gods among the Celtic Gauls. And many Celtic names given by parents to children, especially in the aristocracy, exalted war: Vercingetorix ('King over Warriors'), Cingetorix ('Warrior King'), Boudica ('Victorious Woman'), Ambigatus ('For War') and such like.

Of course, all antique societies were capable of waging wars. But the city-dwelling civilisations of the Mediterranean, among them the Romans, had not, in contrast to the tribal north, vested their identity in battle. Indeed, southern writers constantly hedged war around with qualifications, even producing the concept of a 'just war'. The result was that southern wars often begin (or end) with a laborious attempt by the parties to show that they had been right to fight or that they had been forced to send out armies by a malignant foe. War was not seen as being positive in itself—even if heroism in a good cause was celebrated. It was a means, not an end. It is doubtful, on the other hand, whether the Celtic warriors of northern Europe would have understood the idea of a just or unjust war: though there were conventions that raiders were to respect.

For them war was a way of life. Indeed, time and time again what southerners notice about the Celts is their 'savage and war-loving nature' and how they 'desire strife'. Many scholars today would like us to believe that the southerners overplayed the Celts' bellicosity; and there was certainly room for misunderstanding and exaggeration between two cultures that were so different. But contemporary accounts of the Celtic passion for battle are consistent enough. One Pharaoh, for example, felt himself so threatened by the Celtic mercenaries in his employ that he tricked them onto a river island, removed any boats that would allow escape, and watched amazed as the warband fought itself to extinction. Another Asian ruler, meanwhile, tried to show his gratitude to a Celtic tribe that he had hired as mercenaries by settling that tribe in his territory. But these could not resist raiding the nearby towns and cities and so, in the end, he wiped out every man, and almost every woman and child of them.

These two different attitudes to war produced two very different fighting-styles. The southerners perfected a system that depended on collective effort and careful drilling—the shield wall, the ordered charge, the 'tortoise', the fighting withdrawal. It was not dramatic, but its results against disorganised armies often were. The Celts focussed, instead, on the might of the individual warrior and his prestige—war was about the pursuit of renown and the clash of heroes. The southerners, once they got over the fright of the wild raiders before them, described the Celtic army as being brave, impressive but uncoordinated. Celtic nudity in battle for example, a common feature of northern warfare, might be frightful to look at, but it also made killing Celtic warriors considerably easier. This is not to say that all parts of the Celtic army were judged hopeless. In fact, parts of the Celtic army were extremely effective; the Celtic cavalry was especially admired and even emulated by southern armies. Nor is it to say that Celtic weapons were inferior: it has been argued, indeed, that the metals forged by some of the northern Celts were ahead of those of their southern 'civilised' neighbours. But, in terms of tactics, the southerners were convinced that they were superior to the Celts: a belief that was, at times, tested to destruction.

It was written in the DNA of the Celtic tribes that they would come smashing against the rich Mediterranean with momentous consequences for the northern and southern halves of Europe; for one of the features of this militarised, tribal society was that it was not fixed down, it did not have the anchor of cities. And so tribes moved to wherever there was wealth and land. Nomadism, in fact, was almost as important as war in the Celtic imagination. Even their legends were based upon the coming and going of peoples, Celtic time being measured not in dynasties or centuries but in invasions. So one of the early details of druidic lore to be recorded tells how the first Celts arrived in their homelands in a series of immigrations and emigrations involving the vast expanses of wooded, hidden Europe beyond the Rhine and beyond the sea, from which

30

tribes were driven 'by ceaseless wars and violent floods from the ocean'. And even a thousand years later the last Celts, the medieval Irish and British Celts, would also see their history as a succession of tribal comings and goings. Indeed, the oldest Irish national history is called *The Book of the Taking of Ireland* and describes a series of invasions of gods, humans and intermediate human-god-like beings to the farthest island of the west: including one wearying walkabout that took the ancestors of the Irish from the Black Sea to Kerry via Egypt and Spain.

Now, as we shall soon see, legends are everywhere in the Celtic past, eating through history like rust eats through iron. So it is important to stress, here at the outset, that these migrations were not only imaginary: they also took place in the real world. A particularly striking account comes from ancient Switzerland and concerns the details of the migration of the Celtic Helvetii. We are told that the tribal elders of this people had felt for some time that their lands were too small; and, surrounded by mountainous territory and girded by rivers, they found it difficult to make war on their neighbours, a sport that they loved exceedingly. As a result, the decision was made for the whole tribe of a quarter of a million to emigrate into nearby Gaul. This was clearly not a jaunt to the seaside; something that could be prepared for the day before. The tribal council set a date three years hence and began slowly to buy up wagons and beasts of burden from near and far. Then, when the time finally came, they burnt all their villages and any excess grain—this so that no feint hearts would insist on returning—and set off. It has been calculated that the wagon train—chariots, oxen, mewling infants and guards—would have stretched five or six miles. And

31

we know that at some points—the unforgiving Jura Mountains are mentioned—the road was only wide enough for one wagon to pass at a time.

The planning put into this particular venture is another reminder of how 'primitive' tribal peoples were not as unsophisticated as the southerners would have us believe: the migration of the Helvetii involved, after all, hundreds of thousands of individuals. But not all migrations involved an entire people wrapping up affairs and heading off down the track. One of the realities of life in Celtic Europe was that the tribes themselves were unstable. And failure or, curiously, success could lead to tribes dividing like a cut worm. Often these divisions were between the old tribe and groups of young warriors tens of thousands strong— excess testosterone—who were sent off to find new lands for themselves taken, of course, in wars.

We catch occasional glimpses of these warriors raging across the continent in our histories. But more often we can trace their movements in the placenames of ancient Europe. So there was, for example, a tribe named the Atrebates in what is today northern France, and from placenames and a handful of historical references we learn that in prehistory they had sent warbands to Britain. In Britain there was, likewise, a Celtic tribe named the Brigantes, who dominated the Pennines, and who sent colonists to Ireland where a similarly-named tribe was founded. Or there were the Parisi of Gaul—who gave their name to the French capital—and the Parisi of northern England the offspring of the Gaulish tribe (interestingly both tribes had similar burial rituals). Of course, in some cases we may have got the relations between these namesakes the wrong way around or we may have seen a relation where there was none. So who is to say, for example, that the French Parisii really sent out emigrants to the River Humber in England? Actually, it may have been an early British-Celtic tribe that sent out emigrants to France. There is something peculiarly satisfying about having gruff, tribal Yorkshiremen as the first Parisians. Or, alternatively, there may have been two unconnected tribes who had both been given the same name—'Parisi' likely meant 'the Commanders' in Celtic—and who had adopted, quite by chance, a similar way of burying their dead. But, even with such problems in interpretation, on a tribal map of Celtic Europe we can still make intelligent guesses about relations between widely-separated groups.

Tribes or warbands on the move were looking for two things: booty and land to settle. They could find both in the north of Europe as the movements described immediately above demonstrate. But, from the sixth century BC, as the city states of southern Europe were struggling into existence, they also found booty and land outside the Celtic homelands. In part they will have been brought south by necessity: tribal nomadism was not just a question of heading out in whichever direction you wished. Settlers will have been directed by geography. Mountain ranges and rivers hemmed some peoples in, as they had done the Helvetii. In other cases, though, mountain passes and river valleys acted as natural channels. And the tribal plumbing of Celtic Europe meant that, when population pressure grew in the north, it was down these river valleys and mountain passes that new tribes were swept and out of which they were belched: some of these valleys (the Danube) and passes (especially in the Alps…) leading towards the Mediterranean. But the

33

Celts also had other reasons for moving southwards. The Celts' raiding economy depended on stealing from neighbours. Now there was some pleasure in stealing land and cattle from Celtic-speaking cousins in the forests or the plains of Gaul. But, in the south, there was land that grew grapes, olives and figs: and several southern commentators allege that the Celtic invaders came south because they were so enamoured of the novel taste of wine and olive oil. Then there were also fabulous goods sucked up through the Celts' efficient trading networks: Greek drinking flagons, intricate Mediterranean carving, imported coral and spices that were the stuff of dreams, something like colour in the monochrome Celtic existence of raid and counter raid...

And so the great Celtic invasions of antiquity began. The Celtic tribes, of northern Europe, who had earned a reputation for war-like behaviour, found themselves for the first time pushing over the border into the south of Europe and the urban, luxury-producing oases of literate civilisation in Italy, Greece and Turkey. We will describe other movements of Celtic people and ideas in this book—an exodus of monks in the Dark Ages and an incursion of Celtic legendary heroes in the Middle Ages. These subsequent 'invasions' were largely peaceful—few people died. However, that was not the case with the raids of the Celtic warriors of the age of migrations. The warbands taking part here spilt blood: they were head-hunting, blade-toting galloglass. And between 500-200 BC their raiding and fighting in southern Europe would change the course of history, for these invasions would favour the rise of one of their earliest southern enemies, Rome, and open the way to an Empire on which the sun would not set for a long thousand years. It is only fitting then that we begin with the Celts' first conquests in Italy.

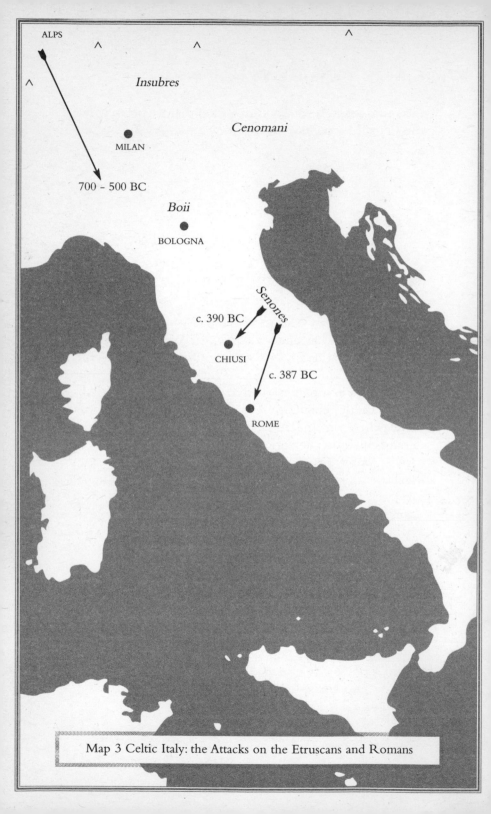

Map 3 Celtic Italy: the Attacks on the Etruscans and Romans

2

THE INVASION OF ITALY

he first Celts to invade Italy came in a fairy tale. The legend was recorded by the Roman historian Livy several centuries afterwards. But it almost certainly originated among the Celts themselves in a period of unimaginable antiquity. It tells of a Celtic chieftain named Ambigatus who lived somewhere in the unknown north of Europe—the continent-wide, unmapped homelands of the ancient Celts. Ambigatus, the tale tells us, had ruled his tribe with ability and his people had prospered. But they prospered too well and for too long until the tribal territory could no longer contain them. And so Ambigatus took two of his nephews aside and instructed them to go and find other lands and found new tribes. The nephews' names—both unmistakably Celtic—were Segovesus and Bellovesus. And to choose the lands that they should colonise, the chieftain made them draw lots. The first, Segovesus, drew a lot that pointed him to the east and the forests of Germany. The second, the lucky nephew, Bellovesus drew a lot that sent him south and, by following a series of curious omens, he crossed the wall of the Alps and made his way into fertile Italy.

As fairy tales go, there is not much to recommend this one. There are no sleeping potions, princesses or magical wishes—Hans Christian Anderson would have turned up his nose. But we are fortunate to have the story of Bellovesus and Segovesus—arguably the earliest myth from northern Europe to have been recorded—because these words echo down from the Iron Age, they are whispers from a time before history. When this story was first told, Christ's birth lay the best part of a millennium in the future, Alexander the Great was still generations away and Italy was not Italy. It was a collection of different peoples and cultures split into tens of city-states, much as it would become again in the Middle Ages. There were the Punic cities, allied to the Carthaginian Empire with its capital in distant Tunisia. There were the Greek cities set up in Sicily and Calabria by Greek colonists intent on taking over the Western Mediterranean for their commerce and their triremes. There were the Etruscans of central Italy who 'do not resemble any other nation in their language or way of life'. There were the Italic cities, among them Rome, barely a regional power at this time, a bantamweight in central Italy. There were the Veneti in the north east, the Venetians two thousand years before the gondola. And there were the Ligurians who dominated the north west of the Peninsula.

It was into this divided world that the booty-hungry Celtic tribes from beyond the Alps forced their way. First came the tribe that claimed Bellovesus of the fairy tale as their founder: the fairy tale was a legendary retelling of a real event whose details have been obscured by northern European mythology. They conquered and settled the lake lands below the Alpine peaks. And, spurred perhaps by their success, other tribes followed. There were the Boii (who gave their name to the Italian city of Bologna and possibly to Bavaria in Germany), the Lingones, the Libui, the Saluvii, the Cenomani and the Senones who settled across the Lombard plain and as far as the coast in the region that Italians call today the Marche: all Celtic names with the taste and sound of the rain-dripping, tribal north. They brought with them their customs: their naked war dances, their woodland gods, their war paint. They brought with them their language: Celtic words started leaking into Italy; for example, 'javelin' and 'chariot'. They brought with them their possessions: among these, the characteristic swords of the north with dragons in spiralled metalwork—though the Celtic tribes of Italy also quickly showed an interest in Etruscan and other Italian goods. They brought with them their folktales: the stories of origins, such as that of Bellovesus, as well as tales of a hero named Raven who brought low the enemies of the Celts in an apocalyptic war. They brought with them the relics of northern society—we have hints of characteristically Celtic tribes and clans. And, of course, the Celts brought with them their violence, annihilating various Italian peoples.

We know virtually nothing of the battles the newcomers fought while settling because this was a time before history—a time glimpsed from fairy tales and the scrapings of archaeological digs. We know only that they appear on the map of Italy in these prehistoric centuries, some time before 500 BC, and that they had tangible connections with the Celtic tribes of the north of Europe. From the beginning these Italian Celts took on Italian customs—some even built towns (or adopted seized ones), something that the Celtic tribes of the north never did. But there were also reinforcements from beyond the Alps—mercenaries and allies sent to war. We hear rumours of these newcomers or find their traces in

Tuscan, Umbrian and Lombard soil. And, even in this antique period, there are occasional sentences that can be culled from the first European writers suggesting the range of the Celts' migrations. It is from one of these that we learn that, at an early date, an alliance of Celtic tribes captured the Etruscan city of Melpum and built there or nearby their Mediolanum, the Middle Place or, as we say today, Milan. An ancient geographer, meanwhile, informs us that the lands of the Ligurians were depopulated by scavenging Celtic armies.

Then, from about 500 BC, the historical light from writing starts to get stronger and is directed with more care. At first, it illuminates only Greece, but afterwards it spreads and by 400 BC much of Italy and parts of the western Mediterranean are also lit up by historians, chroniclers and early thinkers. For the observer of the past it is a magical moment. So far European history has been a play performed with all the lights off, from which only the noise of scuffles on the stage reaches us and the occasional flashes of the usher's torch showing up a face or a prop. Then slowly the lights buzz on and we can see actors and put voices and noises in proper context. The magic moment comes at different times for different peoples. For the Celts in Italy that moment of visibility comes c. 390 BC. The campaign described was certainly not their first in Italy. But it was the first one to be written about in any detail—at least in more detail than the stray sentences described before where 'city X was taken' or 'people Y conquered'; even if, as we shall see, some of these details come from Celtic legend not history.

The Senones or 'the Ancient Ones', the movers of the war, were the most southern of the Celtic tribes in Italy. In a time now forgotten they had come from Gaul and they were possibly related to another Celtic tribe named the Senones in north central France—the French city of Sens is so called from that people. The Italian Senones settled on the eastern coast of Italy around what is today Ancona in a territory that they complained was hot and generally unsatisfying—it is difficult not to think of modern German or English tourists swearing about the mosquitoes and their sunburn. Later writers were keen to stress the primitive nature of Celtic settlements in the peninsula. One, for example, notes that the Celts 'dwelt in unwalled communities, with no furniture, and sleeping on leaf beds and eating meat, interested only in war and agriculture, they led simple lives and knew nothing of the arts or science'. The Senones give the lie to this. Surrounded by older town-based civilisations they took on many of the material trappings of their neighbours so that the archaeology of the region is quite 'Italian'. But we have every reason for believing that in battle the Senones remained true to their roots. In the graves of the Senones weapons typical of northern Celtic Europe are found. And while there are differences—the Senones quickly learnt the value of the helmet, little used in the Gaulish Celtic tribes—our archaeological and historical sources suggest that the Senones warriors, who gathered for raids on their neighbours' territory, would have been, essentially, the same as the tribal armies of the north.

And it was a warband of Senones that marched against the Etruscan city of Chiusi c. 390 BC and that saw the Italian Celts caught in the spotlight of history for the first time. The reaction of the Chiusians to this invasion was naturally one of horror: 'The Chiusians were—when they saw the numbers, the bizarre appearance of the [Celts], and the weapons that [the Celts] bore, and came to know how all the Etruscan armies had often been defeated by them on both sides of the Po—sent into panic by this

41

novel war.' And with 'novel war' we might see, however briefly, the Celts as they were seen by their victims: the long hair and greased-back white mohicans of the invaders, their often naked bodies, their lengthy swords. And also the noise that so many ancient authors refer to in the Celts' marches through enemy territory: 'the awful racket from so many horn- and trumpet-men with the entire force screaming their war-cries together with such a great sound made it seem that not only the horns and the warriors, but also the countryside itself had found voice and taken up the cry'.

In the fourth century BC, Chiusi was an Etruscan settlement: part of the larger Etruscan federation of independent cities, the League of Twelve, centred on what is today Tuscany (in fact, Tuscany comes from a Latin word, *Tosci*, meaning 'Etruscan'). The Etruscans have defeated all historians and cultural pundits, for no one has ever managed to do justice to this eccentric people, though authors as varied as the Italian Renaissance forger Curzio Inghirami and the English novelist D. H. Lawrence have tried. Among contemporaries the Etruscans were famous, first and foremost, for their wealth, importing, early in their history, such luxuries as monkeys and ostrich eggs from the eastern Mediterranean. They were obsessed by music—cooking, beating slaves and even hunting to gentle flute tunes. They loved games and the many ivory dice to come out of Etruscan tombs resemble the ones we use today to play Snakes and Ladders. The paintings that survive from their vanished civilisation suggest that dining among the Etruscans was a less onerous occasion than in the rest of the ancient world and there were some scurrilous rumours about after-dinner sex, 'with the lights left on'. Their funeral urns, meanwhile, with happy couples reclining together in the prime of their lives, are some of the most human and intimate to come down from antiquity.

But, if there are hints of pleasure-loving, there was also a peculiarly morbid and violent side to Etruscan civilisation. Etruscan artists loved to portray scenes of slaughter, far more so than the Greeks, who tended to get a little prudish where blood was involved. The Etruscans perhaps invented gladiator fighting and, at the time the Celts attacked, human sacrifice may have still been indulged in. To their violent nature, we must also add their extreme religiosity that made them fatalistic and that led them to forecast the impending doom of their own civilisation by hammering nails into a temple door every year on the first of September. Then, to these several apparently contradictory features, the Etruscans added one more exotic possession, their language.

Of the forty or so dialects and tongues spoken in Italy at this time, Etruscan stands apart, having no relation to any of the others. Some of its words sound simply strange, *lucomo* ('king') or *tular* ('boundary'), some bizarre *Rasenna* (the Etruscan name for themselves) or *frontac* ('an interpreter of lightening'), and some have the tinniness of words invented by a fantasy or science-fiction writer: so one of the gods of the underworld was *Vanth*, while an official was a *zilath*. Most of these names vanished with the Etruscans into the pit of time, but a handful arrived, via Latin, in English, including the words 'histrionic' for the temperamental behaviour of an actor, and 'person'.

In times even more antique than the invasion of the Senones, the Chiusians had been one of the mightiest of the Etruscan cities. Indeed, one of their early kings had been buried in Italy's most vain-glorious tomb, a mound flanked by four pyramids—and Chiusi is still today riddled with underground Etruscan passages. But, by the fourth century, the city had declined in strength and, though it remained famous for its fine ceramics, its days of dominance had long been over when the Celts approached those high city walls. Yet it was Chiusi's very decline that saved the town from the Celts. In the years immediately preceding the Senones' raid, the Etruscan city of Veii had been involved in a particularly savage war with a still obscure city of central Italy, named Rome, a war that ultimately Veii had lost. But Chiusi had kept itself out of this conflict and so, as the Celts approached, it was not war-weary. It was also able to do something that few other Etruscan cities could have done at this date. It was able to send a message south to Rome, whose reputation for military excellence was growing after its recent victory, and ask for assistance. And Rome changed the course of Italian history by answering that call.

The city on the Tiber decided not to send an army to the north: the Romans were perhaps too exhausted after the recent hostilities or perhaps a march through Etruscan-speaking Italy would have upset the Etruscans and sparked further unwelcome conflicts. It did, however, send ambassadors to see what the Celts were doing in Etruscan territory. And the answer was given as soon as these ambassadors arrived and were welcomed at the camp of the tribesmen. The Senones warriors explained that they wanted land. Either the Chiusians would hand over some of their own territory, or the Celts would take the city by force. The Roman delegation gently reminded the Senones that they had no claim on Chiusi or its surroundings. But the Celts did not take this appeal seriously, laughing uproariously and replying that their claim was in their swords and that everything belonged to the brave. And when the Roman ambassadors tried to talk the Celts out of this illegal act of violence the Celts shouted them down, asking though that the Romans wait and watch the battle to bring back to Rome an account of 'the best soldiers in the world'. This endearingly macho behaviour on the part of the northerners is reminiscent of other ancient descriptions of the Celts. It amuses modern readers, but it irritated the Celts' southern, city-dwelling contemporaries. So Alexander the Great, in the later fourth century BC, would express his impatience with the 'pretentious boasting' of the Celts after one of their warriors had told the Macedonian king that he feared nothing but that the sky might fall on his head.

According to one author, Chiusi was the earliest meeting between the two civilisations: 'this is the first that we have heard of the Romans....', a Celtic leader confided. And given that the various Celtic tribes and the Romans would become the very best and bitterest of enemies in the next centuries, there is something intriguing about looking back over the encounter. It is almost as if we have a privileged account of a young Wellington, on a trip to France, bumping into a presumptuous new Corsican recruit named Bonaparte. Yet this was not only a prelude, but also a beginning. The Roman appeal to justice and the Celtic appeal to martial excellence had already shown that here was not just another encounter between hostile city states. Rather it was a meeting between two different ways of life—one tribal, one urban. And the Roman officials lost patience with what they saw as the lack of reasonableness among the Celts. In fact, so infuriated did they become that they disregarded the law of nations and took up arms along with the Chiusians in the initial skirmishes.

The Roman ambassadors understood that talks

were futile… and they sneaked into Chiusi and encouraged and emboldened the Chiusians so that the citizens of that place would join them in sallying out against the Celts… And the Chiusians sallied out and, in the fight along the city walls, Quintus Ambustus [one of the Roman envoys], charged on horseback against a noble and comely Celt who had ridden ahead of his army. Now the Celts did not at first recognise Quintus because his attack was quick and his shining armour hid his face. But when Quintus had beaten and knocked his opponent from his horse and was despoiling him then [the Celtic general] saw the Roman, and asked the gods to witness how, against all conventions, conventions held good and holy by all humanity, this Quintus had come to the Celts as an ambassador, but had fought them as an enemy.

The Celts, distracted and confused by such an unchivalrous act, withdrew from Chiusi. We have no reason for thinking that they stormed the city—the end of that campaign is not elaborated on by ancient historians. The Senones had, instead, a new enemy—Rome: and after their own ambassadors were sent south, and the Roman people refused to hand over the rogue diplomats— furious public assemblies are reported—the northerners swore revenge. The Senones would march upon Rome and make their own justice. Accounts differ as to whether the warbands set off immediately or a year or two afterwards, but what is agreed upon is the surprising outcome of that war.

3

THE MARCH ON ROME

he Senones who set off for Rome are reported to have had as many as seventy thousand warriors in their ranks. This number has been questioned. But tribes could include hundreds of thousands of souls: one head count of a Celtic tribe in antiquity came up with over three hundred thousand. There is nothing impossible then about seventy thousand, especially if the Senones had been joined in war by allies from the Celtic tribes further to the north. The Senones, irrespective of their precise numbers, will, in any case, have wreaked havoc as they traversed two-hundred miles of central Italy. 'At the sound of their racket... the terrified towns ran for their weapons and those in the country fled' and the Celts were 'given to wild outbursts' and 'their horrible howling and tuneless din filled everywhere with noise'. What shocked Rome most of all, though, was the speed with which the tribal army arrived in their territory, barely giving time for the city government to organise a satisfactory defence. Men of age were brought into the militias and the hastily prepared army rallied out into the countryside to keep the invaders away from Rome itself. A Sicilian historian, Diodorus tells us that the Romans were able to muster close to twenty four thousand good soldiers, plus other less experienced reinforcements.

Battle was joined some ten miles from Rome on the far bank of the Allia, near where that river joins the Tiber. The sheer mass of the Senones need not have particularly worried the Romans, who were later to take pride in winning battles while outnumbered by tribal opponents. But to assure themselves of victory the Romans would first have to resist a powerful attack. For the Celts, after some requisite boasting and offering of challenges, not to mention a little javelin throwing, were accustomed to start their battles by charging madly at the enemy. The success of this charge depended on the Celts' charismatic fury and their long swords that were lifted and brought down in a lethal, shoulder-strong slash on anyone courageous enough to hold their ground. But the charge was flawed. The long Celtic swords proved almost useless for the close-quarter fighting that followed the first maniacal assault. Not only did they sometimes bend on impact— one ancient historian describes the Celts having to step backwards to straighten their blades with their feet, a time-consuming and faintly ridiculous occupation. But they were also poor at the stabbing and thrusting at which the shorter Roman swords excelled. This meant that, if a line of Mediterranean infantry with their shields held carefully together could resist the initial charge, the chances that they would survive the battle rose considerably. After the first sword blows and some furious pushing and shoving, the protected, well-organised infantry could then pick off the often naked, invariably exhausted northerners at their leisure. But that first fanatical, shrieking, Celtic charge was one of the most terrifying moments in ancient warfare and only a trained army would keep its nerve as the tribesmen approached.

The day that the Celts, or 'the Gauls' as the Romans called them, reached the Allia, the Senones proved themselves, if not geniuses on the battlefield, then at least capable tacticians. The Romans had thinned their lines, stretching their units across the river meadows to prevent the more numerous Celts slipping around and outflanking them. They had also placed their least experienced troops as reserves on some hills by the Tiber. The Celts, 'by fortune or design', placed, instead, their fiercest warriors facing these green Roman soldiers and it was here that the battle was decided. Down on the plain the Roman shield walls held against the trouser-wearers' charge. Roman professionalism triumphed over tribal flair and rage. But the inexperienced Roman reserves panicked as the shrieking Celtic line whipped up towards them and turned and fled from the rising swords and blue-painted spearmen. If that had been all, then the battle may still have been won by some speedy wheeling of units on the plain. But for the reserves there was no way out. Running anywhere but in the direction of their war-painted assailants, they were caught between the river and the foe, and moved down towards the unprotected Roman flanks with the bezerk Celtic warriors coming on behind. The Roman army was now being attacked not only frontally but laterally. And within minutes it was all over, the whole Roman battle-line had dissolved in confusion.

The Roman historian Livy, many centuries afterwards, wrote that the disaster was so complete that the Celts could not quite believe what they were seeing. There was even some hesitation to follow up the victory and eradicate the fleeing army. Was this not perhaps a trap? Could it really be so simple to destroy the mighty Romans? But the manner of the Romans' retreat soon left no room for doubt. In the escaping army, discipline broke down almost completely. Most tried to scatter along the river bank, but this route became jammed and those held up there were easily cut down from behind by the Celts. Others dived into the Allia to return home. Either they threw away their armour and weapons to swim the better and escaped, but without the wherewithal to defend their city; or they jealously held onto their equipment and were dragged down by the current to their deaths. As the Romans swam, the Celts, in any case, entertained themselves by showering the drowning with javelins. And, not surprisingly, for centuries afterwards, the Romans considered the anniversary of this battle a particularly unlucky one: a Friday the 13th of the Roman calendar.

The Senones had just worked a stunning victory on one of the most admired armies in the Mediterranean: Rome lay less than a day's march away without any militia to defend it or man its walls. We have countless later examples where the Romans, on achieving such a victory against their enemies, followed up the attack immediately with stunning promptitude, destroying nearby cities or exterminating mauled warbands. But the Celtic army dallied, enjoying their victory. They first ¬heaped the weapons of their enemy into vast piles 'as was their custom': perhaps to sacrifice these to one of their gods or even the Allia that had welcomed them into the territory by swallowing up a good part of the locals. We have the evidence of archaeological digs from northern Europe to demonstrate that tribal peoples there tossed weapons and body parts into rivers as tribute to divine powers. The Senones then spent the next day travelling around the battlefield cutting off the heads of the dead or dying Romans as trophies. If the invaders acted as their northern cousins, the heads will have met varied fates.

Some will have been hurled too into the river. Others will have been brought back to be embalmed in cedar oil and hammered onto tribal gates in the Senones' heartlands, where guests would be ceremoniously introduced to these withered remains before entering for a meal. While a specially honoured few, the heads of centurions and generals, will have been flayed and boiled, and then made into candleholders or wine-beakers for niches in woodland temples.

The Romans should have had some time to organise a defence while the Celts were amusing themselves with these invigorating activities. But geography was working against the defenders. Those soldiers who had fled down the far banks of the river were not easily able to return to Rome and so they took refuge in the abandoned Etruscan city of Veii. Meanwhile, those soldiers who had returned were often unarmed and spread panic about the ferocity of their opponents. The situation was as desperate as any that Rome had faced in its history, as desperate as any that Rome would face in the next thousand years. An enemy army lay mere miles away and there was virtually no one left to keep the city walls. Much of the population fled. Sacred objects were removed from the temples and taken away to safety. The city itself could not be defended: there were too few men of military age left. But rather than surrender the city entirely, the remaining legionaries went up to the Capitoline Hill, the most easily defended of all the hills of Rome, where the heights were prepared for a last desperate stand. Then, poignantly, as the enemy lumbered into sight, the city gates were opened by the guards, who did not want to delay the inevitable. Rome was about to be overrun.

Most of the civilian population had fled. But some of the older senators and officials of the Republic had elected to remain at their posts and, as they were too decrepit for war, they waited not in the citadel, but outside their houses. History (or is it legend?) tells us that the invaders were astounded by these old men who sat stock still on small wooden thrones, and the Celts came to examine them carefully. Finally, unsure whether one was a statue or a living thing, a Senones warrior reached out his hand and pulled at the beard: an impiety that the senator in question could not tolerate. Sharply lifting an ivory walking stick, he snapped it across the impudent Celt's head and the invaders closed in with their weapons. The elders of Rome, even if spread regally and haughtily around the city, had only so much blood to spill and were quickly done away with. The Celts then got on with turning Rome into a furnace.

It is impolite in a historical narrative to write the words 'or is it legend?', as I have done in the last paragraph. But it would be irresponsible not to state again that the story of the war between the Senones and the Romans is one that comes not from an eye-witness, but from writers who were using sources of uncertain value, generations later. We know that the attack on Rome actually happened because Heracleides Ponticus, a near-contemporary, records it. He says that a Greek city with that name—a nice reminder of how little known Rome was at this date that it could be said to be Greek!—was destroyed by the Hyperboreans, one of several ancient terms used for the Celts.

But we also know that, to repeat a key image we used in our first chapter, Celtic legend eats through Celtic history like rust through iron. So the Celtic commander of the Senones was said to have had the name Brennos or 'Raven'. We know though from elsewhere that this Raven was a mythical hero of the Celts, a Celtic Hercules: we will come across him again in the next chapters. And, as sometimes happens in ancient history, myth and fact have been mixed together. It is as if, in two or three hundred years' time, a historian were to describe how Roosevelt and Churchill won the Second World War with the aid of Superman. The ancient Celts were quite indifferent to history as we understand it, distilling their past into legend. And the only explanation for this mix-up is that early Roman historians had listened to a mythic Celtic version of events and included it uncritically in their accounts.

Then if there are Celtic legends there are also Roman ones. Take, for example, the description of the siege of the Capitol. Did a band of brave Romans really hold out on one of Rome's hills to the bitter end: or was this just a way for later Romans to be able to claim that the city was not completely taken by the boastful Celts? A good deal of circumstantial detail has built up around the defence of the Capitol: names, dates and anecdotes—even if this is in itself no guarantee. We are told, for example, that the Celts made an initial charge on the fortress that failed miserably, the Romans counter-charging and sending the Celts smarting back into the smoking city below. We are also told that the Celts remained in and around Rome, while food on both sides started to run low and a siege began. We are told that Romans hidden outside the city sent one of their number, Cominius Pontius, sneaking through the Celtic lines to co-ordinate the defence with his companions on the Capitol. Cominius swam the Tiber and climbed a near vertical path on the cliffs on the north side of that hill.

It was, in fact, Cominius's rash journey up the cliff-face of the Capitol that put the last pocket of Roman defence in danger. Cominius was spotted by the raiders as he scaled the heights and the leaders of the Senones determined to make their own attempt by the same route and so finish the siege once and for all. It should have been a brilliant end to a brilliant war. But, instead, it is remembered today not for its outcome, but rather for the manner in which the Romans learnt of the attack.

At about midnight a large gang of the Celts climbed the cliff-face and scaled upwards in silence. They went on all fours over points that were jagged and almost-vertical, but which were easier to pass than they had expected. And they did this until the first of them had come to the heights, they had prepared themselves and were ready to fall on the sleeping sentries: for neither man nor their dogs were aware of the attack. Close by though there were some holy geese around the temple of Juno, which were usually well fed, but, as there was little food for the garrison, were starving and in a bad way. This bird has naturally sharp hearing and is attentive of all noises, and these, restless and unable to sleep in their hunger, heard the Celts, and flew at them with loud squawks, waking up the whole garrison. The barbarians now that they had been noticed, took no care to be silent but attacked wildly. And the defenders quickly grabbed whatever weapons they could find and did as best they could. First, Manlius... strong in his body and brave in his heart, met two of the enemy together, cut the right hand from one with his sword, as the Celt was lifting an axe, and smashed his shield into the face of the second, sending this one over the cliff. Then, holding his position at the wall with those who had come to help, he drove back the rest of the enemy.

The story of the geese saving Rome is an attractive one. It deserves to be true, even if many modern historians dismiss it as legend. Perhaps we should follow the advice of Livy, one of the historians who records this war, concerning a similar tale: 'In questions of the most ancient times I would be pleased if what seems true is believed. Stories like this one, which are better suited to a stage which offers marvels than to the inspiration of belief, it is not worth either the denying of nor their affirming.' In later centuries, the Roman populace and priests were not so sceptical, to the detriment of the canine population of the Seven Hills. At festivals, for generations after, they would carry geese through the city on golden cushions and crucify dogs in a long drawn out revenge for those dogs that had forgotten to bark on the night of the attack.

Soon after the failed attack, the Senones moved back from the ruins of Rome leaving only 'a funeral pyre' to the inhabitants, who had finally to buy off the Celts with a thousand pounds of gold. But here too legend has got the better of history. There is a story that the Celtic leader fixed the scales weighing out the treasure and that, when the Romans complained, this chief replied with the immortal, unanswerable words: '*vae victis!*', 'woe to the vanquished!' But 'the leader' was none other than the Celtic mythological hero Raven and so this picturesque little episode has to be consigned to the dustbin. We are also told that Raven's band was ambushed by the Romans on its way home. But who are we to say that this too was not invented? Certainly in legend, Raven's campaigns seem always to have finished badly. In fact, what we are left with are only the fundamentals of the attack on Rome, sent like morse code across the centuries with a good deal of interference on the airways—the static of legend and hearsay. The Senones attacked Chiusi and from there came into contact with the Romans. At a later date they turned towards Rome and a Celtic army defeated the Roman army on the far side of the Allia. The Senones then entered and burnt the city, the Romans arguably holding one part, the Capitol inviolate to the very end.

It is not difficult to understand why the Romans had such a long-lasting, almost pathological hatred of the Celts; the Celts alone of the ancient enemies of Rome were able to say that they had entered that city and destroyed it. And the Romans remembered this through the centuries. We have seen how the disastrous battle with the Senones was counted in the Roman calendar as an unhappy day, year after year after year. We have also seen how for generations after the Roman public remembered the defence of the Capitol by rewarding geese and torturing dogs. They also gave an exaggerated importance to any news of Celtic warbands heading south. On one occasion in the third century BC, the populace became so fearful that they actually sacrificed human beings in one of their market places—an extraordinary act for the Romans who looked on human sacrifice as a barbarism. In what was perhaps a ritual borrowed from the Etruscans, Celts and Greeks were buried alive while the people looked on. The Roman state, when it sweated in the grip of a nightmare, did not invoke Hannibal and the Carthaginians or even the Egyptians or the distant Persians, but rather the painted Senones and their warrior brothers from the north of Italy and the Alpine passes.

And yet, for all this antipathy and fear, it was the Celts more than any other people that smoothed Rome's path to Imperial greatness. Tribal raiders—the Vikings, the Huns and, at this early date, the Celts—often play a

Darwinian role, picking off urban civilised states such as Rome. They lack, or do not care for, the administrative structures necessary to set up permanent empires of their own and so, after their invasions and raids, they leave behind the states or kingdoms that were sturdy enough to survive their depredations, to assert their rule over the territory of the losers. And this was what the Romans now did, as one of the survivors of the Celtic raids of those years. They rebuilt, redefended and then returned to doing what Rome and its people did best: dominating failing neighbours. And the Celtic invasions of northern Italy had made this task easier. Many of Rome's old or potential enemies, the Venetii, the Ligurians and the Etruscans, had been weakened or eliminated in the Celtic storm. And the Romans easily swept aside their old rivals. If it had not been for the Celts, the Etruscans might have proved a stumbling block for Roman expansion. It might even have been the Etruscans who conquered Italy and sent out their legions to dominate the Mediterranean and eventually the Arabian deserts and distant Britain. It might have been the strange Etruscan tongue, not Latin, that became the common language of southern Europe... Or perhaps the Italian powers would have remained in stalemate and no Empire would ever have arisen. Or perhaps it would have fallen to Carthage or Greece to conquer the world.

But, as it was, Rome cleaned up the mess left behind by the Celtic hurricane. And once they had won easy victories over their neighbours, the Romans had only to get the hang of defeating the Celts. They had to learn not to be intimidated by the noise and the carnival of Celtic warfare—they were steeled, we are told, by the consideration of how much gold the Celts wore and how much booty victory promised them. They had then to learn to

57

resist the initial Celtic charge. And then they had only to let the lines of legionaries efficiently despatch those Celts still able to fight. With this formula, they were, within a century, dominating the Italian Celts and pushing them towards extinction: at one battle, Telamon, in the third century, the Romans claimed to have killed forty thousand Celtic warriors and taken ten thousand prisoners. And we will come to the bloody end of the Senones in the next chapter.

The balance had shifted and the northern half of Italy now slipped into the Roman sphere of control. Rome had risen into the first league of nations, strengthened, says the historian Polybius, like athletes by their frequent sparring with the tribal Celts. And it was from that strong base in northern Italy that Rome could make war on the Greek commonwealth of cities to the east and the Carthaginian Empire across the Mediterranean. Roman Italy was the Celts' first contribution to European civilisation: and it was one that the descendants of the Senones, both in Italy and the homelands to the north, would have reason to lament. It had certainly not been the intention of those proud northern warriors when they had set off generations before in search of gold and wine in *Italia fertilis*.

4

DOWN THE DANUBE

he next Celtic push towards the south began in the fourth century BC the best part of a hundred years after the events described in the last chapter. And it started along the banks of the Danube, the long river that connects the Alps to the Black Sea and that passes through, to name the modern countries that run beside its banks, Germany, Austria, Hungary, Serbia, eventually forming the border between Romania and Bulgaria. Today this territory is very much central and eastern Europe. But, in the early centuries BC, it was, instead, 'darkest Europe', a vast expanse of forests and plains that, for the most part, lay outside the range of literate southerners.

Material remains offer us a crude overview of the region. From these and the study of placenames we deduce that the upper or the western Danube was within the heartlands of Celtica and that Celtic-speakers dwelt there. The lower Danube, however, was a rather different affair. From Hungary and running on through the Iron Gates where the river, caught between the Balkans and the Carpathians, narrows into a series of gorges, the Danube valley was controlled by other peoples including

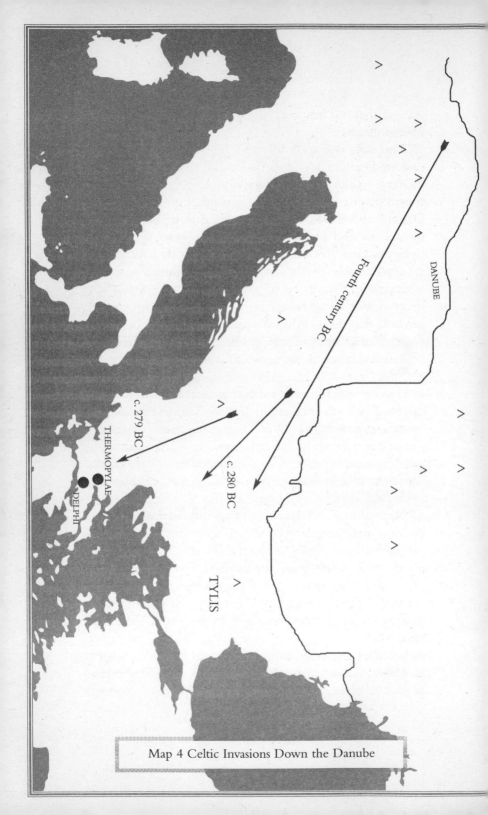

Map 4 Celtic Invasions Down the Danube

the tribal Thracians and the Greek-speaking Macedonians.

The wars that took place as the Celts moved into the eastern Danube are, for the most part, invisible to the modern world. Archaeologists do know that, from the fourth century, the boundary between the Celtic western Danube and the eastern Danube began to shift, items of metalwork and burial styles that we associate with the Celts moving towards the Black Sea. Of course, it is always possible that the Celts, at the pinnacle of their achievement, were being copied by awed non-Celtic peoples. But some fragments of southern writing show, instead, that this eastward spread of Celtic goods and customs reflects an actual eastward migration of Celts.

The evidence is slight but suggestive. We know, for example, that in 335 BC Alexander the Great had dealings with Celtic chieftains based in Illyria (the ex-Yugoslavia) that means that the tribes had infiltrated the Balkans. We know, too, a story recounted by an early writer concerning a trick that a group of Balkan-based Celts played. Inviting local dignitaries to a feast, they seasoned the food with a laxative and then attacked these visitors, easily massacring them in their discomforted state.

Nor were the Celtic invasions limited to the Balkans. We hear from an ancient historian that some Celtic tribes-people settled at Tylis in eastern Bulgaria, and remained there for a number of years, taxing the locals for the privilege of peace. In a desperate attempt to satisfy these parasitical newcomers, these locals took duty from ships passing through Pontus and into the Black Sea. We learn, meanwhile, from the study of placenames and archaeology that the Celts spread into Transylvania and Moldavia: a Romanian stone sculpture from this period has even been said to portray a druid.

Then there are hints that some Celts may have travelled still farther. A single Celtic-style tomb in northern Ukraine, not far from Chernobyl on the border with Byelorussia, suggests that one warband pushed on and into the first of the Asian Steppes, hundreds of green miles to the north. While another warband appears, on the basis of placename evidence, to have been sucked down the Silk Road ending up in what is today Kazakhstan. We cannot be sure quite what such surprising and out of the way finds mean. But what is clear is that, by the fourth century, the Celts had begun the long slide down the Danube corridor: a slide that would ultimately have important consequences for European and particularly for Roman history.

But why did the Celts move down the Danube? Two explanations are commonly given. The first is that the tribes did not jump, but rather that they were pushed. And to understand this we have to return for a moment to Italy. In Italy of the fourth and third century BC, the Romans had begun to defeat and, in some cases, to kill off the north Italian Celts, chief among these the Senones, who had been fighting Rome for the previous century. In c. 283 BC, the leader of the Senones, wantonly killed several Roman ambassadors. And the Romans were not inclined to let such a slight pass unnoticed, any memory of their own diplomatic improprieties at Chiusi having been forgotten. They sent their armies north and defeated the Senones. The Romans sold the Senones women and children into slavery, and slaughtered all the men except the chieftain, whom they reserved for torture.

Any of the Senones who survived must have fled to the north, towards the Alps, the same mountains from which their ancestors had emerged several centuries before. If these wars sent the Senones and other Italian

Celtic tribes scuttling north, then these escaping tribes will have bumped against other tribes, who will in turn have bumped into other tribes, until this tribal domino-toppling ended in the most eastern tribes being knocked along and out of the Danube.

But domino-toppling was not the only factor in migrations, there is also another explanation for the invasions: greed. In this period Celtic mercenaries began to show up on the shores of the Mediterranean to auction off their military expertise: they would soon feature in the armies of Greece, Carthage, Egypt, Syria and the various kingdoms of Asia Minor—bands of young braves selling themselves to the highest bidder for money and the promise of war. And these mercenaries, when returning home, of course, brought news of the enormous wealth of the south: wealth that would also have been reported by raiders and merchants. So the key to the new invasions may have lain not only in the tribal north, but also to the south of the Danube valley.

Greece especially cultivated wine and figs and other goods that reached the appreciative Celts. And its urban civilisation produced crafted items such as flagons or helmets that became fashionable among the tribes—a sign of prestige for those who possessed them. Then the Greeks sold too, in their emporia, red and white coral and spices from the Indian Ocean, not to mention silk from China. Given all this, it would hardly be surprising if a Celtic warrior salivated on so much as hearing the word 'Greece'. And perhaps the invasions that now followed were not the result of population pressures in and around the Alps—or not only. There may have also been the question of warbands along the Danube and in the Balkans being drawn like iron filings from out of the tribal mass towards the magnet of rich Greek cities to the south.

The entrance to Greece, the lock on the Greek gate, was the state of Macedonia. Though Greek-speaking, Macedonia was different from its Greek cousins to the south. It consisted of a series of towns in the coastal east and hundreds of miles of rich agricultural land: while, in the western highlands, the Macedonians were still very much a tribal people. It was perhaps the hybrid nature of Macedonia that meant that the normal Greek city-state model with an assembly and the occasional tyrant had been passed over. Instead, Macedonia was ruled by a king in close consultation with a council of nobles.

Fifty years before the first serious Celtic raids there, Macedonia had been the mightiest kingdom in Europe, possibly the mightiest in the world. Indeed, under its most notable king, Alexander the Great, it had conquered to the Ganges in India and into the mountains of Afghanistan: an achievement that makes Julius Caesar's later triumphs look like small change—Caesar, in fact, wept on comparing his own deeds with those of the Macedonian. But this enormous wedge of territory had been won by the genius of Alexander, not the colonial ability of the Macedonians or their Greek allies, and it fell apart on his death into a series of warring successor states.

Macedonia had previously enjoyed peaceful, polite relations with the Celtic tribes of the Danube: there are no records of early wars. Macedonian coins among the tribes suggest that there was trade and perhaps alliances in the time of Alexander's father, the vigorous Philip. Alexander had himself warned the Celts off his territory at the time of his wars of conquest, and all the indications are that the Celts took him at his word. But, after the collapse of Alexander's empire, Macedonia and Greece returned to their own straitened territories, enriched and weakened by their eastern adventures. For the Celtic warriors who were now on the lower Danube it was a combination of circumstances that they were unlikely to let pass by.

The first raid recorded by history came at the turn of the third century BC under a warleader with the name Cambaules. But, to the best of our knowledge, Cambaules limited himself to an attack on Macedonia's tribal neighbours, the Thracians, and felt, even then, that he had too few men to risk an all out invasion. As to a raid on Macedonia itself—it would have been an act of impertinence to attack a people, who, a mere generation before, had fought close to the Bay of Bengal, on the other side of Eurasia. However, in the next decades Macedonia declined from Empire to regional tough, and the Celtic warbands made a direct attack in the year 280 BC against both Macedonia and its Thracian neighbours, some grizzled veterans from Cambaules's army taking their place in the Celtic ranks.

The Macedonian army had earned a reputation for excellence in the previous century, making short work of even Persian Immortals and squadrons of Indian elephants. Its heavy cavalry was the *hetairoi*, known for routing entire armies, while the Macedonian heavy infantry held the enemy, pinning it down with long pikes and impenetrable shield walls. But the Celts of the Danube also used cavalry in their Greek campaigns and the opinion of the southerners was that Celtic warriors were more effective on horseback than on foot; an opinion shared, incidentally, by later Romans, who would teach Celtic horsemanship in their academies.

In any case, the Celts in their eastern wars had not only excellent cavalry, they also had an unusual system of reinforcement that caught the attention of the Greeks.

Each horseman was accompanied by two mounted grooms who would send another horse forward if their master's horse was killed or injured, or, when necessary, take the place of the rider himself. In this way Celtic warleaders would be able to guarantee a constant number of horses in the field, and also have effective reserves if there was a sudden retreat or any danger of outflanking. This detail of Celtic military organisation is a reminder of the potential sophistication of tribal armies and a warning that the Celts about to descend from the wilds were a worthy opponent for the Macedonians.

It was Macedonia's misfortune that they were ruled at this date by a monarch who was uninterested in such considerations. In 280 BC the first rumours of violence reached the Macedonian court, where one of Alexander's more mediocre successors, young Ptolemy 'the Thunderbolt', as he was rather absurdly styled, listened impatiently to reports of burnt settlements. Then, while preparations were being made to march out his troops, an embassy from the raiders arrived. The message was simple. The Celts would spare Macedonia if they were given money.

The Macedonian court and the leadership of the Celts were the representatives of two very different civilisations. And one of the dangers in any meeting between peoples with such different mind-sets was that the two sides, even with good translators and the best of intentions, simply would not understand each other. And this is what, in fact, happened in Macedonia in that fateful year. The Celts had asked for money to leave the territory of the Macedonians in peace: call it blackmail, bullying or Dane-geld—it was what it was. Ptolemy, instead, took it as a sign that the warbands had already been unnerved by the might of his kingdom and wanted out as quickly as

66

possible. He told them—and one can only imagine the haughty terms in which this was put—that he would accept their peace terms and let them go, if they handed their leaders over as hostages. The message was reportedly greeted with hilarity in the Celtic camp and Ptolemy decided to settle the matter martially.

> Only Ptolemy, king of Macedonia, heard of the coming of the Celts without concern... and he rallied out with a few untrained men to meet the Celts, thinking that wars might be carried out as easily as murders.
>
> There had come an embassy from the Dardanians [a tribal neighbour to Macedonia], with an offer of twenty thousand troops as allies. But Ptolemy turned them down insultingly, saying that the Macedonians would be in a poor state if they needed help from the Dardanians to defend their homeland—the Macedonians who had once conquered all the east, they who had the sons of the soldiers of Alexander in their force, that same Alexander who had won wars across the whole world! When this answer was brought to the King of the Dardanians he observed that famous Macedonia was about to be sacrificed to the imbecility of rash youth.

And the King of the Dardanians was right. Within days the Thunderbolt's head was being jolted around on the tip of a Celtic spear, while the Macedonian army had not only been humbled but humiliated in the field.

> When the news [of the defeat] was known throughout Macedonia, the Macedonians shut the

gates of their settlements and all mourned. Sometimes they lamented the death of children, sometimes they were paralysed with dread in case destruction be wrought on their cities; and, sometimes they called on Alexander and Philip [Alexander's father] as gods, asking them for protection, remembering that under these two they had not only been safe but had been world-conquerors. Would Alexander and Philip not defend their own country, a country whose name they had made famous by the glory of their deeds, and help the desperate people, ruined by the madness and impetuosity of Ptolemy?

But while all despaired... a Macedonian nobleman, deciding that prayers would do nothing, gathered those of fighting age and drove back the celebrating and victorious Celts, so saving Macedonia from utter devastation.

The invasions in Macedonia went no further. For the most part, the Celts crashed uselessly against the strong walls that protected the Macedonian cities in the east. But it had been an extraordinary campaign, the Macedonians, at best, fighting the invaders to a draw. Splitting into several war bands, the Celts had proved that they were quite the equal of the southerners, while the Macedonian army, that had once careered through half a dozen eastern empires, had been knocked to the ground by tribesmen. For Athens and Sparta and Corinth, meanwhile, and for all the other Greek cities to the south, here was the first sign that the Celts had designs on their possessions. And, in fact, the raid proved to be but the first tiding of a new war that would not now be long in coming.

In 279 BC, two years after the king-killing attack on Macedonia, a pair of Celtic raiding parties, each numbering tens of thousands, descended from the hills. The Macedonians, quickly saw their revived national army brushed aside and were able to do nothing but close themselves in their towns and cities and wait. The first of the Celtic warbands ravaged Macedonian territory determined to finish off what had been begun at the time of Ptolemy's death. It is possible that they had been so encouraged by their previous success that they now wished to conquer and settle. However, far more dangerous for the delicate balance of power in the region were the movements of the second warband that may have been as many as two-hundred-thousand strong. This second warband passed into Greece proper, tempted by stories of rich cities and wealthy temples.

5

INTO GREECE

n the early fifth century BC, the Persian Empire had sent two separate armies to beat the Greeks and especially the Athenians into submission. The resulting wars and sea battles checked Persian expansion into Europe before it had begun and were the subject of Herodotus's *Histories*. It was the boast of the Greeks for centuries, and it is the boast of many Greeks today, that they alone of all the peoples of the Eastern Mediterranean had been able to halt the Persian steam roller. And understandably enough, the Celts who came down into Greece were now compared to the Persian invaders of two centuries before. Here was a new challenge from outside the bounds of civilisation, a new invasion to be heroically blunted and broken. But the Greeks also noticed a difference. The Persians had wanted dominion over the Greek lands. They had wanted the symbolic gifts of earth and water that would show that the Greeks accepted Persian rule. If the Greeks had ever given these gifts, they would have been welcomed into the Persian Empire and the war would have ceased and taxes begun. But, from the outset, it was understood that the Celts were not interested in domination. There was no empire to join, no imperial ambassadors to surrender to or even to negotiate with, no taxes to be levied. The Celts wanted only to destroy and pillage. This was not a warband sent out to settle, but one that was to raid for gold and other goods.

Against this kind of violence, concerted action was necessary. In other circumstances it would have been Macedonia that offered leadership: the Greek city states had been, for most of the previous century, dominated, even ruled, by Alexander's kingdom. However, as the Celts rode so easily over the Greeks' northern suzerain and down into the Greeks' own valleys, the city states realised that if they were to act they must act alone. It was then Athens, the major power in central Greece and, arguably, still at this date the mightiest Greek city, that took the lead and gathered armies from the different Greek communities. And Athens collected these troops at famous Thermopylae, the rocky gateway to Greece. Two centuries before, when protecting their country from a Persian invasion, the Greeks had found that this narrow mountainous pass acted as a bottleneck that could be easily defended. (Indeed, three hundred Spartans led by the Spartan Leonidas had temporarily held the pass against a Persian army several hundred times its size.) Then, when the fortifications at Thermopylae had been secured, the Greeks confidently rode out and destroyed bridges on the Spercheius, the river to the north of Thermopylae, so that the Celts would have to fight even to reach the peaks beyond.

Usually records of wars between the northern barbarians and Mediterranean peoples break down into patronising accounts by the southerners about the superior tactics of their fellow-countrymen against hordes of irrational, hysterical savages. But as Pausanias,

71

our best source for this invasion, notes, the Celtic leader 'was not entirely stupid nor without experience for a barbarian'; and this, given the unwilling praise of the Greek, perhaps meant that the Celtic warleader was a gifted general. The Celts detached as many as ten thousand warriors from their army, the tallest and best men, and sent them at night to a higher part of the river. There these warriors, either by swimming or paddling across on their large shields, came to the far bank without any resistance and threatened to get around the Greeks who had rallied out to meet the invader with such optimism. The first trick of the campaign had gone to the Celts and the Greeks rapidly retreated to the cliffs above. The Celts did not manage to sack even a city in this territory: like many barbarians they were better at battles than sieges. But they did kill any Greeks that they discovered working in the fields, and then set themselves resolutely towards their enemies in the mountains to the south.

Thermopylae, which had held up even the mighty Persian army for a time, was to prove more challenging than a mere river however. The warbands, at first, did not take the defences very seriously. Starting at daybreak they swarmed towards the narrow pass, with their accustomed noise. But the Greeks had prepared their positions and were not intimidated by the howling warriors, no matter how numerous, because only a few could reach them at a time. The polished stone of the pass made the Celts' horses slip and rendered them useless in the battle. Then, when the Celtic foot-soldiers smashed into the regimented hoplite lines, they hardly dented these lines, distracted by javelins, stones and arrows sent by the enemy standing behind the vanguard. Aiming at the pressed crowds of northerners, the Greeks could hardly miss. In fact, the Celts suffered terribly as they moved in, protected only by bucklers, having little armour and few helmets and being crushed in the unforgiving confines of the ravine. But this was, in no way, the end of their woes as the Athenians sailed their triremes close to the coast and showered arrows onto the northerners from behind.

The Greeks were impressed by Celtic courage—we hear of injured northerners pulling out spears from their bodies and hurling them back at the enemy. But, at the same time, the Greeks saw in the disorder of the attack the blind, furious rage of the barbarian that would be his undoing. This anger was a commonplace in southern writing on the Celts: one author even suggested that to defeat this people it was first necessary to make them lose their temper so that they would lose with it the little reason with which nature had endowed them. We may doubt that the Celtic warriors were quite so in the thrall of rage. But there can be no question that their first attempt on the pass of Thermopylae had been a miserable failure and, as they disengaged and limped back in their desire to get out of the reach of Greek missiles, many were trampled to death by their fellow tribesmen. Forty Greeks died in this first battle. No number is given for the Celts, but we gather that many, many times more perished in their failed advance—hundreds or even thousands. The Greeks, in the meantime, awaited messengers for a parley. The Celts might now wish to leave their territory, they would certainly wish to collect their dead and give them a respectable burial. But no ambassador came to the Greeks, underlining the horrible strangeness of this northern people who cared not even for the corpses of their comrades.

The Celts, if dispirited by the failure of their hammer-blow attack, were clearly satisfied that their dead would not need burial to make their way to the battlegrounds of eternity. Instead, they set about planning a further assault, showing now rather more cunning than the Greeks would have wished to give them credit for, even if it was cunning of a most diabolical kind. Knowing that an important part of the Greek coalition came from Aetolia, on their side of Thermopylae, tribesmen went to turn over that city's territory and to destroy the town of Callia. The resulting acts would be described today as racial cleansing: 'the fate of the inhabitants of Callia is the most evil ever heard of... every male was slain, killed both the old and children on the breast... those [women] who survived suffered under tyrannical violence every form of abuse from men lacking pity or love.' The Aetolians were lured away from the pass by these terrible reports. They did reach their home and did punish the invaders, but the Greek army had been compromised and weakened at a dangerous moment. And, shortly after the Aetolians departed, the Celts at Thermopylae managed to 'persuade' a group of locals to show them a secret path to slip around the defences. It would not be force but guile that would allow them to conquer the pass that had defied the Persians for so long. And, as little as a week after the initial, disastrous battle, the Celts crept around the Greek hoplites and poured down behind them, hidden by an unexpected summer mist that had rolled across the hills.

That innocent detail concerning the mist, which finishes the account of the Celts at Thermopylae, gives the historian pause for thought. Mist, of course, appears in mountainous zones all the time. But the production of mist on the battlefield was said by certain later writers to be the prerogative of the druids, the priests of the Celts. So was this mist a meteorological fact, remembered by one of the trapped Greeks? Or is it a Celtic fiction or half fiction taken from a tribal informant in the Balkans, interviewed when the Greeks themselves were writing up the story of this epic war? As we have seen with the question of the sack of Rome, the ancient Celts did not remember things historically. They mythically arranged the past and this meant that legend and fact easily blended together. The southerners did not, however, appreciate the danger of false history and uncritically took up details from the oral sagas of the north as if they were historical truth. That is why a Celtic Hercules, the mythical Raven, was believed by the Romans to have been the leader of the Celtic attack on Rome. The Romans had listened to Celtic stories about that event and they had taken too much on trust.

The same thing happened with the Celtic attack on Greece. Yet again in this war, the Celtic leader was said to be named 'Raven'. And just in case there is the doubt that perhaps this was a second Raven, a historical Raven named after the original Celtic hero, this Greek-raiding Raven is actually credited with some of the deeds that Raven is known for in Celtic legend. There is only one conclusion possible. The Celts in the fourth century were already including their divine heroes in the oral retelling of the invasion of Greece. Several other names of Celtic chieftains from the raid seem to be taken from Celtic mythology. And when the Greeks came to recount what had happened, they evidently took these names from their Celtic informants, as the Romans had done when Raven was found at the head of the Senones.

The invasion of Greece certainly took place. But how many of the incidental details such as the mist are true? For example, when Pausanias mentions the expertise of the Celtic leader at the river Spercheius he is speaking of Raven. Does this mean that we should discard the information, or should we suppose that there was another Celtic leader behind the mythical name who was a fine tactician? It is now, as we reach the climax of the invasion and the Celtic army moves towards the Temple of Delphi, that such questions become especially urgent.

Delphi, the most famous of all the temples of Greece. The first temple there had been built, according to antique accounts, to the south of Thermopylae with the branches of bay trees. The second was made—and here we are reminded that the Greeks had no need of Celtic legend to confuse their own histories—by bees using beewax and feathers: but blew away to the north of Europe in a gale. The third was of bronze with supporting pillars and strange bird-like creatures perched atop who sang epiphanies—the gods destroyed it, concerned that worshippers would become hypnotised by such unearthly music. The fourth temple had been built by two Greek heroes Trophonius and Agamedes, only to be burnt in 548 BC. The fifth and the last temple was constructed in impressive marble—its supporting wall survives to this day—with phrases of Apollonian wisdom written over the portals: 'Avoid Excess' and 'Know Thyself'. The site on which these different incarnations of the Temple had arisen was the same: a natural fortress on Mount Parnassus surrounded by vertical drops. It would have been almost as easy to persuade bees to build another temple there as to haul the necessary marble up to its heights. It was and is a dramatic location. 'The central place has the form of an amphitheatre and, as a result, if you shout or trumpets are blown, the sound echoes and re-echoes on the rocks and is heard many times, louder than at first. The effect on those ignorant of the reason is one of overpowering awe…'

Delphi was the premiere religious centre of the

Greeks. It was believed to be the *omphalos* or belly-button of the world and pilgrims came here to pay their respects to Apollo, the god of sunlight and of genius. And when these pilgrims had trod the weary paths towards the heights, Apollo spoke not to them, but to one of his servants, a woman who lived there. The medium would, on payment of a fee, go to a large tripod and sit on its top. From a distance an official would then announce the question of the supplicant and the medium, hearing the god's voice within, would shout back Apollo's riddling reply that had to be rendered into hexameter verse by a priest. Scholars have argued for years about whether this divine communication was caused by hallucinogenic bay leaves, mineral gasses, auto-suggestion or sheer dishonesty. But what mattered was that the Greeks believed, sending embassies there to ask questions of Apollo and leaving gold for the god's trouble—and that eventually they were mimicked by other nations, including the Romans, various Asian and African peoples and allegedly the Celts themselves. In fact, it is an irony, considering what was about to befall the temple, that Apollo was said to spend half the year among the Celts. He flew north—it was claimed—to their distant homelands and dwelt in the temple of bee's wax and feathers that had been blown to barbarian Europe centuries before.

We cannot be certain why, Thermopylae behind them, the Celts showed such enthusiasm to sack the Temple of Delphi when there were so many other Greek cities and towns close by. It is unlikely that they made the journey to see the gnomic phrases written over the portals: words that they would not have been able to read. Perhaps there was, instead, a desire to stand at the centre of the world and blow an enormous raspberry. Or, more likely, it was

77

that Delphi's reputation for wealth had gone far beyond the borders of Greece. Already in perhaps 700 BC the warrior hero Achilles was made to speak admiringly in *The Iliad* of the riches that had been left over the years in the temple. And, by 279 BC, though Delphi's reputation had fallen away somewhat, the gold kept rolling in and 'many were the rich gifts of kings and peoples that are to be seen there, which in their magnificence, bear witness to the gratitude of those that have paid their vows.'

The Celts may too have made the assumption that a temple would be easier to raid than a city or town. But if the Celts did make that assumption they were mistaken. The facts about what happened at Delphi are rather difficult to get at because here, suitably enough as we near the sacred confines, legend grows at the expense of history. But some points can be established. First, the weather turned against the invaders: it snowed. Second, there are hints in our sources that the chieftains had lost control of the army by the time they reached the temple. The tribesmen hungry, and presumably cold, beat their way around the countryside looking for food and wine on which they got drunk, the attack having to be delayed as a result. Then, third, when the final assault came, the temple authorities had managed to gather as many as four thousand Greeks together to defend the heights against the tribesmen.

> And so the Delphians supported by the might of their allies prepared their settlement, before the Celts, holding their wine-skins, could be brought back to their battle-lines... Raven, to give courage to his men, pointed out the enormous spoil before them, telling them that the statues and four-horse chariots [of the temple], of which many were

78

visible at that distance, were made of purest gold and that they would prove greater prizes when weighed than they appeared to the eye. The Celts, excited by these claims and yet without order, a result of the wine that they had drunk the day before, charged into battle without any fear.

In this contest between the two armies, the priests of the temples along with the priestesses with their hair hanging loose... came frantically forward trembling, to the very vanguard, to tell how the god [Apollo] had come and that they had seen him jump into the temple from the roof... and that two armed virgins coming from the nearby temples of Artemis and Athena had met them. These they had seen not only with their eyes, but they had also heard the noise made by a bow and the rattling weapons.... Excited by these encouragements, the Greeks all went keenly to the battle where they also saw the proof of divinity for a part of the mountain loosened by an earthquake, smashed down on a party of the Celts.... The warleader Raven unable to stand the pain of his wounds, killed himself with a dagger...

This will not be to the taste of those who prefer descriptions of wars without gods wading among the mortals— we have here not only Apollo, but also Artemis and Athena ('two armed virgins') making an appearance for the Greek side. But it communicates the ferocity of the battle and its outcome. The author, Pausanias, goes on to tell us that, after the assault had ended in failure, the warbands killed their own wounded and turned back towards their Balkan homes.

In the words quoted above, lurks a mythological

version of events that is, in its way, far more remarkable than our few facts. The priests of Delphi, so the story goes, had asked their god what they should do as the Celts moved towards them. And the answer came that Apollo himself would take care of the Temple. Not surprisingly, then, the Greeks tell of long dead heroes, gods and goddesses striding onto the battlefield. Apollo, Artemis and Athena are seen, and priests actually hear the twang of a divine bow. But it is a peculiarity of this battle that the Celts and Greeks both summoned their divinities and immortals to war—for, on the other side, we also have Raven.

Of course, in legends gods often fight other immortals either directly or through proxy human allies. But here, uniquely in ancient record, we have a battle where representatives of two different pantheons, two different religious systems, meet and cross their magic swords. These events and their outcomes justly reflect those in the tangible world. Apollo and his sisters went back to their perpetual frolics, whereas Raven was to be carried away dead. Another source reports he had been mortally wounded by an arrow, perhaps one of Artemis' darts. And the fates of Raven and the children of Zeus give a more satisfying idea about what actually happened at Delphi than the muddled historical details that have been passed down to us—drunk armies, snowstorms and the like.

The most beautiful memorial of the Celtic attack on Greece is a hymn. Though written two decades after the attack, the part quoted here was composed as if a prophecy, looking forward, rather than backwards to the invasion. Its tone captures admirably the terror of the war, the impression of countless tribesmen, not to mention their intimidating size, and the final disintegration of the warbands. 'I tell you that there will come in the future a struggle in which we [Greeks] will all fight together, when the lifting of the savage sword and Celtic battle, today's titans, will fall upon us like snow from the farthest west, as many as the stars when at their thickest they cover the sky... And we will see smoke come up from a neighbour's burning home, not just hear of it. Then, at the Temple [of Delphi], there will be the armies of enemies... And the hated spear that will drag on their owners, the mindless tribe of the Celts on a journey which ends in pain.' Pain, that is for the Celts who were racing back through the Greek countryside towards their own lands, the enemy, emboldened now that all danger was past, closing in on every side.

The mountainous terrain, the unfriendly weather and the constant, stinging charges in their rear quickly took effect on the retreating northerners. On one of the first nights of their retreat, the tension, instead of draining away, was exacerbated to the point of hysteria. A troop of warriors heard, or thought that they heard, horses galloping and, believing themselves attacked, rose up in the dark with their weapons. Somehow, in the confusion, they fell upon a neighbouring band. By now men were, in any case, also dying from lack of food: 'fate was not kind to the pathetic fleers, mercilessly hunting them down with cruel nights, terrifying days and punishing them with endless rain, snow and hungry exhaustion.' The Greeks kept the tribesmen away from the pastures and fields where they could gather food. And, as the Celts passed north, more and more were caught in attacks. A Celtic warband had been left near Thermopylae to guard booty and leave the door to Greece ajar. But the Greeks routed this troop so that it would have proved difficult for any of the Celtic warriors returning from Delphi to make their way into Macedonia. The Greek writer Pausanias states that not a single one of the invaders returned home from the attack on the Temple—cursed as they were. This is probably an exaggeration, but may have been tolerably close to the truth. It had been a campaign that the Celts would have done better to forget.

And yet, the curious thing is that they did not. We have already seen how Raven was smuggled into the story of the attack on Delphi. This can only mean that the Celts themselves were telling stories about the Greek raid in the generations that followed. The survivors, or those who had been too young to join in the war, wished to immortalise the warriors that had died. This Celtic retelling of the war echoes down through the centuries. It has even been suggested that details from it appear in *Branwen*, a British-Celtic folk-tale written down fifteen hundred years later—though with the Balkans replaced by Wales and Delphi replaced by the palace of the king of Ireland.

Another curious memory of the invasion of Greece is found in a Roman account. A century later, a Roman general Caepio fought against a Celtic tribe in Gaul and triumphed over them. Part of his spoils included a pool that the tribe had used to throw ritual objects in. Pools like this were clogged with valuables—'rocks of hammered silver' are mentioned—and, in other cases, the Roman state had actually auctioned off ritual lakes to the highest bidder. Caepio greedily sent divers and dredgers and took what treasures he could and there he found items from the shrine at Delphi stolen by the warbands a century before. It is an unlikely-sounding story—the shrine was, after all, not taken. But there is the fact that this treasure was recovered in the territory of a tribe in Gaul, a branch of which is believed to have taken part in the raid on Greece. The curse of Delphi was said to have engulfed the avaricious Roman general: he died in exile and his daughters were reduced to selling themselves as prostitutes.

However, the invasion of the Celts into the Balkans and Greece had far more important consequences than the ruin of Caepio's daughters. The first and the most important concerned Rome. This may at first seem strange as the city on the Tiber has barely figured in this narrative. Yet Rome, the master of Italy, still not an empire at this date, but already looming over the ancient world, was one of a series of regional superpowers in the Mediterranean. At the beginning of the third century BC Rome would have identified the Greek world—especially united under Macedonia—as a danger to its imperial ambitions and a guard keeping the legions out of the east; at the very date of the Celtic invasion Greek soldiers were fighting the Romans in Italy. But the Celts had put an end to any pretensions of that kind by killing a Macedonian king and harassing the entire territory twice. Macedonia was now nothing more than the first among equals in the Balkans, standing a little higher than the various Greek city states that had seen off the invasion. Again Celtic raids, invasions and migrations had worked in the Romans' favour. The Greeks would not, from then on, be a serious preoccupation for the Senate and People of Rome. Indeed, they would be greedily sucked up after several one-sided wars. Barbarian-inspired confusion had brought Europe and near-Asia a step closer to Roman rule. The second effect concerned the Celts themselves. The Celtic migrations of the third century, whether driven by ambition or necessity, had opened up the east to the Celts. Celtic warriors would now cross the Bosporus, moving into Asia Minor, present-day Turkey, destabilising yet another region.

83

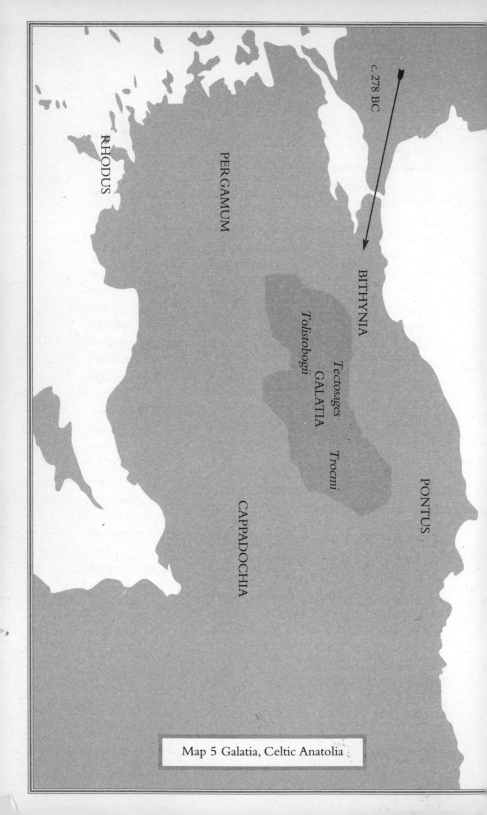

Map 5 Galatia, Celtic Anatolia

6

INTO ASIA MINOR

he Celtic warband that crossed the Hellespont in 278 BC was not the first Celtic grouping to pass into Asia, nor even the furthest travelling. They had possibly been preceded by Celts in the Ukraine and central Asia and, a half-century before, a party of Celtic ambassadors had gone to distant Babylon (just outside modern Baghdad) and had amazed the court there with their strange north European weapons. But the warband of 278 BC was the most significant of all the Celtic-speakers who would visit that continent. Their warleaders were to carve out a kingdom, Galatia, that would enjoy generations of independent rule in Asia Minor. Their descendants would continue to speak a Celtic tongue for perhaps a millennium. Alone among the Celtic-speaking peoples, the Galatians, as the Asian Celts were called, insinuated their way into the New Testament and the works of Asian writers of antiquity. They are, too, a warning against the idea that the Celts as a tribal people were no match for their southern city-dwelling cousins on the Mediterranean. While southern writers—Asian and European—tended to portray the Galatians as a savage and ineffectual people, the Galatians' impressive record in war and, above all, the fact that they prospered in an alien territory, tells a different and altogether more interesting story.

That alien territory in which the eastward-migrating Celts found themselves was Asia Minor or Anatolia (from the Greek word for east), in effect modern Turkey. Asia Minor has been, throughout its history, a meeting place between orient and occident and this was especially true in antiquity. On the western, Europe-facing coast of the peninsula there were various Greek cities—a Greek-speaking population would survive there until the Greco-Turkish wars of the early twentieth century. These cities were in constant interaction with Greece and were governed by popular assemblies and the occasional tyrant. Inland, on the first of the Anatolian Highlands, were the 'decadent' Lydians, whose most famous king had been Croesus. His reputation for riches owes something to the Lydians' extensive mining of precious metals (they were said to have been the first people to mint gold and silver coins). In the inner Highlands there were the Phrygians, a people who had come as raiders from the far north: but who had settled down into a quiet and undemanding town life—their earliest king was the legendary Midas whose touch was cursed. Then, in the east, there were various other peoples, Asian and otherwise, including Hittites, 'White Syrians', Thracians and Jews—indeed, one of the most famous of all Jews, Paul of New Testament fame, was born in Tarsus in Asia Minor.

Cicero later wrote approvingly, as might be guessed of a territory that had hosted both Midas and Croesus, of the wealth of Asia Minor. The land, he said, 'was so rich and so fertile that in the greatness of its harvest, the variety of its goods, the size of its herds and flocks and the numbers of its exports it stands above every other country'—a reputation assured by its saffron, its figs and its incense exported to all corners of the Mediterranean. But the mix of different peoples also produced an extraordinarily variegated culture. So there were the castrated priests of the mountain goddess Cybele, a wide-hipped divinity who wandered the peaks of Anatolia, throwing worshippers into ecstasy. There were the peasants who began 'legal action' against the Meander—the endlessly turning river from which we get our verb 'to meander'—because it changed course and so stole their land. There was the flesh-eating lime-stone of Phrygia, the *sarcophagus*, that was used extensively in *mausolea* (two other words that comes from the region) to reduce the dead to hard skinless bones. And there were the obscene pottery trinkets sold in the city of Cnida where the temple of Venus had been built, so that the goddess's nude, stone-carved form could be enjoyed from every angle. The ruins of Troy could be visited, too, not to mention three of the seven wonders of the world, including the Colossus, a statue over the harbour at Rhodes that had been finished the year before the Celts arrived in Asia and that stood almost as high as the Statue of Liberty.

This territory had been overrun by empire after empire in the early centuries BC, the Persians and the Hittites among them. But when the Celts landed on the shores of Anatolia the most recent magnate to control the land mass had been Alexander the Great. On Alexander's death, Asia Minor had broken free from Macedonian control, as almost all the rest of the collapsing empire. Then it had fragmented into four different kingdoms: Pontus, Cappadochia, Bithynia and

Pergamum. It would be a relief to write that these four kingdoms corresponded to four different ethnic groups. But they did not. History in ancient Asia Minor was never that simple. These four were a reflection rather of the ability of local monarchs to intimidate the inhabitants of the valleys and plains in which they found themselves. This was a world, in fact, of fractured and fracturing fiefdoms, trying to get one up on their kingly neighbours, to ignore threats and blandishments from the east and the Greek-speaking world to the west, where Alexander's successors hovered like greedy vultures, and sometimes there was the difficult job of putting down rival claimants within the kingdom itself. In these wars for survival and aggrandisement, it was natural that the monarchs of Asia Minor—kings who, as we have seen, had a reputation for wealth—would look outside their own realm to strengthen their armies with foreign mercenaries.

A divided country, large sums of money and regular wars—it would be difficult to write a tour guide that would have made Asia Minor more alluring to a wandering Celtic tribe. In fact, the people that were to become the Galatians either sailed to Anatolia as mercenaries or they were employed as hired swords shortly after their arrival. There was nothing exceptional about this, but hiring Celts was a risky business. The problem was not merely the characteristic self-interest of mercenaries. In the ancient and medieval world mercenaries were responsible for the fall of scores of dynasties and realms. There was also the obsessive Celtic love of war as an end in itself—war for war's sake—that was so unfamiliar to anything that the near Asian world knew and that made any relationship between an urban, urbane employer and a tribal chieftain a tense and potentially dangerous affair. So, for example, the Carthaginian general Hannibal used Celtic allies, but would disguise himself with wigs when in their presence to avoid being attacked.

The Asian king who invited the Galatians into the peninsula was Nicomedes, lord of Bithynia, the north-western kingdom, the forested plain along the Black Sea. Bithynia had several important cities, but tribes also lingered on, tribes of Thracian descent that can never have been easy to rule. Then, to add to problems of ungovernable subjects, Nicomedes was being threatened from the east by the Seleucid Emperors of Asia who had, the year before the Celts arrived, marched an army into his territory. He suffered too from family difficulties. His brother Zipoites had risen in revolt against Nicomedes' rule. And Zipoites, who may have taken exception to the fact that Nicomedes had killed two of their brothers, had enjoyed some success. In this grave situation, facing enemies on every side, Nicomedes made the decision to have a Celtic warband move into his territory and help him restore order. We are told that these Celts—the future Galatians—were over twenty-thousand strong, though this included non-combatants (wives, the old, families...) dragged along in the tribal migration. But even if there were only ten thousand warriors, Nicomedes must still have watched the approach of this mighty army with mixed emotions.

As it happens, Nicomedes did not regret his choice. Certainly his reign was impressively long by the standards of Anatolia—he defeated his brother and his armies were to threaten neighbouring states for several decades more. But Nicomedes' heirs must have often cursed the decision to invite the mercenaries in. For this Celtic warband did not remain under the control of the kings of the north west. Instead, within a generation of arriving in Bithynia, the Celts had decided to put down roots. The kingdoms of ancient Asia Minor ran to the centre of the land mass like spokes of a wheel. And it was here, at the very axle, that the Celtic warband settled in a land that was called Galatia after them from the Greek word for 'Gaul', a synonym for 'Celt' in antique writers. But Galatia—the Gaul of Asia—was a land like no land the Celts had visited before. Verging on desert, its mountainous terrain where few crops could grow and only ravenous sheep survived was something new even to those far-travelling warriors who had seen the Danube, Thermopylae and the Black Sea. Its two most important exports were wool and slaves and, we are told by the Roman historian Livy, that, as there were not trees or kindling, locals had to burn sheep droppings to keep warm.

But the choice of this territory proved an inspired one. The highlands offered excellent defensive opportunities. This land also had wonderful potential for booty-hunting; for the newcomers, by placing themselves in the middle of Asia Minor, had created a raiding paradise with good stealing at every point of the compass. And, from this raiding paradise they divided up the surrounding kingdoms—giving them out to their various chiefs as tribute territory—much as mafia dons today assign each other city districts to milk, even bullying money out of distant Syria. 'So great was the fear they inspired in all nations west of the Taurus, that even those who had no experience of the Celts as well as those who had met them before, the most distant as well as their closest neighbours, all alike submitted'.

It will come as no surprise to learn that among the more pacific Asians these raiders quickly earned a reputation for violence. Recent digs at Gordium in Galatia (where, a century before the Celts' arrival, Alexander had cut the Gordian knot) have suggested that the Celts brought their rituals of human sacrifice to the region—several skeletons have been found buried with dogs in a characteristically north European fashion. With such terrifying customs and their readiness for war, the Galatians were able to fleece the kingdoms of Anatolia.

Tellingly, only a handful of Asian monarchs managed to force the Celts back without ransom. One of these was Antiochus 1st, the son of a general of Alexander, who was given the title of *Soter* or 'Saviour' for his rare victory over the Galatians. Antiochus stunned the warbands by bringing an unfamiliar animal, elephants, onto the battlefield. One other of the Galatians' rare failures is recorded in the most famous of all antique representations of a Celt: 'the Dying Gaul.' The statue of a naked warrior crouching, living through his last moments, agony written across his face and his twitching muscles. This work was likely made in Pergameum, a Greek coastal city in Asia Minor, to celebrate a failed Celtic attack. But, even if the Celts were sometimes defeated, they were a constant irritant and their commanding position effectively frustrated all attempts to unite the territory. If the normal rules of ancient history had been followed in Anatolia, eventually, one of the kingdoms would have started to absorb its neighbours and build itself into a pan-Anatolian power. But the Galatians standing at the very heart of Asia Minor, kept all their neighbours weak. The effects of this for both the history of Anatolia, and for the increasingly Roman Mediterranean, would be important.

So far we have referred in a generic way to 'the

Galatians'. But the ancient geographer Strabo, himself from Asia Minor, tells us that the warband hired by Nicomedes had originally included three tribes: the Trocmi, the Tolistobogii and the Tectosages. Here are words that bring us far away from Asia and back to the Celtic heartlands. The name 'Tolistobogii' also belonged to a Celtic tribe on the edge of Marseilles in southern Gaul. And, given the way that tribes divided and migrated, it is only natural to assume that the Galatian and the Gaulish tribes were related in some way.

Even more interesting is the name Tectosages that is best translated into modern English as 'the Searchers for Booty', a reasonable enough title for a raiding band. There was a tribe named the Vosges Tectosages in south-western France: this was the same tribe that had allegedly thrown gold from the raid on Greece into their sacred lake. There is evidence too for a Celtic tribe known as the Tectosages in southern Germany. And, as we see here, the Tectosages had settled in Asia Minor. One of the chief cities in their territory was modern Ankara. Had the Gaulish Tectosages sent out a group of their young warriors who had conquered in Germany? And had this tribe in turn sent out a group of young men who raided down the Danube and then into Asia Minor? Things may not have been as neat as this, but there is the possibility of some link between these groups.

Of the kingdom of Galatia we know a surprising amount. In fact, we know more about how the Galatians organised themselves than we do about any other part of the Celtic world at this early date, because they settled in a region with literate neighbours on every side. We know, for example, that each of the three tribes was divided into four smaller groups. These would have been the clans or sub-tribes that we also find in Britain, Ireland, Gaul and other parts of Celtica. Each of these clans had its own chief, its own judge and a warleader. And there were also three hundred councillors or tribal elders— presumably one hundred for each tribe—to be consulted for decisions. These likely represented the next step down in Celtic social organisation, for, if each tribe was made up of a series of clans, then each clan was made up of a series of large, extended families. In the medieval laws of Celtic Wales and of Celtic Ireland we can just pick out the traces of an ancient Celtic legal system. This system was based squarely on the extended family and included all those who shared a common great-great-great-grandfather—easily a hundred or a hundred and fifty individuals in a tribal society.

It is tempting to say that the tribe was the yard, the clan the foot, and the extended family the inch of ancient Celtic society. In outline, this was true. But things were not as simple as these suspiciously symmetrical numbers would have us believe. So we know that different clans typically fought among themselves for influence and, above all, to head the tribe as a whole. We know that extended families also fought among themselves for domination of the clan. And we know that there were conflicts between brothers for control of important families. Not all were equally strong. Indeed, some clans and families were so weak that they were permanently in submission to others. When we think of Celtic social organisation, instead of yards, feet and inches, we need therefore to think of an irregular and ill-fitting series of shifting numbers and units. We should also remember that by definition any Galatian born into such a society will have felt loyalty to three different groups. Sometimes his or her loyalty will have been strained in one direction or another as civil war broke out.

This already fragmented and chaotic world was criss-crossed by other ties of loyalty. Battle-leaders gathered around them warriors who came from their own families and clans, and also warriors from others. These warriors were bound to this leader by his aristocratic blood and his ability to provide feasts, drink and gold. Or as Caesar put it: 'those most distinguished by birth and wealth have the largest number of vassals and clients about them. [The Celts] acknowledge only this as influence and power.' We do not have any straightforward comments for such vassalry in Galatia. Most of the descriptions of such relations come from Gaul or from Dark Age Celtic Ireland. But there is one especially interesting passage relating to Asia Minor that reports how a noble set up feeding points around the country, inviting the local population and passers-by to partake of 'every kind of meat' for a year in a series of temporary feasting halls that each seated over four hundred. In this report we likely have the attempt of a Galatian leader to bring warriors into his personal retinue by showing that he could share the bounty of his fortune with them. With traditions like this no wonder that, in the region, 'to eat like a Galatian' came to mean 'to stuff yourself'.

We learn that at certain times the twelve Galatian clan leaders and the three hundred elders came together to discuss issues of common concern and to judge murder in an assembly. Did then the Celts in Asia Minor operate something akin to a democracy? Again we know from other parts of the Celtic world that tribes did have such meetings. But one man, one vote this certainly was not and it is extremely unlikely that the three hundred repre-sentatives had been chosen by ballot. There were, though, rules and debate. In Gaul, Celtic tribesmen who spoke out of turn in assemblies were approached by an assembly official, the speaker if you like, and told to be quiet. And if · they persisted in their rowdiness their weapon was cut from them as a sign of dishonour. And rowdiness there evidently was. One Greek author reports that, to soothe the attendants in assemblies, calming music was played as the different factions spoke out. This kind of tribal democracy proved not only noisy, but wide open to abuse as when, for example, one Celt appeared to be judged for a crime, but brought with him ten thousand sworn-warriors to ensure that he was not found guilty.

There is another detail about the gatherings of the Galatians, the name of their meeting place: the Drunemetum, a quintessentially Celtic word that meant the Holy Glade of Oaks and would be better suited to the Celtic west than remote Turkey. Regrettably, we do not know where in Galatia this place was, but an educated guess would be that it was near the centre of the territory so that representatives of the three tribes could easily go there. Certainly, in several Celtic regions there were such central meeting places where tribal representatives could talk together. So, for example, in Gaul there was Carnutes (modern Chartres in France) where the druids met once a year. It has been suggested that Oxford (of all places) served a similar purpose in Britain, and Milan or 'the Middle Place' in northern Italy, and Tara in Ireland. At these meetings at the Holy Glade of Oaks in Galatia, we might even wonder if there were not druids among the elders, perhaps as judges (the druids did sometime act as judges in Celtic Gaul), as the oak was a tree connected with the druids. One medieval source even tells us that the druids would eat acorns

95

before prophesying, and the tribes settled in Galatia had ultimately come from lands where the druids were respected and wielded power.

7

THE GALATIANS AND ROME

he first generations in Galatian history, from 280-190 BC, grew up with seasonal raids and vain defensive efforts on the part of neighbours. However, rumbling on the horizon there was a more serious foe, one that threatened to end the independence of Galatia—Rome. The Romans had come a long way from the bumbling city army that had failed against the Senones two hundred years before. They had taken up the burden of empire in Italy—that by this date they controlled completely. They had smashed the power of Carthage, their most convincing rival in the southern Mediterranean, and now they were turning against Greece and the successors of Alexander in the east.

And, for these imperially-minded Romans, wealthy Asia Minor was as tempting a proposition as it had been for the Celts, so much so that in 189 BC their legions arrived to conquer it. The Galatians were unconcerned when they first heard the rumour that Roman arms had arrived in the region, they reasoned that they lived too far from the sea to be endangered by the invaders. The Romans, on the other hand, were unnerved by the thought of an encounter with the Galatians. The Celts, after all, were among their oldest and most dangerous enemies. The only enemy that had ever managed to burn Rome.

The Roman general Gnaeus Manlius Vulso, preparing his men for campaign against these eastern Gauls, is said to have admitted as much in a speech: 'I know all too well, men, that of all the peoples of Asia the Galatians have the finest military reputation. This ferocious nation, after wandering and fighting their wars through almost the whole world, have come to dwell among the most peace-loving of all races. Their height, their cascading red hair, their massive shields, their fantastically long swords... their songs as they move off into battle, their war cries and dancing, and the horrible smash of weapons as they rattle their shields... All these are done to appal and terrify.'

In ancient histories the speeches of generals before battles are rarely, if ever, even approximations of the speeches that those generals actually gave. But they are often useful barometers of attitudes and preoccupations among the audiences who listened to these histories. And reading these words, written two centuries after the war between the Romans and the Galatians, we come as close as we ever will to understanding what the Roman legionaries and their allies likely felt as they started their march into the unwelcoming mountainous interior, to places where the warbands ruled.

The Roman march began uneventfully enough. As Manlius moved into Galatia proper some small villages came out and showed no hostility. A Celtic elder, probably a clan chief, even allied himself with the Romans and offered to go and persuade his fellow-countrymen to give up before it was too late. His mission was granted. And, as the country became rougher and rougher, the Romans sought protection in a fort: a useful precaution as they came for the first time here into contact with Galatian cavalry that surprised the Romans and that almost caused a rout.

A difficult few days followed as the Romans passed still deeper into enemy territory: we read of unfordable rivers, empty towns and religious oracles. They did not see any more of the foe, but the news eventually came that the Galatian leaders would not parley and had removed themselves to mountain strongholds with their women, children and livestock. The Tolistobogii, it transpired, had decided to defend Olympus, a mountain where geo-thermic vapours had convinced the locals that the Chimera, an Asiatic dragon, lived. The Tectosages had, instead, decided to defend the mountain of Magaba where they looked after the women and children of their tribal friends the Trocmi, who elected, instead, to assist the first part of the Galatian federation on Olympus.

The Romans marched at their fastest towards the bulk of the Celts on Mount Olympus, where the Chimera breathed out her fire, and camped at its foot while the Galatians above prepared themselves for the novel experience of an attack on their own homes. And here we see again the contrast with the Romans who had been overrun by the Senones all those generations before. The Roman army had become, in the meantime, the finest fighting force in the ancient world: there would be no more careless retreats or hysterical reserves. Not only were the legions the best heavy infantry in the Mediterranean, but Roman conquests and that city's deep purses meant that a whole series of allied soldiers, with varying speciali-ties and characteristics, had been enlisted. And these were picked out for use by Roman generals against particular enemies as carefully as a modern craftsman picks out a tool with a particular lock or screw in mind. Certainly

99

Manlius chose well. He had brought with him archers, javelin throwers and sling-shots. And these he separated from the rest of the army knowing that, for all their much vaunted courage, the Celts had little armour to resist such weapons. Then he split his men into three columns to storm three paths to the Celtic fortress near the peak, leaving behind elephants and horses on the plain as reinforcements. If the gods gave him victory, he wanted none of the enemy to escape.

There follows one of the saddest descriptions from all the annals of ancient warfare—reminiscent in some ways of the colonial adventures of the eighteenth and nineteenth centuries, where technologically- and tactically-superior Europeans marched against outclassed native armies. The Celts ran down from their fortifications and into battle, probably surprised that the Romans were attempting to storm their invulnerable defences. But, as they came towards the Romans, confident that their higher position and a customary charge would help them tear apart the troops sweating upwards, the Roman missile troops, who had been placed in front, began the assault.

> On every side [the Galatians] were hit by arrows and slingshots and javelins which they were unable to keep off. Blind with fear and anger they did not know what to do, and they found themselves fighting the kind of fight that they were least suited to. In melee where they could receive, but also give wounds, this fury makes for courage; yet now hit by missiles from afar, by an enemy that was not even visible, with no one to charge, they ran up against each other like savage, speared animals.
>
> Their manner of fighting—always naked— makes the wounds they have all the more visible;

100

their bodies are white and full of flesh as they never undress in this way except for battle. As a result more blood gushes out, the gashes appear worse, and the whiteness of their skin shows up the blood all the better. Open wounds do not worry them overly. When it is a surface wound instead of a deep one, they slash at the skin, and, in this way, win greater glory... But when an arrow-head or a leaden slingshot buries itself and tortures them with what seems a little wound and cannot be got rid of, they throw themselves down with shame and anger...

And now they were lying everywhere, and some who had chased down on their foe were being struck with missiles from every side; and those who came in close were killed by swords... Few of the Galatians had made it through and when they were bested in this way by light infantry, the legions coming up behind, they ran back to their fortress without order, where the women and children were in panic, all crowded together.

The end of the siege of Mount Olympus followed. The Romans came up to the camp and let fly a missile volley over the walls. The screams of the combatants and the civilians within are said to have mingled and the trapped Galatian warriors fled, many falling from the heights, as there was no escape free of Romans and none were allowed to get away: 'as [Manlius] believed that the war would end if as many as possible were slain or made prisoners.' Estimates of those who died range from ten thousand to forty thousand. Certainly forty thousand prisoners (including the families of the warriors) were said to have been taken and all were sold into slavery. There was inevitably maltreatment and abuse. One historian tells

101

us of a Celtic matron caught and raped. She did, however, clean the stain on her honour by bringing her assailant's decapitated head home and throwing it at her husband's feet.

The Tectosages determined to fight on. But after hearing the accounts of the siege of Olympus they realised that brute force would be of little help against the Roman army: they would have to resort, instead, to cunning. They arranged a meeting to surrender to Manlius and hid a thousand crack cavalry troops in the wings, hoping to avenge the defeat of their comrades.

Once [his deputy] had assured him that the [Galatian] kings had promised to come and that the negotiations were close to completion, Manlius set off from his camp... He rode for almost five miles and was nearing the pre-arranged meeting place when he spotted the Galatians riding hard at him, intent on attack. He had his escort stop and ordered them all to prepare themselves for battle and they were ready for the first attack and were not bettered. But, as the number of Galatians started to overwhelm them, he had his men retire slowly while holding their ranks and then finally, when remaining was more dangerous than fleeing, all the Romans turned tail.

The Celts now rode hard behind the scattering Romans, slaying them, and the escort would have been in the direst straits had it not been for 600 Romans who were close at hand to protect foragers... The 600 had heard warning shouts from the escort and grabbing their weapons and horses as quickly as they could they had charged energetically into the fight when it was ending.

In this way the battle turned and it was now the conquerors, not the defeated Romans, who panicked. The Celts were pushed back and [the rein-forcements], coming from the fields, pressed in on every side so that there was no way out open to the Celtic Gauls. The Romans with mounts, not yet tired from fighting, went after the exhausted Galatians and only a handful escaped; while, of those left behind, no prisoners were taken. Almost all paid with their lives for their treachery and the entire Roman army, angered by this trick, set off the next day against the enemy.

And 'when [the Romans] approached the Galatians all that had happened in the previous battle [on Olympus] was repeated except that the bravery of the one was added to by their recent victory and that of the other depressed, for though not yet defeated, they saw the defeat of their co-nationals as if it had been worked on themselves... A cloud of missiles rained down on the Galatians.' The Romans marvelled at the treasures they had gained from these two successful sieges. But, after all, a hundred-years worth of raiding had likely been brought into the confines of these camps. And perhaps Gnaeus Manlius Vulso muttered a quick *vae victis* ('woe to the vanquished') as he stood over the piles of booty, remembering the story of a Celtic leader named Raven who had visited his own city, Rome, five generations before.

Was this the end of the proud Galatians—the most easterly of all the Celtic nations? It was certainly the end of an independent Galatia. With even the central steppes and mountains of Asia Minor open to tramping Roman legionaries, and with many of the Celtic nobles enslaved or killed, there were unlikely to be any tribal meetings in the

103

near future. In fact, all that had to be settled was the time-table for absorption into the Empire. For a while the Galatians were governed by an individual ruler and there are signs that the Romans favoured them in the region when there were disputes between kingdoms. In the first century BC there are accounts of some Galatian raiding in the west. This was, however, quickly stamped out. Then, after that, the evidence of Celtic civilisation become scarcer and scarcer. If no historical references had come down to us concerning Galatia, we would by the third century BC only have some placenames and the sparsest collections of north European jewellery and weaponry to convince us that the Galatians had once ruled here. By the time of the Roman conquests, these traces too are lost: the archaeological record becomes increasingly difficult to identify with the Celts, and the few Celtic placenames were twisted out of shape by non-Celtic speakers.

The Galatians had probably never taken control of the cities of their region where the older Phrygians dwelt or they had done so partially. It is interesting, for example, that the capital of the Trocmii, Pessinous, had two conflicting legends to explain its origins: one Phrygian and one Celtic. And, already in the early generations, there was intermarriage with locals. These Celts were, after all, surrounded by a sea of predominantly Greek speakers. It was only natural then that the Celts would start to take on Greek customs and Greek manners. So we have cases of men with Celtic names giving their sons Greek names. There is also early evidence that they worshipped at the shrines of Asia Minor, at the altar of Cybele above all, whose priests castrated themselves. There is no convincing proof for a Celtic god or goddess anywhere in the region, though these there surely must have been. When Paul of Tarsus arrived in Galatia in the first century AD, he preached to its inhabitants in Greek. Arguably the earliest book to be written in the New Testament was his letter to the Galatians.

There are many cases from history of a people getting cut off from others of their kind. We know of the Greek communities founded by Alexander the Great in Afghanistan that got left there. Some of the early Indo-European clans that came to Europe and India 'got lost' and turned up in the Tarim Basin in central Asia. There are doubtful rumours—fuelled by the Chinese tourist industry—that one Roman legion ended up among Mandarin speakers. There are the Vikings that settled in Greenland and Canada and, for a few generations, kept up contact with their homelands and were then never heard of again. A party of crusaders, allegedly, found themselves in near Asia, where they lost touch with western Europe only to resurface as a community in modern Georgia...

We have every reason for believing that soon after the Roman conquests the Galatians followed the same melancholy trajectory: assimilation and loss of identity. The most interesting index of Celticness was perhaps language. But we have mere fragments of the only Celtic tongue to have been established in Asia. Indeed, of the twenty or so Celtic languages that we know of from history, Galatian is one of the worst preserved. (A rival for 'worst preserved Celtic language' is Cumbric the British-Celtic dialect of the north-west of Britain). We know a few personal names of Galatian clan-leaders and warriors, a handful of recognisably Celtic placenames such as *Drunemeton* ('the Holy Oak Glade') and one noun from Celtic Galatian, *taskos*, that probably meant 'badger'—not much to write a dictionary with. This language may already have been in decline in the glory days of the third century when the Galatians were raiding and terrifying their

105

neighbours. It will certainly have suffered under the Romans' invasion of the early second century BC. By the time that Paul came to evangelise the 'hard-headed' Galatians two decades after Christ's death we have no reason for thinking that any inhabitant of Galatia was still speaking Galatian. Nor have we any evidence for the next two hundred years. But then comes a surprise. In the second century AD an Assyrian writer, Lucian, describes how translators were sometimes needed for the locals who spoke Celtic. In second-century Galatia, then, the language of the Tectosages was still being shouted across the gorges by shepherds going home to burn dung in their stoves.

The truth is that ancient writers rarely show any interest in languages other than Greek or Roman, and it is easy then that a language can go unnoticed in this way for four centuries. Lucian's is the last cast-iron certain reference we have concerning a Celtic language in Asia, but it need not be the end. If Celtic had gone unnoticed from the time of the battles with the Romans to Lucian, almost half a millennium later, who is to say that it did not struggle on a little longer yet? Galatia was, after all, isolated and perhaps for three or four more centuries Celtic survived in the relatively stable eastern Roman Empire. Perhaps it even survived the coming of Islamic invaders in the eighth and ninth centuries and Galatians were called to their mosques and to the worship of the one true God by a tongue that a millennium before had been muttered by the druids over their sacrifices under spreading oaks.

8

DID THE CELTS PAVE THE ROAD
FOR THE ROMAN EMPIRE?

et us turn again to the question of Rome and the Celts, starting with the former. In the fifth century BC Rome was a pugnacious city state in central Italy, one of perhaps twenty major city states in Italy, at this date, and one of between a hundred and a hundred and fifty city states dotted around the Mediterranean. And, yet, by the late first century BC, a mere four hundred years later, Rome had knocked all its rivals in the region to the ground. Put in the most vivid terms possible, if an Italian sailor in 400 BC had found himself in a maritime storm, and was blown to some unknown point of that sea, he would fear for his life. There was no telling in whose jurisdiction he might have been blown. But if an Italian sailor, at the time of the birth of Christ, had been through a similar experience, he would have felt no such fear once the storm had abated. Wherever he might land in the Mediterranean, he would know that he, a Roman citizen, was landing in Roman territory. Rome produced other triumphs: a form of government capable of controlling and taxing imperial gains; and later victories in the north of Europe. But it was the conquest of the Mediterranean that made Rome:

and upon which Western civilisation was built.

Was this empire really the creation of the Celts, a tribal, Iron Age people, despised as backward savages by the Romans themselves?

That question is and will, of course, remain an open one, as with any other explanation for the rise of Rome. But the case for the Celts is a compelling one. In Italy they had swept Rome's enemies out of the way and allowed the first major victories of that city; in Greece they had smashed their way through Macedonia and ended any convincing attempt at the formation of a single Greek nation capable of taking on Roman Italy. And in Asia Minor their constant raiding had acted as a check on the kingdoms around them, preventing any from rising to prominence and offering defiance to Rome and Rome had, by the second century, its noose around the region's delicate neck. The major effect of the great Celtic invasions of antiquity had been to open the way for a single Mediterranean Empire and that Empire was Rome.

This is not to say, of course, that these Celtic raids would have been enough: far from it. If Rome had not had a strong and resourceful leadership, it never would have been in a position to take advantage of the Celts' scourging of Italy. It would never have recovered from the burning of its capital. If Rome had not developed an outstanding infantry, it would not have been able to overrun the Celts in northern Italy, let alone defeat its rivals in the southern Mediterranean, the Carthaginians, including Hannibal and his elephants. By the time that the Romans went to battle against the Galatians, the legions had amply proved themselves. In Livy's description we are seeing one of the most efficient and brilliant armies in human experience. Rome had, too, stumbled upon a form of government—balancing popular democracy with the powers of a public-minded aristocratic class—that produced stability through its early history, and that, at the same time, left space for conquests. Then there was Roman ambition, Roman self-belief, Roman religion, Roman righteous anger, Roman arrogance, and an endearing lack of Roman imagination. All of these things went into the mix of what made the Roman Empire possible: they have all been claimed as vital ingredients.

However, they should not detract from that initial burst of Celtic-inspired instability along the northern edge of the Mediterranean in the years 400 to 200 BC; the tribal helping hand to an upwardly mobile city in central Italy. For the truth is that we are too inclined to follow the Romans' lead on the Celts, to see them as half-frightening, half-fascinating savages, static and unimportant victims awaiting the arrival of the master race. But the march of history was rather different. The Celts in Italy, Greece and Asia Minor were a serious threat, quite capable of beating war-tested Mediterranean armies—think, for example, of the humiliated Macedonians. That does not mean, of course, that they were co-ordinated in these different attacks: how could they be when tens of different tribes and *ad hoc* coalitions of war were the driving force behind these invasions. But we should not confuse their lack of co-ordination or even their lack of motive—clearly the Celts did not want to help Rome—with the fact that these invasions stand as a watershed in Mediterranean history. This is something that is easily forgotten as the tide of invasion turns and the Romans eclipse the Celts' earlier achievements by sending their legions north.

And the Romans, however much they owed to the tribes, would be composing no thank-you letters to their Celtic enemies. Indeed, in the next centuries it was the Celtic homelands that would pay the price for their misplaced generosity, for now the invaders would be invaded. And if we want to think of Celtic-Roman relations in the next centuries we should think of the noise that a chainsaw makes as it passes through a pine trunk. In the third century BC as part of their wars with Carthage, the Romans had defeated the Celts of Spain. In the second century BC the Romans moved over the Alps and conquered the near parts of Celtic Gaul. In the first century BC, under Julius Caesar, they conquered northern Gaul, what the Romans called Long-haired Gaul. Then, in the first century AD, after several false starts, the Romans would turn to Britain and conquer that island. Of the ancient Celtic commonwealth of nations, tribes and clans only some very few cases around the periphery, notably in Ireland and what is today Scotland, survived. The ancient Celts ceased to exist as a free people by the mid-first century AD. They then ceased to exist as a people in the next generations as they were assimilated into the Empire. Only in partially conquered Britain and unconquered Ireland did Celtic civilisation survive in any significant fashion to re-emerge at the end of the Roman Empire in a surprising Christian form.

They had their lodges in the wilderness,
Or built them cells beside the shadowy sea,
And there they dwelt with Angels, like a dream
So they unrolled the volume of the Book,
And filled the fields of the Evangelist
With antique thoughts, that breathed of Paradise

The Quest of the Sangraal, Robert Hawker

II

Saving
Dark Age Christianity

c. 400-500	*The conversion of Ireland to Christianity*
c. 521	*Birth of Colum Cille*
c. 550	*Birth of Columbanus*
561	*Civil war among the Uí Néill (Battle of Cúl Dreimhne)*
562	*Colum Cille goes to Iona*
562-597	*Cormac's Voyages*
c. 570	*Mohamed born in Mecca*
c. 577	*Brendan the Navigator dies*
590	*Columbanus arrives on the Continent*
597	*Colum Cille's Death*
597	*Roman mission begins in Kent (England)*
611	*Columbanus's second exile*
611	*Columbanus at Bregenz*
614	*Columbanus at Bobbio*
615	*Columbanus's death*
627	*Abortive Roman mission to Northumbria*
633	*Battle of Heavenfield and Irish mission in Northumbria*
c. 640	*Jonas writes the* Life of Columbanus
642	*Oswald's Death*
651	*Finan becomes bishop*
661	*Colman becomes bishop*
664	*Synod of Whitby*
c. 700	*Adomnán writes the* Life of Colum Cille

9

THE DARK-AGE CHRISTIAN CELTS

aving conquered all the Celtic peoples bar the Irish and the most northern Britons, the Roman Empire reached its greatest extent at the end of the first century AD. However, from then onwards Rome would be on the defensive against barbarians from beyond its borders. By the late fourth century AD, the pressure on the Roman frontiers was becoming intolerable. Rome in the last difficult decades of its existence resembled an ostrich egg in a vice. The Empire was surrounded by hostile tribal peoples who envied its wealth and lived according to the logic and for the excitement of the raid. These different peoples pushed inwards across the borders and exerted ever more pressure, turning the handle of the vice millimetre by millimetre.

The Empire, of course, reacted. It spent more on defence and militarised government. Ancient liberties were taken away in an attempt to regulate its citizens. For example, sons were to follow their fathers in their profession—so the sons of legionaries were obliged to become legionaries. The economy was channelled to serve the army. Barbarians from beyond the frontiers

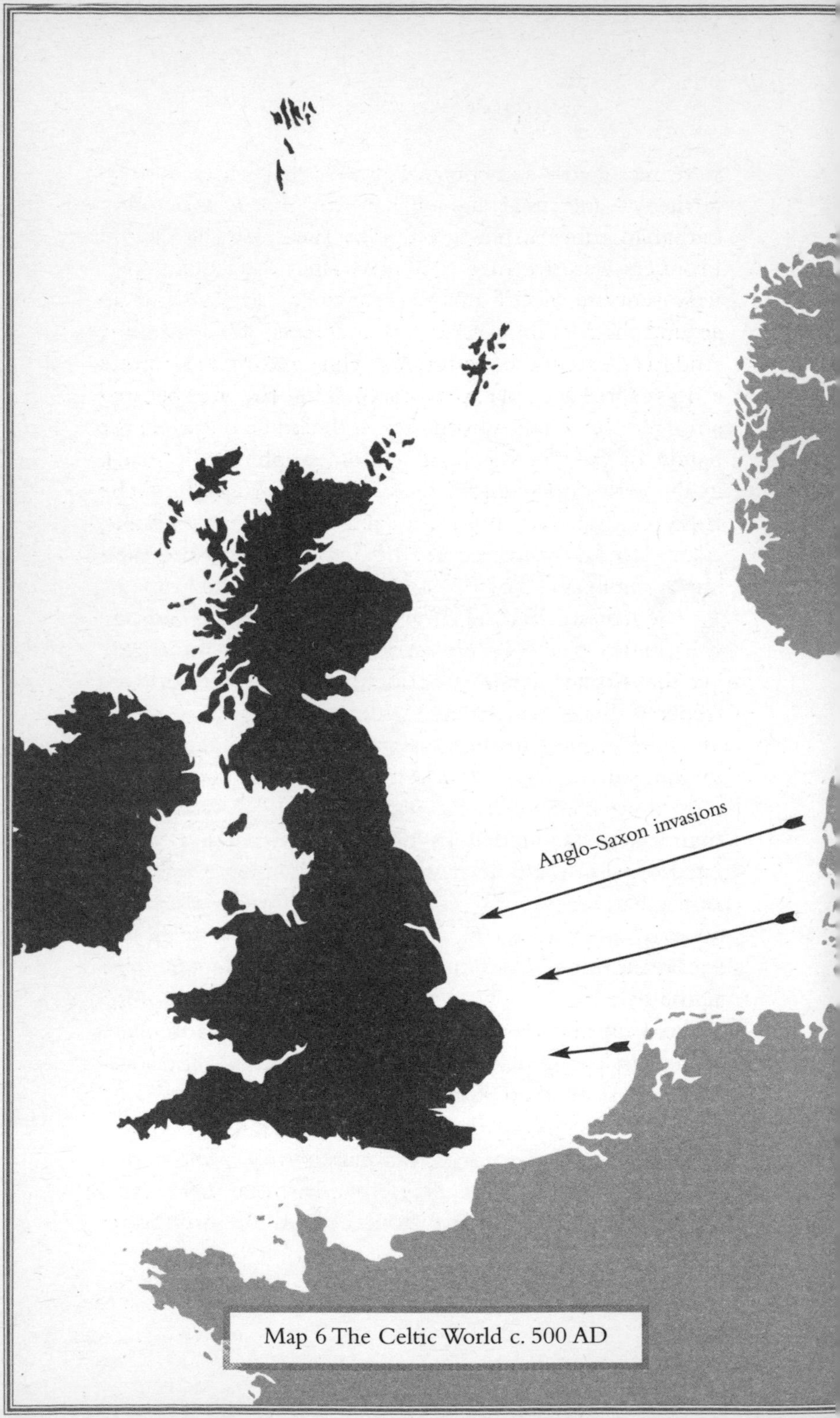

Anglo–Saxon invasions

Map 6 The Celtic World c. 500 AD

were recruited—sometimes being settled within Roman
territory—and used as auxiliary troops against other
barbarian tribes in an attempt to stave off the enemy.
Frontiers were fortified, defensive lines were built, spies
were sent into non-Roman lands, cities had walls put up
around them even in relatively safe areas of the Empire.
And to an extent these attempts, while making the Empire
a less agreeable place, worked. The Empire became
stronger. But it was a brittle strength and all the while the
handle of the vice was turning. Catastrophe finally struck
in the early fifth century when the western half of the
Empire was overrun by the barbarian: Goths, Franks,
Alans, Vandals and the Celtic Irish, to name only the most
important of the foes of Rome.

The new world that emerged after the Roman Empire
collapsed was a fragmented one, a return to something
like the tribal societies of antiquity. But, in two important
respects things had changed since the Iron Age Celtic
invasions. First, Christianity had come in the late Empire
to dominate much of southern and western Europe. And,
second, very few of these tribal successors to Rome were
Celtic-speaking—the Celts had been largely assimilated
into Roman society in the previous centuries. Only in
Britain and Ireland and in Brittany (a British-Celtic colony
on the north-western coast of France) would Celtic-
speakers survive in any significant numbers. Yet negligible
as these Celtic territories were at the fall of the Roman
Empire, an important number of Celtic and particularly
Irish Christian travellers—monks, priests and abbots—
departed from their homelands, pouring out into what
was left of Roman as well as non-Roman Europe.

If the invasions of the first part of this book were a
warrior's story, the coming of these Irish travellers was a
religious mystery. And the mystery is easily stated. In an

117

age of unprecedented danger and instability, when every other monk or priest aspired only to remain at home in the relative safety of a monastery or church, why did these dandelion seeds of the Lord allow themselves to be blown over so many acres of land and ocean?

The simple answer is that the Irish Celts were, with the British Celts, different from their Roman and non-Roman neighbours in the Christian customs that they followed. Like other Christians in other ages and places, Celtic Christians became experts in the art of self-harm and abnegation. But, detached from the mainstream of medieval Christendom, they developed new ways to cauterise the spirit and body. For instance, they did not stop at fasting but immersed themselves in freezing lakes and streams—a form of asceticism well-suited to the last island of the world. Wrinkled hermits lay out in beds with naked girls to test themselves, a form of sexual temptation known nowhere else except among the antique Christians of Syria. We have cases where human faeces were eaten to shatter the pride of the faithful, and one saint, Fursa from Munster in the south-west of Ireland, is said in a revealing legend to have deliberately swallowed a lizard so that, for the long decades of his life, it scratched cruelly at his guts.

Of course, if the Irish had restricted themselves to cold water, sex games and revolting diets, these peculiarities would be nothing more than a curiosity and one of history's billion footnotes. But they also chose another form of flagellation—exile. For the most spiritually ambitious directed their bodies to ports and deserted their own lands, swearing to never return, swearing that for the sake of God they would remain abroad for the rest of their lives and so deprive themselves of their family, their friends and others who spoke their language. The stimulus for this migration was an act of religious sincerity—a freak invention of ecclesiastics. But it served not only God but also Europe, for the exiles brought with them physical artefacts, their ideas, in some cases intellectual brilliance, their prejudices and most of all their revolutionary energy. In our sparse Dark Age sources again and again we trip over references to the ancient Irish, passing down roads, rivers and across seas. These men—Irish women did not seem to undertake exile—had a certain genius for bringing themselves to the attention of usually inattentive Christian neighbours.

The Christian Celts did not look outwards as they passed across the waves and down the highways and byways of their new homelands, but always backwards to their much missed birth-lands. Their longing can be found in poems composed by the exiles and in the tormenting details of their lives. They were not hoping to change the world around them. Half of their minds was always somewhere behind in the cemetery of their family in Ireland where they should have been buried, and would vainly wish themselves one day to be buried. If there were a picture of this monkly migration, it would show a cross, naturally enough. It would also show, at the base of the cross, a small man carrying that cross and his steps would take him across the geometric square waves found in Celtic sculpture. His head, with a melancholy parched face etched into it, would be twisted in the opposite direction back towards Connaught or Ulster—the unattainable home that he carried with him as other pious Christians wore spikes or chains that bit into their flesh.

But as they were staring backwards, dreaming not of change, but of the holy confines of the churches of Kildare and Armagh or of their tribe and kin, they certainly did institute a revolution. As missionaries among the pagan, explorers in the frozen northern seas and Dark Age intellectuals in monastic libraries, these exiles, time and time again, exerted their power, rescuing Christian Europe in its most difficult centuries.

10

COLUM CILLE AND IONA

olum Cille, or Columba as the most famous of the Irish-Celtic exiles is also known, was born into the royal line of an Irish tribe, the Uí Néill, in the early sixth century. At that date, Ireland had as many as two hundred tribal kingdoms, constantly warring and jostling for land and reputation. The Uí Néill in general, and Colum Cille's own Uí Néill clan the Cenél Conaill in particular, boasted the foremost warlords in this rural island. If you had lived in sixth-century Ireland—Colum Cille perhaps came into the world in 521—you could therefore have done far worse than be born into one of the aristocratic halls of the Cenél Conaill, within an arrow-shot of the endless Atlantic and within ear-shot of its breakers and waves.

There were still surprisingly close parallels between Colum Cille's Ireland and the Celtic Iron Age of a thousand years before. One Dark Age Irish story describes warriors coming together and arguing at a banquet over who should get to eat the choicest part of a boar that had been brought to them. The warriors take turns to boast of their bravery and intimidate others into sitting down, until finally one warrior out-insults the others and finishes his speech by hurling a decapitated head at a rival seated on the other side of the hall. The custom of arguing over the cut of meat from a boar or swine was also attested in Iron Age Celtica, while references to head-hunting are frequently found in descriptions of the ancient Celts (as, of course, headhunting is found in many war-obsessed cultures). Colum Cille grew up then in a world of chariots, duels, cattle-raids and glorious golden trinkets, not so terribly different from the world enjoyed by the Tectosages and the Senones in the Celtic Europe of 400 BC.

Or was it? In one important respect Colum Cille's Ireland was different from the Celtic nations of ancient Europe, and that was in the religion of its people. Colum Cille's great grandparents and his grandparents had been brought up to believe in Celtic gods. Some of these had the same names as those worshipped by the Iron Age Celts on the continent. But Colum Cille's parents had probably—and Colum Cille had certainly—been brought up according to the teachings of the Bible, for in the fifth century British-Celtic missionaries had brought the cross to the furthest island of the west, and had had success weaning the Irish tribes away from their Iron Age gods. Indeed, by the time that Colum Cille was taking his first communion, pagan Ireland was in its last doddery years. We have only fleeting references to the druids, one of whom is recorded as trying to convince a monk that he could turn himself into a bird.

The tribal and warlike nature of Irish society remained, though, and the young Colum Cille would have had the jarring experience of being told stories from the Gospels about turning the other cheek and loving neighbours, while his family was out stealing heifers from farms over the hill and firing barns and granaries in feuds that had their origins in pagan times. Every civilisation has its fits of schizophrenia, of course. But in Ireland the new religion and the old tribal realities made especially strange bed-fellows. One imagines a wife chastely muttering psalms before lights out, lying next to her husband, a barrel of a warrior with chest-hairs like wires and a broad-sword under his pillow. As we shall see, Colum Cille's life contains this contradiction in his personal history. That Colum Cille was to be a lord of men was decided by his royal blood. That he became a master of a congregation rather than a small Irish kingdom depended, instead, on his talents and inclinations. So we read of prophetic signs that are said to have occurred while he was still in his mother's womb. From his early years he showed great promise following the path of matins and mass rather than warriors and warbands. And in his early adolescence he was not sent to learn how to fight, but handed over to a priest with the intimidating name of Cruithnechán to learn the ways of God.

At that young age miracles are recorded of Colum Cille, miracles reported by later pious writers, who were more intent on sanctifying Colum Cille's childhood than telling historical truth. For many of Colum Cille's biographers cared little more for fact than those early Celtic story-tellers who had made the god Raven into a living, breathing general. But, we are reliably told that, in his late adolescence, Colum Cille left Cruithnechán behind and travelled to distant Leinster, on the other side of Ireland, and there studied holy scripture, determined to make his way in the Church. However, for all that he was a priest, Colum Cille, now in his twenties and thirties, also remained a member of his kingroup the Cenél Conaill. It is in his full adulthood, a well-respected member of the Irish Church, that we have the first glimpse of his own personal version of schizophrenia. For, in the year 561, civil war broke out within the Uí Néill and this war included the Cenél Conaill.

Quite what Colum Cille did when the Uí Néill crossed swords has long been discussed. At this remove, the facts of the matter are impossible to recover, though the various claims do, at least, make for intriguing reading. One ancient legend, for example, has it that the saint used his powers to blow away a magic mist that had been lain across the battlefield by the enemy. Ireland's last druids, it seems, were casting spells for the other side. Another account says that Colum Cille did nothing more than pray for the success of his family. Or, perhaps, he fought alongside his clan. In later centuries Irish monks were famous for their fighting skills, even raiding rival monasteries. So this is not as unlikely as it might at first seem. Yet another account blames the battle on an argument over which of two saints—Colum Cille or Finan—owned a manuscript.

It is such confusion and such ample luxuriant growths of Irish legend, both obscuring and ornamenting, that caused one Dark-Age writer to note that nothing concerning Irish history could be trusted. Fifteen hundred years later, we know only that this civil war among the Uí Néill coincided with Colum Cille's going into exile. He may have been escaping condemnation at home—there are hints that he was excommunicated by rival churchmen. Or he may have decided that it was impossible to carry out his Christian vocation with the bitterness that remained after the war had ended.

Colum Cille, then, decided to leave Ireland. The problem was where he would go. And here it is important to dwell for a moment on the legends that inspired the early Irish monks in their acts of exile, for among those Irish clergymen who wished to pass abroad, one of the most important sources of inspiration were the writings of the Desert Fathers.

The Desert Fathers were the early Christian mystics who had travelled into the expanses of the Egyptian and Arabian deserts in search of a place where they could live alone, away from the rush of civilisation, and pray to God while doing battle with their own and other demons. There was Anthony, who lived for thirteen years on a dune in the sands of Egypt, and allegedly had no contact with man in that time. Or there was Simon the Stylite who climbed a pillar in the Syrian desert and remained atop for half a lifetime, visited by heathen Bedouin and pilgrims from as far afield as the Latin west. These solitary hermits attracted followers who would build huts in the sand nearby and sometimes small villages of these praying Christians would be set up in inaccessible corners of the desert—communities that would evolve into the first monasteries.

Irish monks, including Colum Cille, were tremendously excited by the stories of the Desert Fathers and wished to imitate them. They, too, wanted to pass out into the sandstorms and find God there. But the Irish had an overwhelming problem. They had no desert. And so Irish monks were condemned to invent deserts for themselves and they did so in one of two ways. The first and simplest was to call Irish wildernesses 'deserts'. A piece of bogland or the empty side of a mountain

125

might be made to work for any Irish hermits looking for a place to live in peace and think on God. And, in fact, there are several modern Irish placenames that include the word *disert* and that recall spots where Irish monks once played at make-believe, becoming 'desert-dwellers' in the heather and the bogs with butterflies and songbirds flying around their cells.

However, the second Irish solution, and the one with which Colum Cille experimented, was far more original—a brilliant act of lateral thinking. Instead of making Irish wilderness into 'desert', other Irish monks had chosen the one truly uninhabited expanse available to them—the ocean. These Irish monks would set out into this 'desert' in their boats and sail until they came to an abandoned or unknown island where they might decamp and praise God. Here the idea of exile from Ireland and the search for a desert fused perfectly. And it was to this marine desert that Colum Cille gave himself up.

Islands appealed to the medieval Christian imagination. Certainly, throughout their history Irish-Celtic exiles sought them out, whether small coastal isles close to Ireland or islands in other countries, including Lindisfarne off the coast of England, or Honau, an isle on part of the Rhine which was so buffeted by torrents that it eventually collapsed. We know, for example, that, in Colum Cille's lifetime, monks were already crossing the wild waters between Munster and the piles of ocean rock known as Skellig Michael about twelve miles from the Kerry coast. This plug of granite was a paradise for seabirds, but also proved a paradise for monks who wished to get away from it all and build stone shacks in which they could pray. This Skellig ('Rock' in Irish) was named for the

Archangel Michael, probably because like many coastal islands it was frequently struck by lightening, the 'fire from heaven' associated with God's warrior angel. And the image of Irish monks humming prayers to themselves in their stone huts on a summer evening as electric storms resolved themselves overhead (and perhaps sometimes on their heads) is a memorable one.

It was only natural that Colum Cille also decided to search for an island. But, as befitted his high station and reputation, he wanted an island to call his own, a piece of earth where he could set up a foundation that lived according to his rules. He had already gathered around him twelve disciples who would be his monks. And the island that Colum Cille found is today one of the holiest sites in Britain, Iona, the little brother of Mull in the Inner Hebrides. It is, true, a very different proposition from rocky Skellig Michael, but in its own way as impressive. Over two thousand acres of mostly heathered land, it has been described as 'a thin place', one where the barrier between this world and the world to which Christians aspire has almost broken down. In later centuries it would become the burial ground of the kings of Scotland. This was mostly, of course, through the association with Colum Cille, but also owing to its tremendous natural charisma.

Colum Cille arrived on Iona in 562 AD. And within a generation the monastery would be the most famous in all of Britain and Ireland and its founder the most feted holy-man. On one occasion, when Colum Cille visited another monastery, he had to be protected from pressing crowds by bodyguards who placed a square of wood around him to keep the curious at arm's length. Within a century stories would be told about him in England, and within three centuries he would be a well-

known saint on the Continent in France and in
Germany. But what interests us here is that initial burst
of enthusiasm in the late 500s, when his name came to
be known above all in north Britain and Ireland. As
perhaps the earliest poem to survive in Irish would have
it, a poem that describes Colum Cille's piety and
achievement and that dates to shortly after his death:

> The north it shone,
> The westerners blazed
> Colum Cille illuminated all the east with
>   the pure holy
>   ....
> Most lovely and most special
> His talent in priestly ways.
> Unknowable to the people:
> A shelter to the naked,
> A breast to the poor.

On Iona, the island that became the physical manifesta-
tion of the saint's fame, none of the original buildings
of Colum Cille's time survive. There is so little of those
times, indeed, that when eighteenth-century writers
looked at the few ragged remains of his settlement they
believed them to be of druidic origin—not something
that would have pleased the saint.

But we do, at least, have detailed written accounts of
life on Iona in the first generation. We know, for
example, that monks from the British Celts, the Picts,
the English and, of course, the Irish themselves, came
to live here under Colum Cille's rule. Iona ultimately
became the capital of a monastic empire, for Colum
Cille founded, too, various sister monasteries in Ireland.
We hear of a bustling library where works were

copied—one of Colum Cille's most famous miracles concerned the clairvoyant proof-reading of a manuscript—and poems and original works of Irish scholarship were penned out. Works written on Iona would become some of the classics of early medieval Irish literature. We hear of a guest house where visitors were allowed to stay and were frequently set upon by Colum Cille, who accused them of multiple sins and demanded penance from them. We hear of a hill where angels congregated—a hill that in more modern times was known as the Fairies' Hill. And there was the dairy where an old work horse brought pails back and forth, the same horse that would many years later cry and foam at the mouth when it understood that its master Colum Cille was coming to the end of his life.

Iona was a Celtic monastery built according to the tradition of exile. Colum Cille had left Ireland behind him and had gone to search for a place to be at peace with God outside his homeland. But Iona also became a nursery for other Irish exiles wishing to pass abroad. Indeed, many of these exiles came to Iona and stayed in the monastic house there. Some were absorbed into the monastic community. But others were sent away by Colum Cille to points of exile near and far. One man named Librán of the Reed Bed, for example, was instructed to go to another Hebridean Island, Tiree, to expunge his sins in monastic discipline and poverty. A scholar named Fiachnae also arrived on Iona to ask for penance for his sins before the saint likewise sent him away. An Irish warrior, who had both killed his brother and slept with his own mother, was banished by the saint to the British Celts in a life-long penance. But all these sins and penances pale beside the acts of Colum Cille's fellow saint, Cormac Ua Lithláin. He brought to

Iona his own stronger form of exile and introduces us to the next outward ripple of Irish holy journeys.

11

CORMAC &
THE DESERT IN THE OCEAN

s the exiles were spreading out and populating the islands close to Ireland and Britain, mythical stories began to arise about their deeds on the ocean. One early Irish exile from Munster, who may have visited Skellig Michael, was Brendan, nicknamed 'the Navigator', and Odyssean tales were told of Brendan's trips into the ocean in search of an island. There was the time, for example, that his disciples came upon a rock in the midst of the sea and disembarking realised that it was a sea-monster's back, a sea-monster named Easter no less. On another occasion they came across Judas Iscariot bobbing in the ocean, for Judas had been let out of hell for a day on a furlough. On one island they came upon some giant blacksmiths, who stoned them, and, on another, three choirs of divine singers dressed in blue, white and red. Here we have an early Irish version of the 'island-hopping story' that has been worked over by such dissimilar literary associates as Jonathan Swift, C.S. Lewis and Homer.

These legends may not tell us about historical voyages. But almost as an aside, they tell us something that is just as useful for understanding the biography of Cormac Ua

Lithàin, the most dedicated of all the exiles to come to the court of Colum Cille. They tell us how the Irish exiles went about finding islands where they could give themselves over to God undisturbed. (They wished to pray alone, not to minister to others.) In the case of a known island like Skellig Michael or Iona they employed fairly conventional methods and sailed and rowed to where they were supposed to be going. But, when wanting to discover new places of prayers, new 'deserts in the ocean', they took up a technique that simply astonishes the modern reader, as it also astonished medieval neighbours who witnessed it. The monk intending to become an exile would place himself in a small craft with two or three companions and a few days worth of food, be dragged out into the waves and hoist the sail. They would then let 'God' (the currents and the wind) decide where they should go. And, if 'God' did not carry these determined exiles to an island, they died from starvation or the great waves of the sea opened up, somewhere far out of sight of land.

So bewildering is this custom as it is described in the legendary accounts of Brendan the Navigator, so surprising and unexpected, that it is tempting to dismiss it altogether. Sat by a warm fire with a story-teller such a tale would have great effect, but real monks would, of course, never adopt this way of searching out a place for meditation. However, we, in fact, know that they did. Indeed, we have solid historical sources that describe exiles doing just this in their attempts to find an island on which they might settle and pray.

It is unlikely that Colum Cille himself resorted to such a strategy, because Iona, like Skellig Michael, was well-known by Irish sailors and there was no need to discover it. But the future Saint Cormac Ua Lithàin certainly did.

Indeed, the first time that we come across Cormac is in a history concerning Colum Cille, where we learn that Cormac failed to find a suitable island because God had chosen not to show him one. And the reason for God's refusal? Colum Cille explained to one of his juniors that Cormac had taken a monk who had had the impudence to tag along without asking permission from his abbot. Reading between the lines it seems that Cormac was blown out to sea, perhaps near his home, in the west of Ireland, and then blown back to the coast.

On a second attempt, though, the currents, at least initially, treated Cormac and his crew more kindly. They were blown out into the ocean and, after several days of travel towards the north, they were washed up onto the shore of some flat heath lands. Unfortunately these were not another Iona, an uninhabited demi-paradise. They were the Orkney Islands, the small chain off the northern coast of Britain which were very much inhabited at this date. We have talked in this book of Iron Age customs surviving into Roman and medieval times. But in Orkney it was not so much a question of Iron Age customs as Bronze Age or sometimes Stone Age customs that had been passed down the generations.

These were the islands that time had forgot. Archaeologists have shown that their population lived in extreme poverty for all that Orkney was fertile. Inhabitants often still used bone and stone to cut when the rest of Britain and Europe had graduated onto metals. Their landscape was indented with brochs, the thousand-year-old tapering towers where families would run to hide in times of war. By this date—we are in the late sixth century—Christianity had reached India and Eastern Africa, and it may have reached China and Tibet. But Christianity had not come to these last extremities of

133

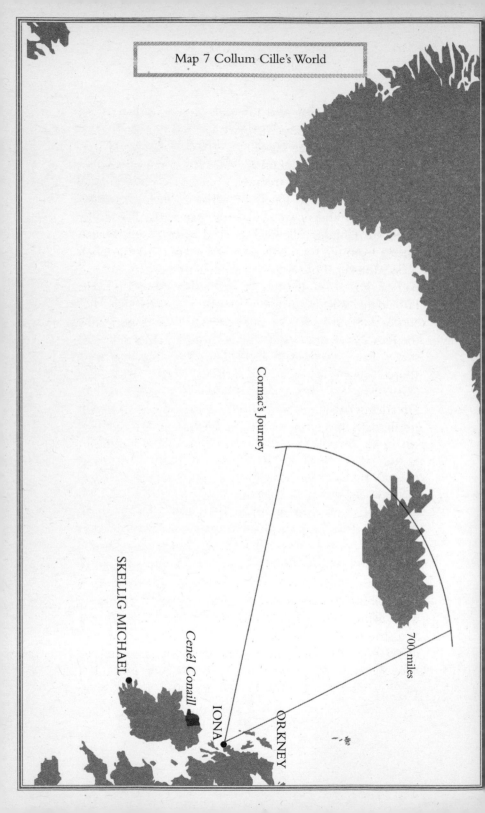

Map 7 Collum Cille's World

Cormac's Journey

SKELLIG MICHAEL

Cenél Conaill

IONA

ORKNEY

700 miles

Britain, and Cormac and his crew were brought to the
pagan king of a pagan territory.

Cormac's prospects would not have been good if it
had not been that Colum Cille pulled some strings for
him. The saint was in frequent contact with the King of
Pictland, master of much of what is today Scotland.
Indeed, so frequent were these contacts that already by
this date Colum Cille had duelled with pagan Pictish
priests from the royal court, had frightened off the Loch
Ness Monster (Loch Ness lay in Pictish territory) and had
had a go at converting the Pictish King himself.
Historians still argue about whether Colum Cille was
successful in that respect, but he was at least respected by
the Pictish monarch. And when Colum Cille sent warning
that some exiles were on the sea and asked that they
should be. protected, he was listened to. Luckily for
Cormac the Pictish King was overlord of Orkney and had
Orcadian hostages in his court. So Cormac was sent back
south with his monks and eventually arrived on Iona
where he was able to show his gratitude to Colum Cille in
person.

Two times Cormac had risked his life on the ocean,
and two times he had failed. A lesser man, it is tempting
to write a saner man, would have given up at this point.
But, for a third time, a boat was prepared and dragged to
the beach and, perhaps from Iona itself, Cormac once
more gave up his life to the waves. Before describing the
course taken by Cormac on this trip into the unknown, it
is important to understand the kind of ship that Cormac
was using. The monks on their sail-abouts were
accustomed to employ boats that were made of leather
not wood. Typically bull-hides would be treated to
become waterproof and were then sewn around a
wickerwork base. The result was a *curragh* or a floating

surface on which several men could perch—it would be too much to say 'sit'. It is a boat that had already been recorded several hundred years before, when a Roman author tells us that the ancient Britons resorted to such vessels. And it was employed routinely a century ago by fishermen in Donegal. The fact that it was used for at least two thousand years can only mean that it was easy to construct and that it served its purpose admirably. But it served its purpose admirably in the bay where the British or the folk of Donegal caught fish. It was not designed for ocean travel. Indeed, we might reasonably ask whether any ship constructed in Ireland or, indeed, in Europe at this date was suited to the places where Cormac was about to go.

> [Cormac's] ship blown by the south wind drove with full sails in a straight course from land towards the region of the northern sky, for fourteen summer days and as many nights. Such a voyage appeared to be beyond the range of human exploration and one from which there could be no return. And so it happened, after the tenth hour of the fourteenth day, that there arose all around them a terrible thing, such as no one had ever before seen, exceedingly dangerous small creatures covering the sea…; and these struck with terrible impact the bottom and sides, the stern and prow, with so strong a blow that they were thought able to pierce and penetrate the skin-covering of the ship. As those that were present there related afterwards, these creatures were about the size of frogs, very injurious by reason of their stings, but they did not fly, they swam. They were a terrible impediment to the oars as well… The Irish were

terrified and most perturbed and weeping prayed to God, who is a true and ready saviour in times of trouble.

It is first important to situate this incident on the map. We cannot be sure from where Cormac set off: his home in Munster is one possibility, as is Iona if this third attempt immediately followed the abortive landfall in the Orkneys. But, from either of these, fourteen-days full sailing takes us far to the north: way beyond any British islands and probably beyond Iceland. A sailing boat today can travel as many as two hundred miles in a day. If we grant that Cormac had travelled only quarter as far—this is a conservative estimate corresponding to modern recreations—then we are speaking of about seven hundred miles that would have taken him into or close to the Arctic Circle. If the reference to the south wind is only approximate and Cormac had been blown north-west, he would have covered much of the distance between Ireland and Greenland. If to the north-east then he would have found himself on the coast of Scandinavia. That such a voyage was 'beyond the range of human exploration' suggests that the wind blew him north or north-west. It is records such as this that have led to speculation that the exiles found their way to North America in the Dark Ages (see the Appendix).

A more immediate mystery is the animal that is being described here. The description of these creatures is inadequate. But we must remember that the monks had never seen anything like this before. There is a long history of explorers being faced for the first time with creatures familiar to us from film and from zoos and making a poor job of describing something that shocked them. An early Carthaginian expedition to north-western

Africa, for example, got gorillas mixed up with humans. The Irish themselves described a squid that washed up on their shores as a giant woman. But, reaching behind these words, can any credible suggestion be made as to what these creatures were? In fact, many taxonomic suggestions have been made over the years including flying fish, jellyfish and, bizarrely, Greenland mosquitoes. But the most sensible explanation would be a species of young dolphins unfamiliar to the Irish monks: dolphins, juvenile and otherwise, do travel in groups and do jump.

In freezing waters the Celtic monks were understandably terrified that these creatures would pierce the leather surface of their boat. It was for this that they concentrated on the evil-sounding 'terrible impact', while the 'stings' were likely the protruding noses of these creatures that will have been responsible for the blows. It is curious that an animal that is thought of as the friend of sailors should have become the inspiration for this nightmarish episode.

> St Colum Cille was with them in spirit, there in the boat with Cormac, even if his body was far away. At their point of worst trouble he rang the bell to bring all his monks to the church. And, inside the church, he gave this prophecy to those standing about… saying: 'Brothers, pray now most earnestly for Cormac, who is drifting and has gone beyond the limits where any man has gone before. In that place he suffers awful horrors, monsters that have not been seen before and that are almost impossible to describe. Let us all then come together and take part in the terror of our friends…who find themselves in this awful danger. Now I see Cormac and his crew asking Christ for help, crying all the while. Let us too help them with

our prayers and ask Him to have pity on our brothers so that He might change the direction of the wind that has sent them fourteen days to the north and let Cormac's boat be brought back to safety.'

And saying this he fell to his knees before the altar, praying to God, who rules the winds and everything. Then, after having said these prayers, he rose quickly, brushing away some tears, and most happily thanked God saying: 'Now, brothers, we can all be thankful for our loved ones for whom we are praying. God has turned the wind back from south to north and this wind will carry our brother monks out of danger and carry them here to us again.' And, at that time, the south wind stopped. And, for many days, the wind blew from the north and Cormac's boat sailed back to land. Cormac came to Colum Cille, and… each could look once more on the face of the other, while all marvelled and celebrated greatly.

The above was Cormac's last recorded adventure on the ocean. We must assume that afterwards he resigned himself to a monkly life in Ireland or Iona. But this final passage concerning the failed holy mariner remains, leaving us with a mystery even greater than the location of the boat or the identity of the stinging frog-like beasts— Colum Cille's supposed telepathic powers. After all, the saint is said here to see Cormac in a vision, for all that he lay several hundred miles away. So far in our description of Colum Cille we have brushed such things to the side. As, though, they fill ancient accounts, it is only proper that we give space to what his contemporaries most remember about him. Take, for example, the story mentioned above

139

how Colum Cille knew that Cormac's first voyage had failed because of a disobedient monk who travelled with him. Colum Cille claimed to know this even though Cormac was setting off on his voyage on the other side of the Irish-Celtic world. Likewise when Colum Cille asked the Pictish King to warn his Orcadian underking that Cormac might land among them, we stated it as a simple diplomatic fact. But the saint's biographer says that Colum Cille went to the king because he knew that Cormac would land on Orkney as he had seen it in a vision.

Usually, historians do not take such miracles very seriously. Such accounts typically appear in works written hundreds of years after the death of the saint, where the author had to 'create' the miracles associated with said saint. But what is striking about Colum Cille's biography is that it was written—using excellent material only a century after Colum Cille passed away—by a man who had very possibly met and interviewed some who had personally known the saint. One of the most important living Celticists has even suggested that Colum Cille was believed to have *imbas for-osna* ('the embracing vision that illuminates') a second sight more typically associated with Celtic pagan seers and prophetesses. Certainly, Colum Cille's contemporaries were convinced of it.

And any modern book-reading visitor to the world in which Colum Cille dwelt is constantly shocked by its supernatural charge. This was, after all, a world of portents equal to those of Cormac's adventures. One where otherwise sober historians describe fairies, genocidal lightening storms, ships floating through the heavens and flying moles. When we pass into those lost early medieval centuries, it is as if we have strayed off the edge of the map into the margins where the map-maker has written 'there be dragons'. And it should come as no surprise to learn that two centuries after the death of Colum Cille, dragons were, indeed, claimed, by marvelling Gaels, to have flapped their way across the Irish firmament.

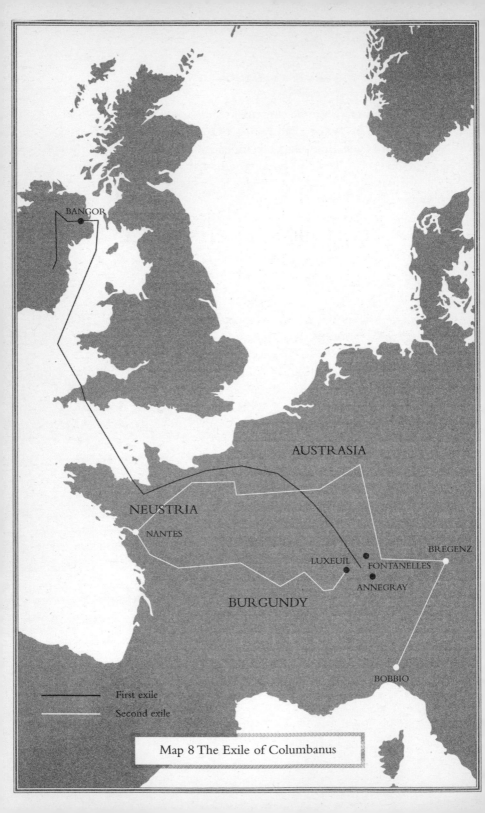

BANGOR

AUSTRASIA

NEUSTRIA

NANTES

BREGENZ

LUXEUIL

FONTANELLES

ANNEGRAY

BURGUNDY

BOBBIO

First exile

Second exile

Map 8 The Exile of Columbanus

12

COLUMBANUS'S FIRST EXILE

he Celtic invasions of the early centuries BC involved hundreds of thousands of individuals. But, with the Celtic monkly migrations of the early Middle Ages, we are speaking of much smaller numbers. Colum Cille established himself on Iona with just twelve disciples. And another example of quality over quantity comes in 590, seven years before Colum Cille's death, when a crew of thirteen Irish monks made landfall on the north-western coast of what is today France. We know the names of several of these thirteen. There was, for example, a Celt named Libranus who would be abandoned in France twenty years later. Another, called Gall, would found a monastery in the Swiss Alps—St Gallen, to give that monastery its German name. But these lesser figures would have been quickly forgotten had it not been for the extraordinary personality that led them.

The monk-commander of the little group, Columbanus, was an Irishman, a native, in fact, of Leinster in south-eastern Ireland, whose piety and righteous rage were to strike all he met in the next years. This future saint had been born, a generation before, c.

550, in Leinster, within perhaps a day's walk of the boggy lands where a settlement named 'the Black Pool' or Dublin would one day be built, the region of Ireland from which accounts of the first recorded Irish tribal conflicts come. The young Columbanus had refused the temptation of battle that excited so many young Irish males in those first Christian centuries. Instead, as a boy, he had been caught up in the stories of the holy of Ireland, stories about men such as Colum Cille who had, a mere decade before, established his monastery on Iona in the Scottish Hebrides.

And, in fact, in his early twenties, Columbanus had headed towards Colum Cille's home province of Ulster, passing to the monastery of Bangor, to follow a religious vocation. There he had laboured as a monk under Comgall, a famous abbot, and by the age of thirty he had won a reputation for excellence both in his writings and his prayers. If he had remained at Bangor it is quite possible that he would have become abbot when Comgall died. But, instead, Columbanus was haunted by an episode that had taken place when he was still a teenager. At this age he had been uncertain how to best serve God and so he had searched out a holy woman to ask her advice. She was emphatic. He must become an exile and leave Ireland.

Seeing the growing strength of the boy, she said: 'I have fought the good fight as I was able. For the last twelve years, I have lived here far from my home, in this place of exile [within Ireland]. If it had not been for the weakness of my sex I would have gone out across the seas and chosen another place of exile among strangers. But you, full of the fire of youth, remain here on your native earth;

and, weakling, you listen, against your will, to your own flesh and think that you can mix with a woman without sin!... Flee, flee!... Leave this path that has led so many to the gates of Hell!'

Early Irish Christians, as other medieval Europeans, show a streak of woman-hating that shocks us today. Women were temptation personified, the Devil's proxies, and were felt to be 'unclean'. Not only this, but women themselves, as here, often indulged in the barracking of their own sex. Near where Columbanus had grown up another Irish ecclesiastic, visiting a female hermit, described how the female anchorite drove a brooch pin into her own cheek, pushing out a little green puss and told her visitor that, while there was that much fluid in a woman, her sex were not to be trusted. (For all this misogynist bluster, it is striking that nuns and holy women were often chosen as advisors by Irish holy men. Indeed, time after time, in early medieval Irish writings, we read of how Irish saints went to holy women to ask them in what direction their devotion should take them.)

It was the advice that Columbanus was given on this occasion, namely that he would best please God by leaving Ireland and by going into exile abroad, that stayed with him through his time at Bangor. Columbanus ruminated on the hermit's words and eventually in his thirties asked permission of Comgall to do just this, to leave the monastery behind and pass into the ocean. However, Columbanus stands as a milestone not only in Irish but also in European history. For he refused to follow the model of earlier Irish monks like Cormac who gave themselves up to the waves and all too often the abysses of the sea, or those like Colum Cille who went more deliberately, limiting themselves to islands close to home.

Columbanus decided instead in 590 on a distant and planned destination—Continental Europe. His intention, we are told by a medieval biographer, was to convert the pagan and to bring the healing salve of penance to sinning Christians. But, as this same biographer informs us that there was no war in the war-obsessed Ireland of Columbanus's youth, we should be suspicious of such pious, apocryphal hand-me-downs. Conversion and penance for sinners were probably secondary in Columbanus's mind to the hard penance he had chosen for himself: that of leaving his beloved homeland forever. If pagans or sinners were to get in his way then so be it. Columbanus's was, first and foremost, a mission to purify himself and his companions through exile in the wreck of Roman Europe.

It would be untrue to say that Columbanus came to an entirely devastated continent. But this was certainly no longer Europe as it had been under the Roman Empire, one able to project its power into Africa and Asia. These were the Dark Ages when the various Roman Christian peoples turned in on themselves. As Columbanus passed through continental Europe, he will have become aware that his contemporaries were living in a shrivelled-up society. If nothing else, the ruins of impressive Roman engineering and building works will have convinced him of this. There were no longer messages carried up carefully-maintained roads to Britannia sent from an Emperor in Trier or Ravenna. There were deteriorating tracks, and local warbands doing the bidding of regional kings. Though Columbanus could not have known it, things would get a lot worse before Europe would rise again a millennium afterwards.

Twenty years before Columbanus reached the continent, a child named Mohamed had been born in

Mecca (c. 570), a child whose later visions would lead to the birth of Islam and the destruction of the old Christian order in the Mediterranean. Spain would be invaded at his heirs' bidding and Egypt, once the most Christian of all countries, would become Muslim. The invasion of Spain dates to the eighth century, and afterwards Christian Europe would be hit by the attacks of the pagan Vikings in the north, in the ninth century, and, in the tenth century, by the invasions of the pagan Hungarians from the east. Indeed, the period from the seventh through to the tenth century is the only one from the death of Christ to the present day when the total number of Christians in the world actually shrank, perhaps by as much as a half. And, not only was there a decline in numbers, it was a time when the Church, often identifying too closely with local monarchies, lacked independence and hence energy and initiative.

Columbanus and his disciples decided to settle in the Vosges mountains, the age-old barrier between the Latin-speaking (today the French-speaking) and the Germanic-speaking worlds. The Vosges offered a wilderness well-suited to a party of Irish monks in search of a 'desert', for these diminutive Alps, famous today for their wildlife and their *ballons*, the local word for the Vosges peaks, are among the wildest regions in Western Europe. True, Columbanus and his disciples made their way not into the mountainous heart of this range, but to the tamer Lower Vosges: high plateaus covered in immaculate woods and lakes that have an almost Scandinavian feel. In Columbanus's day, however, beautiful landscapes—be they plateaus, mountains or valleys—invariably meant difficult survival. In the Middle Ages, the more lovely a land was to look at the more difficult it was to cultivate. Not only was this a difficult land for man, it was also a

147

derelict one. In the fifth century the Lower Vosges had been in the front line of the barbarian wars. As a result Roman civilisation, which had once been established in the area, had fallen into confusion. Whole regions, including those that Columbanus had come to settle, had been left depopulated as the tide of Empire drained away.

To get some idea of just how far the Vosges had gone to seed in the years between the fall of the Roman Empire and the coming of the exiles we need only look at the descriptions of the three monasteries that Columbanus and his disciples founded in the area. The first of these, Annegray, was built on the ruins of a Roman fort. The second, Luxeuil, was built a mere eight miles distant in the ruins of a Roman village: the exiles were amazed to find statues of pagan Roman gods and temples grown over in the nearby woods, like Inca remains in the jungled valleys of the Andes. The third, meanwhile, was that of Fontanelles, as the name suggests, a set of springs that had been used by the Romans for bathing.

The most important of Columbanus's foundations was not though one of these three. It was, rather, the retreat that the saint made for himself in the deep woodland seven miles from Annegray. Columbanus had, one day, been wandering in the forest there when he had stumbled on a series of cliffs with caverns, caverns that were—and this was what really interested Columbanus—difficult for men to arrive at. He would not be mobbed by the curious. Deciding that this would make an excellent hermitage, he climbed up the cliffs and entered one of these caves only to discover a bear inside: 'He ordered the beast to depart and to not return to that place ever again'.

Celtic saints are often associated with animals, who are made, by monastic writers, to love and respect holymen: it is even tempting to say that the love animals were said to

148

show to Celtic saints was the litmus test of these saints' piety. And some of the many stories about Columbanus and animals are perhaps just Christian dross, sneaked into his biography by the well-meaning. Did, for example, Columbanus really allow a pack of wolves to nibble at his tunic or persuade a flock of birds to stay away from the grain in the fields? But others are credible: including a vignette where squirrels moved across his body 'as cats frisk about their mistresses', even creeping into his cassock and nestling in his bosom. While others still we might wish to be true: notably a second bear episode where Columbanus trains a European black bear to take fruit only from certain trees in an orchard.

But, if Columbanus's authority over these animals was proof of his religious power, so too was the time that he spent in this retreat on the contemplation of God. It was there, in this cell in the wild, on his own or with a small boy to fetch him water, that Columbanus earned his reputation as a holy man. The hermit's cell was at the centre of his mystique, his holiness that rose up like a perfumed smoke and that soon engulfed the whole region. It is not necessary to have any Christian sympathies to see that among a God-fearing people this kind of Godly solitude, especially when attended with a fierce and righteous character would guarantee Columbanus a following that went beyond his original Celtic disciples and British-Celtic hangers-on.

And the establishment of three monasteries for twelve disciples would have been an absurdity. It was possible, instead, because of the impression that Columbanus made on notables throughout the region. When it was heard that he was to build Luxeuil, 'At this news, people came in from every direction to consecrate themselves in works of religion... The children of nobles... burnt to go

149

there, hating the cast-off illusions of the world and the fame of present wealth, they sought after eternal prizes'.

This fragment admittedly comes from a party document, a life of the saint written a half-century later by one Jonas, an avid supporter. But the fact is that, wherever we look in the later seventh century, disciples of Columbanus—'Columbanus's children' they might be called—appear as bishops, as abbots and as holy men. In this case, Jonas's pious details were correct. Columbanus did have an enormous impact on those around him and soon aristocrats and kings were queuing up to give him gifts and trade favours. Indeed, Columbanus emerges from descriptions as a healer, at one point an expert on birth-control, a *consigliere* for the local aristocracy and, when necessary, a voodoo witch-doctor cursing his or his friends' enemies. And it was, in fact, because of this darker, more righteous side of the Christian tradition that Columbanus lost his home in the Vosges.

As we mentioned, while discussing Colum Cille, it was the British Celts who had undertaken the task of converting the Irish, and the British Celts had brought some eccentric Christian customs with them across the Irish Sea. The result was that, by the time that Columbanus was established in the Vosges, the Irish followed the same version of Christianity as the British Celts. But the Irish also followed (along with the British Celts) a different form of Christianity from that of the various continental peoples. They were differences that would have set Columbanus and the British Celts apart. Both the Irish and British Celts, for example, shared the same half tonsure—the back of the head being entirely shaved, while the Continental tonsure was the classic Benedictine one with a continuous band of hair. They read the same Old Latin version of the Bible that had been abandoned generations before elsewhere. While the British Celts and especially the Irish celebrated permanent exile as a form of religious devotion. Continental Christians limited themselves to tamer pilgrimages, a journey to a shrine with, crucially, a return home afterwards.

The differences between the Irish- and British-Celtic churches, on the one hand, and the Continental churches, on the other, were not dogmatic. They might be compared to the differences between the modern Catholic Church and 'Catholic' Protestants, High Anglicans or Episcopalians. But, as is the case today between 'Roman' Protestants and the Catholic Church—and as was even more the case a century ago—much was made of those differences. A fine example, which would mark Columbanus's life, was the question of the celebration of Easter—a defining Christian custom—or rather the date when that celebration should take place. The Irish and British-Celtic churches were accused of dating Easter by a Jewish system, while the Continental Christians had a different way of determining when Easter fell. The result was that different Christians celebrated Easter on different days.

Today this problem may seem irrelevant or even quaint. But to sixth- and seventh-century Christians it became an issue of overwhelming importance, one that led to excommunications, papal letters and furious synods. And it must, of course, have been unsettling for members of different churches to find brethren of other nationalities celebrating Easter at different times. We have one account of some Irish churchmen in Rome bemused that a Scythian staying in their pilgrim hostel followed an alien timetable for the commemoration of Christ's resurrection. And an early royal marriage in England saw the

151

queen still fasting, while the Irish-educated king was at chapel celebrating the risen Lord. These kinds of inconsistencies made an unfortunate impression on the faithful and called into question the truths of a supposedly universal religion.

If Columbanus had kept his head down, then probably nothing would have come of the contrast between his own Christian traditions and those of the continental Christians. But once ensconced, Columbanus did something that surprised the Continental churches of the sixth century. He boldly declared ecclesiastical war. Not for Columbanus 'when in Rome do as the Romans'. Rather, the ex-Romans would have to learn to do as the Irish, for one of the most remarkable facts about Columbanus was his belief in the superiority of the traditions that he brought from his homeland. Indeed, judging himself to come from a special, blessed, superior, civilisation, Columbanus lectured his Christian neighbours, notwithstanding the fact that these neighbours viewed Ireland as the most barbarous corner of Europe. Nor was this confidence a simple quirk of Columbanus's character. He came from a people that, in the Dark Ages, thought themselves a special race. One fine example of this is the medieval-Irish belief that the language spoken by the people of the earth before the Tower of Babel was Irish, as was the language of the angels. The Irish also modestly peopled Christian history with Celts. In their writings it transpired that Simon Magus, a figure in the New Testament, had been the student of an Irish druid, while the Roman soldier that stood below Christ on the cross was also said to be from the furthest island of the west.

Nor had Columbanus any intention of limiting his attacks to the Church in the Vosges. He, in fact, turned against all Continental Christians by writing a letter to the pope of his day, Gregory the Great. Without any embarrassment (and in a smooth, impressive Latin), the Celt from the edge of the world told the Pope, one of the most famous to ever occupy the papal throne, that he really should sort out the question of Easter. Columbanus explained to Gregory in this letter with irony and impatience—this was, after all, only the head of Christendom that he was dealing with—how the thinkers and philosophers of the British Celts and Irish had already mused over this question and worked everything out to their own satisfaction and that others should now follow the Westerners' lead.

Columbanus gradually understood the limits of his 'war' over Christian practice. Within just a few years of his arrival in the Vosges reality had broken in, and the Celt was trying to make peace with the Continental Church. By then, in fact, Columbanus was so obviously losing the argument that he became an advocate of religious multiculturalism. 'Let Gaul contain whom heaven will contain together', he wrote in a letter, whose pious tone is very different from his first to Gregory. But the 'war', while it had lasted, had earned him fame, and many disciples who were impressed by his certainties, and Columbanus might have successfully resisted the calls of hostile clergy to have him repatriated. However, in the early seventh century, Columbanus created a new problem for himself with a more dangerous foe—the rulers of the Vosges.

The Vosges were at this date a part of Frankia, named for a barbarian people, the Franks, who, as the Roman Empire collapsed in the fifth century, had taken control of much of Roman Gaul and part of what is today Germany. The Franks governed this territory with a combination of the Roman and the barbarian. They proved, for example, tolerant of Roman bureaucracy. There was nothing wrong, from a regal point of view, with an efficient tax-collecting machine. Their first leader followed Roman customs, imitating the Roman Emperor by throwing gold from his chariot to passer-bys. He was also baptised into the Roman Church. But, at the same time, the old tribal ways kept coming back—in this the Franks had something in common with the Celtic Irish. Early Frankish warriors took part in human sacrifice on their campaigns, and Christian citizens seized in raids were not sent back to their homes, but had to be ransomed by anxious relatives.

The Frankish kings would slowly smooth out these hangovers from a tribal past. But, perhaps to make up for their more Roman behaviour, they let off steam through civil war. The ins and outs of Frankish dynastic politics were confusing and bloody, a cross between the Forsyte Saga and a snuff movie with fathers, mothers, sons and daughters plotting against each other and frequently slaying inconvenient relations. One royal dame, for example, was attached to four oxen and then torn apart on the orders of a grandson, while a royal father placed a disobedient son, his daughter-in-law and several grand-children in a hut and set them on fire. And so, when Columbanus had arrived in Frankia, it was, as so often in its history, divided into regional blocks—the product of civil war and divisive laws of inheritance. There were, in fact, at that date, not one but three Frankish kingdoms, which were bitter rivals: Neustria, Austrasia and Burgundy. Columbanus in the Vosges was under the authority of Theuderich, king of Burgundy.

In all three parts of Frankia the clergy had been taught that kings and aristocrats, unless they committed extraor-dinarily anti-Christian acts, were to be left alone. The clergy owed their position to these powerful men, and would certainly lose their positions if they challenged them. However, in Ireland and among the British Celts, a different tradition had emerged. Leaders were to be criticised whenever they merited it—and sometimes when perhaps they did not—with public denunciations and even curses. In the Celtic homelands we have saints' lives that tell us quite routinely of kings being swallowed by the ground for daring to anger holymen, and Irish monks took a keen interest in 'maledictory psalms' to increase their cursing potency.

Here was another area where Columbanus, with his uncompromising view of the world, was to import attitudes that were to put his rule over the three Vosges monasteries in jeopardy. The saint was bringing with him Irish traditions that revelled in king-baiting to a land where no king would tolerate this kind of behaviour. It was only a matter of a time before a serious clash erupted between the newcomer and the Frankish rulers of Burgundy. And anyone who has even a passing knowledge of Christianity will not be surprised to learn that the argument, when it came, concerned sexual morality in the Frankish royal courts.

The problem was that some Frankish kings ran what were essentially harems in parallel with a royal marriage to a Christian wife so that a little pagan exuberance could make its way through into the icier world of Christian monogamy. The Frankish clergy did not push this issue. Their posts and perhaps their lives depended on not making a nuisance of themselves. And so it was doubtless a surprise to Brunhilda, the grandmother of the king of Burgundy, when she presented some royal bastards for a blessing to Columbanus and the Irish exile refused out of hand: 'Know that these boys will never bear the royal sceptre, for they were begotten in sin!'

This was not how the Frankish royal family was used to being treated by members of the clergy, but the family seems to have tried to make allowances for the—by this date—most famous of their holymen. The king sent Columbanus a gift of food and drink, to which Columbanus dryly responded: 'the Most High is not pleased with the offerings of the wicked.' Any Frankish priest who had taken it upon himself to make these kinds of comments would already be in the executioner's dungeon. Theuderich, however, noting perhaps a suicidal streak in Columbanus, refused him the satisfaction of martyrdom. Instead, he instructed all the Irish and British Celtic monks based in the saint's three monasteries to leave his lands immediately.

Driven out of his spiritual 'desert' in the Vosges, Columbanus would have to find a new place of exile.

13

COLUMBANUS'S SECOND EXILE

fter their falling out with the Frankish king Theuderich, Columbanus and his Western followers were forced from their homes and escorted back towards Nantes on the Atlantic coast, where they were instructed to board a boat to Ireland. Yet, somehow, the Irish gave their escort the slip. A miracle is given to explain this escape that may have been used to excuse baser tactics on the part of the Celts. And here begins the most difficult part of Columbanus's continental life. The saint had so far set up three important monasteries: monasteries that would continue to flourish after he had been banished and that celebrated his name for generations. But Columbanus himself was forced to wander.

Irish exiles had a reputation as wanderers in the Middle Ages. They were said to be endlessly-moving ecclesiastical gypsies, unable to settle in one place. There is, for example, one medieval story that tells how a group of Irish monks attempted a break-out of a monastery in the middle of the night so as to return to the open road. But stories such as these are the result of disgruntled Continentals complaining about religious customs that

157

they did not trouble to understand. In fact, if the exiles necessarily travelled a good deal on their way to find a place of final settlement, afterwards they were immobile, staying holed up for years in one island or one valley or sometimes a room or cell. If Columbanus had not enraged Theuderich, he would have remained in the region until his death. Indeed, he complains in one of his letters of the seventeen bodies of his monks who were already buried in the Vosges and whom he had no wish to leave behind.

But, after his evasion at Nantes, Columbanus was unable to turn back to the monasteries that had nourished him. And so, without ties, and with just a handful of his disciples, Columbanus headed to the north and to a second of the Frankish kingdoms, Neustria, ruled by Chlothar, a cousin and—this being the Franks—bitter enemy of Theuderich.

Chlothar wished Columbanus to stay in his lands for in a superstitious age a good saint was a resource for a country, much as we might think today of petroleum or platinum. Time and time again in our records, we learn of communities that did everything they could to stop 'their saint' escaping, or that saint's corpse, which, as a source of miracles, was just as important. We even know of one case where a community killed their saint to prevent his exit. But Columbanus, to prevent further problems with Theuderich, Chlothar's neighbour, instead passed on to the third of the Frankish realms and its monarch, Theudebert, 'who received him joyfully'. Columbanus was by now the most celebrated living saint in Europe, and Theudebert promised the Celtic monk 'beautiful places' within his own kingdom where Columbanus could re-establish his monastic life.

Columbanus, given his pick of the glories of

Austrasia, chose another ruined Roman settlement, Brigantia, modern Bregenz, on Lake Constanz at the western extreme of Austria. It was and is a scenic place. But it was also more dangerous than the Vosges for many of the locals had not yet been converted to Christianity. There are tens of accounts from the early Middle Ages of determined saints walking into glades where pagans were celebrating their (often bloody) rites and taking on the enemy directly, either through a duel with a heathen priest or by the simple expedient of chopping down a sacred tree or laying into a pagan shrine with a hammer. Columbanus himself will perhaps have heard, while growing up, of Colum Cille's visit to pagan communities in the north of Britain, where Colum Cille is said to have played games of weather magic with northern shamans. Columbanus certainly will have heard of the stories of St Patrick who, when he had arrived in Ireland two centuries before, according to legend, had shared a series of challenges with druids to prove his God's superiority.

Columbanus's first confrontation with the local pagan community was at a beer festival given in honour of the highest of the Germanic gods, Odin. In accounts like this, where marvels press in on memory and sometimes crowd it out, it is difficult to know quite what to believe. Columbanus's medieval biographer claims that Columbanus strode among the surprised Austrians and, walking straight to a beer cask, he breathed over the cask and watched it crash onto the ground, spilling all the sacred beer. This was the key moment. Would the pagans be amazed that Columbanus had dared to destroy such a holy object and note that Odin had not intervened against the audacious newcomer? Or would they surge in and destroy the blasphemous foreigner, who had come unasked into their midst? The account tells us that, instead of killing, they marvelled at the saint's 'powerful breath', and then bowed before the power of the cross. Is there any historical truth at the bottom of this account? It is certain that Columbanus came to Bregenz, where he founded a monastery, and it is likely that there were pagans who will have excited the saint's ire. But was there ever a beer-festival? Perhaps all we can take back from this legend is some memory among his monastic community of success against the heathen.

But success was not able to guarantee Columbanus the permanent sanctuary that he wished for. Change was afoot in the kingdoms of Frankia. Burgundy under Columbanus's enemy Theuderich was about to declare war on Austrasia, ruled by the saint's protector Theudebert.

> ... The peace treaty which Theuderich and Theudebert had made was broken, and each, assured in the number of warriors, attempted to kill the other. Columbanus then went to king Theudebert and told him that he should give up his kingdom and move into a monastery, so as not to lose both his earthly crown and also eternal life in heaven. The king and his household laughed, however. They had never heard of a king of the Franks who, while on the throne, had decided of his own volition to become a monk. Columbanus said that if the king did not willingly take up the profession of priest, then the king would be made to do it, even if he did not wish to.
>
> Afterwards the saint went back to his cell and his prophecy was confirmed. Theuderich attacked Theudebert without delay and defeated him near Zulpich, and went after him with his great army.

Theudebert then brought together a new army and fought a further battle near Zulpich. Many men were cut down on both sides, but Theudebert was, in the end, the loser and fled... Theuderich chased after Theudebert and Theudebert was taken by the betrayal of his own men and was sent to his grandmother Brunhilda.

As we have seen Frankish family members did not treat each other with any special respect. It should come as no surprise that Brunhilda 'in her anger, because she was allied to Theuderich, shut Theudebert in a monastery and, a few days later, had him mercilessly murdered'. Austrasia ceased to exist as a kingdom and now that Columbanus's old enemies Theuderich and Brunhilda controlled the territory, the saint had to start his wandering once again.

Columbanus fled the Frankish realms and passed into the lands of the Slavs, with the intention of converting them. He may even have been tolerably close to Salzburg where, one hundred years later, a bishop, another Irish exile, would scandalise his fellows by preaching about other-worldy beings who lived on the moon and sun. Columbanus himself, to the best of our knowledge, did not indulge in such speculations. Instead, once established among this entirely pagan people he had an altogether different vision—one that would drive him still further away. An angel came down to his side and drew out a circle, a map of the world, 'as the circle of the universe is typically drawn by a quill in a manuscript'. The angel then revealed to Columbanus that much of the world remained in ignorance of Christ and that the saint could usefully go wherever he wished.

Columbanus meditated on which direction would be

161

best. There was the upper Danube, the Steppes, Chlothar's kingdom, the last of the Frankish lands to hold out against Theuderich. In the end, he determined to head south across the Alps and into Italy, following the same passes that about a millennium before the first Italian Celts had taken. The saint had decided that his advanced years and his years of service to God had allowed him the right to some respite from the work of a missionary. He was going to gentler climes with his followers to live out his last years among the vines and olives.

The site that Columbanus chose was a hill, Bobbio, in the Trebbia valley on the edge of the Dolomites near modern Piacenza. From the Vosges to Lake Constance and now in Italy Columbanus had showed a talent at picking dramatic locations. Here, close by, so local tradition said, to where Hannibal had passed with his elephants at the time of the wars between Rome and Carthage, Columbanus discovered the wreck of an old church dedicated to St Peter. He sent out his monks to gather lumber to repair its roofs and walls and predictably enough miracles are reported about how these heavy trunks were brought up the steep valley side to his new church.

It is striking that after Columbanus reached Bobbio his miraculous powers seem to have dissipated. At least, his medieval biographer Jonas records extremely few marvels. And, in reading Jonas's account, the impression the reader has is that, enjoying the fruits of his labour, Columbanus was no longer playing the Christian druid. In fact, the dominant theme of those final months is quiescence. True, while in Italy, Columbanus wrote a stern letter to Pope Boniface IV complaining about heresy in the peninsula—shades of his letter to Gregory the Great. But when Chlothar, who had now triumphed over Columbanus's arch enemy Theuderich, sent messengers to bring Columbanus to him, wishing again to have the holyman in his kingdom, Columbanus refused pleading that he could not undertake the journey. His old bones were not up to the Alps and German forests and everything else that stood between him and his first continental home, Luxeuil. He did, however, write a letter to Chlothar asking him to protect his early monasteries. Then, in the winter of 615, Columbanus died and was carried down to the tomb where his remains rest to this day: 'blessed among saints'.

It is often claimed that Columbanus transformed Christianity in Europe. But this is to misunderstand what Columbanus was and what he represented. Columbanus's Christian customs that so scandalised Gregory the Great and other Europeans quickly got lost following the saint's death. For example, the exotic Celtic tonsure was kept by his monks in his lifetime, but it vanished afterwards.. *Ditto* the Celtic dating of Easter that Columbanus had brought out of Ulster. And in this Columbanus was not unusual. The customs of Irish exiles were, as we will see in the next chapters, typically abused or ignored by their flocks. In fact, the only possibly 'Celtic' custom that caught on was private confession and penance: it was likely Irish monks and quite possibly Columbanus himself who introduced to continental Christianity the custom that a man or woman confess their sins to a priest. But, more importantly than private confession, what Columbanus and other later exiles gave to Europe in these critical generations, when the Christian world was buffeted by hostile forces, was their energy.

Columbanus's life that at first can seem a series of failures—chased from kingdom to kingdom, settling only through desperation in the north of Italy—looks rather different from the crypt where the Celtic monk is buried. His forced wandering had spread his name much further than the Vosges so that by his death he had become a European personality, one of the most renowned saints of the Middle Ages. His monasteries, which he scattered behind him wherever he went, would survive him. Several including Bobbio and Luxeuil would survive the Middle Ages, only to be undone by enlightenment, revolution and invasion. Most significantly, his students and disciples, 'his children', would rise through the seventh century into positions of power: as bishops, abbots and kings.

It was Columbanus's children, not the fading customs of Irish Christianity, that matter to the modern world. In a very real sense, it would not have made any difference if the name of Columbanus had been forgotten. The mighty old tree, to borrow a Victorian image, had, before being brought down and chopped up for firewood, given birth to a forest of saplings. These 'saplings' would define seventh-century Christianity in France, in Italy and in Germany. And, even if Columbanus's time was over, the outpouring of exiles from Ireland had only just begun. In the next four centuries thousands more Celtic churchmen would stream out of the West in search of a 'desert' where they could live and pray, drawn by the examples of Colum Cille, Cormac, Columbanus and other Celtic holy men. Most would remain anonymous, lost in the blank, holy monotony of monastic lives spent hunched over a manuscript in a library or bent over a hoe. But all would buttress a failing continent and a failing religion in their worst centuries, as invaders pressed from without and monarchs and lords such as those in Frankia stifled Christian development within.

And among these soldiers of Christ, twenty years after Columbanus's death, came Aidan, a monk of Colum Cille's old foundation on Iona, to the mission fields of pagan England.

Map 9 The Irish Mission in England

14

AIDAN AND ENGLAND

British-Celtic and an Anglo-Saxon army met in 633 at the wreck of Hadrian's Wall, abandoned more than two centuries before by the Romans. Though all but forgotten today, the battle of Heavenfield must rate among the most important ever to have been fought on British soil. To understand its significance it should be remembered that Britain at this date was not ruled by one or even four or five kings. This is the period of English history often referred to as the Seven Kingdoms or the Heptarchy, though that too is an optimistic, simplifying count. In fact, Britain in the early 600s was ruled by perhaps fifteen different kings, some with territories no bigger than a modern British county. And, if we included sub-kings as well—warrior chiefs and clan leaders who often had considerable local power and sometimes almost total independence—we might easily triple or quadruple that number.

These kingdoms, of course, fought among themselves. The Anglo-Saxons, the early English, fought each other. And the British Celts, the ancestors of the Welsh and Cornish, also indulged in civil war. But some of the most

167

memorable campaigns were between the two ethnic communities: the Anglo-Saxons attempting to secure the parts of Britain that they had already conquered and the British Celts determined to drive them back into the North Sea from out of which the invaders had come two centuries before. And Heavenfield, in fact, was not only a battle between kingdoms, but also between peoples.

The leader of the British Celts at Heavenfield was Cadwallon, son of Cadfan, one of the most successful battle-lords of the Dark Ages. In the previous three years this Welsh warrior king—Wales by this time was the principal British-Celtic region—had created a veritable empire in Britain. He had, first, united the multiplicity of small tribal kingdoms in Wales itself. Second, he had defeated a coalition of Anglo-Saxon armies in the mountains of Powys—the Severn was said to have run red from its source to the sea. Then, third, he had moved north of the Humber, conquering as far as the Tweed, enemy kingdoms tumbling before his orders and violence. He had chosen the north because it was there that the Northumbrians—the people of the North of the Humber—the mightiest of the Anglo-Saxons—dwelt. And, for a number of years, he reversed the humiliations of the fifth and sixth centuries, when the Anglo-Saxons had seized much of Britain from the island's original Celtic inhabitants.

On the other side, the leader of the Anglo-Saxons was a member of one of the aristocratic families of the northern Anglo-Saxons: Oswald son of Aethelfrith. Oswald was too young and untested at this date to have had much of a reputation—but the very fact that he was Aethelfrith's heir must have meant something to his peers. Aethelfrith—'the Twister' as he was called by the British Celts who had fought him—had dominated the north at the end of the sixth century. And it was his armies who had been among the first Anglo-Saxons to break into what is today Lancashire and Cheshire on the west coast, previously British-Celtic territories.

Oswald was, by no means, the obvious choice for resistance. And the Northumbrian Anglo-Saxons had been so battered by Cadwallon's ruthless form of warfare—the burning and massacring of entire settlements—that only a small group of faithful henchmen had come to fight with Aethelfrith's son. Nor had Oswald been first in succession to the throne of Northumbria. But, by this date, other heirs had either been killed or brushed aside by Cadwallon. In fact, Oswald was perhaps the last hope of the northern Anglo-Saxons in what had become a struggle for survival.

Oswald and Cadwallon were the leaders of communities that despised each other: the memory of the Anglo-Saxon 'thugs' that stole the British-Celts' Britannia or of the 'perfidious' British-Celts was to last for many centuries, and still colours English-Welsh relations. We need have no doubt that the generals shared in this dislike—though Cadwallon was not beyond allying with one Anglo-Saxon king to fight another. But, as well as a probable hatred for each other's people, the leaders had two other things in common. The first was that both Oswald and Cadwallon had spent many years in Ireland. In their early careers, both had been driven from their own kingdoms and forced to flee across the Irish Sea. There, indeed, the two had joined Irish warbands until they were able to gather an army large enough to force their way back into their homelands.

The second biographical detail that the leaders shared was their religious affiliation: both were Christian. This was unremarkable in the case of Cadwallon. By the

169

seventh century, all British Celts were brought up in the
faith. But Oswald came, instead, from a people that was
still overwhelmingly pagan. He had only converted during
his sojourn in Ireland with twelve henchmen—perhaps
being baptised on Colum Cille's Iona. And it is likely that
he was one of very few Christians in his small army,
indeed, one of the few Christians among the Anglo-
Saxons of the north. It is this unusual affiliation that
explains a dream that Oswald is said to have had on the
night before the battle of Heavenfield.

> King Oswald… was waiting for battle, sleeping on
> a pillow in his tent when, in a vision, he saw Colum
> Cille glowing angelically with a body so great that
> the saint seemed to touch the clouds. Colum Cille
> having introduced himself to the king, stood in the
> middle of the king's camp, and covered all that
> camp with his shining cloak, except for one small
> portion, and, as he did so, he gave the cheering
> words… 'Be strong and be brave: for I will be with
> you'. Then Colum Cille having spoken… added:
> 'You must march tomorrow night to battle, for the
> Lord has granted that your enemies will be routed
> and that Cadwallon will fall into your hands and
> also that after the battle you will come back
> triumphant and reign most happily'.
>
> The king having woken with these words,
> brought his council together and told them of the
> vision, so encouraging them. All the people
> promised that, after battle, they would believe and
> be baptised, for the Saxon land had been shadowed
> over until then by ignorance and heathenism, with
> the exception of King Oswald and his twelve men
> who had been baptised while among the Irish in

170

exile… And, on the next night, King Oswald, as he had been instructed in that vision, went out from camp to battle and though having the smaller army… was given a straightforward and easy victory by the Lord with Cadwallon being slain…

The old northern gods of war did not resent Oswald's disloyalty—or so his pagan troops must have thought. For, in 633, at Heavenfield, the smaller Anglo-Saxon army won this surprising victory against the invaders.

Those historians who include Heavenfield in their works often restrict themselves to a lyrical note to the effect that if Oswald had not defeated Cadwallon, if Cadwallon had had a chance to secure his earlier victories, then today the north of England from the Humber to the Tees would be Welsh-speaking. It is an intriguing alternative history and one that has understandably captured the imagination of scholars. It would have created in the Dark Ages a Wales so large that it would have been able to defend itself from the English in the Middle Ages; an early modern, independent Wales able to send colonies to the New World—a Welsh-speaking New Hampshire, a Welsh-speaking Virginia; and a contemporary Welsh-speaking Liverpool and Manchester producing Welsh pop music. So intent, however, are historians on such speculations that they sometimes forget the one serious consequence of history as it happened. The newly-crowned king was determined to convert his subjects to the religion that he had been given by the Irish, for 'he was concerned that the whole race under his rule should be blessed with the grace of Christian faith'. And his first recorded act as king involved the sending of a message to Iona and the monastery of Colum Cille there, asking for missionaries to come and teach his people.

Oswald had lived among the Dal Riadans while he was in exile, the Irish tribes that controlled both eastern Ulster and the Hebrides where Iona lay, so Iona was a monastery known to him, and hence the vision of Colum Cille before battle. Though Colum Cille had died thirty four years before (597), already in his lifetime the monks of Iona had gained experience in missionary activity among the Dark Age Highlanders, the Picts. Colum Cille himself had crossed 'the spine of Britain', to speak of his faith with the high king of the Picts in Moray, in the east of Scotland. But the monks of Iona had only limited success there, despite an energetic visit from their leader, and they knew that sometimes attempts to enter pagan territory could end disastrously. In 616, on an island not far from Iona, a pagan queen had had an entire community of monks massacred for their effrontery in setting up a monastery on land that she had set aside for sheep. The monks of Iona can have had then no illusions about just how dangerous work among the godless could be. And, in fact, the first Irish experience of the Northumbrians proved to be a strained one. An Irish bishop was sent to work their conversion, but quickly returned to Iona complaining of Oswald's 'obstinate and barbaric' subjects.

It is worthwhile trying to understand for a moment just why the first Irish contact with the Anglo-Saxons resulted in this uncharitable conclusion. And the answer is to be found in the Anglo-Saxons' pagan religion which most of Oswald's subjects followed. When we think of paganism today we think most easily of Mediterranean temples where togaed men and gowned women prayed to their gods or made very occasional animal sacrifices. Greco-Roman paganism was, by historical times, a tame religion: red in neither tooth nor claw. But the barbarian paganism that the Irish had practised until a century before—and that Oswald's Anglo-Saxons were still enjoying in the seventh century—was a bloodier, northern version, a religious primal scream. We know that human sacrifice was worked among the Anglo-Saxons, and their gods were certainly not the lounging A-listers of the Greek and Roman pantheon. Take the Germanic deity Odin, whose beer festival in Dark-Age Austria Columbanus had so rudely interrupted twenty years before and who was also worshipped by the Anglo-Saxons. Odin—the name means 'turmoil'—was a violent, unsubtle being who had gained the wisdom of ages by plucking out one of his own eyeballs. His symbol was the spear, his creature the raven and we learn from later Scandinavian sources that, at regular intervals, males of every species (including man) were sacrificed to him.

The reputation of Odin, who was said to be Oswald's ancestor, would have been enough to send any Irish missionary scuttling back towards Iona. But this early crisis in Iona's attempt to convert the Anglo-Saxons of the north was dealt with effectively by the monastery. On the missionary's return—as so often in the case of failed saints we do not know his name—a general assembly of the elders of the monastery was brought together to consider the problem of the conversion of the northern Anglo-Saxons. The monks listened politely to the description of the mission to date and the impossible nature of the Northumbrian heathen. And there followed 'a lengthy discussion for they desired to help that people and were saddened that the one that they had sent had not been accepted'. Then, at the end of this discussion, a monk, by the name of Aidan—who later tradition says had come to Iona from Connaught, in the west of Ireland—spoke up: 'It seems to me, my brother, that you were too hard on your unlearned flock. You did not...

first give them the milk of softer instruction so that, nourished by the word of God little by little, they could take on more perfect and more sublime precepts…' And the historian who records this, the Venerable Bede, says that the assembly was so struck by these words that it made Aidan bishop to the Northumbrians on the spot. After a false start the conversion of the Northumbrians was about to get underway.

In much of history, Christian conversion has involved discussions and persuasion. Missionaries reason out the existence of God and the Trinity; or, at least, reason enough space for faith to do its work. This is the case today in the west when someone with a Bible in hand rings the doorbell. And the early history of Christianity amounted to a similar kind of conversion, a long series of acts of persuasion as Christianity slowly worked its way around the cities of the Mediterranean basin. But in a tribal society, Christianity could not spread in this manner. It was not enough to arrive in an Anglo-Saxon clan in the Pennines, knock on the door of the nearest shack and talk about God.

Any attempt to reach the members of the tribe had to come through the ruler in a given area, and conversion was only likely to succeed if this ruler himself embraced Christianity. If he did, then his entire tribe would typically follow suit or, at least, the part of the tribe that was most loyal to him. When, a generation before, Gregory the Great, the pope with whom Columbanus had had a lively correspondence, sent a mission to the Anglo-Saxons of Kent, he had made sure that his missionaries had gone straight to the king's throne. And the success of the mission to Kent had depended on the conversion of Aethelbert, its king.

The missionaries to Kent—missionaries who, as we

will see, were to have a devastating effect on the Irish mission in the north—had had the difficulty of convincing Aethelbert to convert. But Aidan was in a privileged position. He was coming to a kingdom whose king was already Christian and who would support his mission. (Aidan's success after the first Ionian failure has been explained in many ways, but may have depended on his excellent relations with Oswald. Knowing Irish from his stay in Ireland, Oswald even helped to translate Aidan's sermons.) Of course, there was a risk with this kind of tribal conversion. Should Oswald be killed in battle and replaced by a pagan, then, there was the danger that the northern Anglo-Saxons would switch their allegiance back to one-eyed Odin and his court of maleficent gods.

Nor was this just theory. Less than a decade before, in 627, an offshoot of Pope Gregory's mission to the people of Kent had come to Northumbria and, at first, had had startling success after persuading a king to convert. A letter from the then Pope had followed. Anglo-Saxons in the north were bustled along to rivers for baptism. Working on a conveyer-belt principle, a handful of Italian monks took mere days to make thousands of new Christians, though there must be the suspicion that the Anglo-Saxon peasantry who were being 'converted' understood very little of what was happening to them— the missionaries did not speak the converts' language or spoke it badly. But, when this king died—killed by Cadwallon—Christianity disappeared almost as quickly as it had come. Tribal conversions were, by their nature, shallow conversions: easily planted, easily uprooted.

Then Aidan had another challenge. The sheer size of the territory left to him. The kingdom of Northumbria is today covered by fourteen different Anglican bishoprics,

175

centred on York: and this in the age of the car and train. Northumbria in Aidan's time included the wild recesses of the Dales, the plains of East Yorkshire and Cheshire, the Cheviots and much of what are today the Scottish Lowlands. Nor would Aidan make his life easier by travelling over this vast area on horseback. Irish clergy believed that this sullied their spirit and would only go on foot, much to the frustration of other clerics. Indeed, one seventh-century Archbishop of Canterbury became so annoyed with such behaviour that he picked up an Irish-trained bishop and threw him onto a saddled mount.

And this was also a dangerous territory. We have spoken so far glibly of 'Northumbria': but really Northumbria was a series of loosely amalgamated Anglo-Saxon tribal territories with a few conquered British-Celtic kingdoms hanging off its side. And, in Aidan's time, there were perils almost inconceivable to modern Northumbrians. Bears, boars and wolves still ranged across the countryside and tree coverage was such that we can talk of forests as opposed to the tame woods that characterise the region today. Then this was a time when the laws spoke quite routinely of robber bands and where one northern king's boast was that, in his time, it was possible for a mother to carry a new born child from one side of England to another without being attacked—the implication being that normally it was not.

Aidan had his work cut out for him in this lost and singularly wild part of Europe that he had undertaken to bring to salvation. His early success was deceptive and things could go wrong, and the Celtic monk would have to set down the foundations of a church in this enormous territory that would last the vagaries of kings and dynasties. His first step was the creation of the seat of his bishopric on the island of Lindisfarne on the eastern coast of Northumbria. Lindisfarne is another example of the exiles' talent for picking locations of exceptional natural beauty as their 'deserts'. Windswept and haunted by the constant worry of the encroaching sea—the island is tidal—Lindisfarne already had a reputation in the Dark Ages. According to the storytellers the first northern Anglo-Saxons had been trapped here for three days and three nights while a British-Celtic coalition besieged them.

However, for Aidan Lindisfarne was a conveniently-sited island—it was near Oswald's court—that must have reminded him of Colum Cille's Iona. And, in Irish style, he soon found some smaller islands to the south-east, the Farne Isles, and used them as his place of escape and communion with God, just as Columbanus had searched out his bear cave in the Vosges. There, surrounded by the waves and nesting terns—terns that still dive at visitors, often attacking them—he gave himself up to prayer and fasts. Aidan was a bishop and hence an administrator. But, as with many of the exiles, his authority was based on Godly retreats away his flock. He did not go as far as one later Irish exile who closed himself in a single small cell in the Alps for forty years. Aidan will have moved backwards and forwards from the Farne Isles to more worldly matters. But much of his time in England will have been spent in contemplation among the crying gulls.

Aidan also had another thing working in his favour: assistants. Some of these he had recruited on the spot by buying slaves and then converting them to his own service. And Lindisfarne, in fact, became a school of saints, educating English-born men to the church: men who would go off, in turn, and convert parts of southern England in the next generation. But Aidan also came with brother monks from his homeland, other exiles who had vowed to spend their lives among the English heathen and whom he began to spread around his diocese to govern its vast bounds. Assistants to saints—and Aidan was already well on his way to becoming one—are often overlooked by historians: much as the first failed missionary from Iona has been all but forgotten. Indeed, if we did not have some chance references we might think that they had never existed at all and that Aidan had turned up in the territory alone.

But these assistants sometimes stray across the frame of history. There is, for example, an Irish exile named Diuma, who later appeared in the English Midlands; while one of Aidan's successor in Northumbria, Colman was also possibly part of the original mission. Then, just occasionally, we have placenames from the north that suggest the residence of an early Irish monk, who was remembered by a local population long after he had been buried. One such place might be Mankinholes a heathered height near the town of Hebden Bridge in the South Pennines. This was originally Manchán's *Hol* or, as we would say, Manchán's Hollow and Manchán is an unmistakeably Irish name, while the poor hilly land in which the *Hol* is found—it stands on the edge of a peat bog, towering above the wooded valley—would have proved an excellent retreat for one of Aidan's priests. These are, true, mere scraps of evidence. But they are a reminder that, though Aidan is the only certain name we have from the first generation of Irish missionaries in England, he will not have been alone.

15

THE ROAD TO WHITBY

Oswald, who had brought Christianity to the north, died on the battlefield challenging the pagan Anglo-Saxons of the Midlands in 642, a little less than a decade after the Irish mission had begun. Tradition says that, as the end came, the Northumbrian king, instead of fighting, prayed for the salvation of his fellow warriors. And, whether this is or is not a true record of his last moments, Oswald had, in any case, a Christian victory: one of which Aidan would have approved. For, soon after his death, the faithful began to travel to the spot where he had been 'martyred' to pray and take a little of the blessed dirt on which he had bled. Miracles were reported and stories told, including the legend that a bird had flown with the king's severed arm into an ash tree and that, where the arm had dropped from the bird's beak, a spring had welled up.

But appealing as all this may be—and a more trustworthy account tells us that the defeated monarch was dismembered by his foes—Oswald's death also had consequences in a more tangible and material world. Oswald, in his time as lord of the north, had shown himself a master general, cementing together various kingdoms under his control. However, on his death, all this changed. Oswald's empire dissolved and Northumbria itself split temporarily into bickering parts.

To Aidan and his fellow Irish missionaries it must have seemed, for a time, that Oswald's death presaged the end of their mission. Would the tribal Christianity that they had nourished really have the strength to survive the *interregnum* or would it wither as an earlier Christianity had with Cadwallon's invasion? In fact, their mission held. Though for a number of years storms lashed the north, Northumbria reformed under Oswald's successor Oswiu.

But, with Oswald's death, an era had, nevertheless, come to an end: and Aidan belonged to that time not to the next. The bishop of Lindisfarne grew old adding to his reputation with the years: kindness and moderation being ascribed to him by all. Bede recalls how Aidan would often dine with Oswiu, but would eat little and leave early with his followers before, as was accustomed to happen in an Anglo-Saxon court, 'the carousing broke out and the household became merry with wine'. Aidan clearly lacked the alcoholic tendencies of some later Irish exiles, including one ninth-century Celt, based in Liège, who used to write poems requesting beer from a local dignitary.

Like Oswald, tee-total Aidan was in fact soon a saint. Indeed, to this day he is the patron of firemen—an honour given for a miracle where he is said to have prevented a pagan army from burning the town of Bamburgh. He died almost ten years after Oswald on 31st August 651, leaning against a wooden support of a church near the same town. True to the profession he later represented, that Aidan-touched wood was afterwards held to have an asbestos-like quality, being quite invulnerable to fire. Aidan had governed his enormous diocese in the north of England for seventeen years and had created a Christian community, bringing it successfully through the trauma of the death of Oswald.

He was replaced by Finan, an Irishman who had also been trained on Iona and who may, in his boyhood or teens, have known Colum Cille. Finan does not stand out in the history of Northumbria in the same way as Aidan. One of the few insights that we have into his character are references to furious theological arguments between him and another Celt. The only other deed he is remembered for in the north was the rebuilding of the modest church that Aidan had constructed on Lindisfarne, a church Finan made into a cathedral, constructing it 'in the Irish way, not with stone but from oak, thatching it with reeds'.

Finan's real significance lay, instead, outside his own bishopric. Northumbria, notwithstanding Oswald's death, was, at this time, still the most powerful of the British kingdoms, and by far the biggest. But, while parts of the Home Counties and East Anglia were already Christian, converted by the Papal mission sent by Pope Gregory the Great, at the end of the sixth century, most of the Anglo-Saxons of central and southern England were not. There was then a Northumbrian overlord dominating his neighbours, some of whose peoples were Christian, but some of whom were still very much pagan.

It was too much for the pious Northumbrian kings who were not able to resist the temptation to meddle, convert and generally flaunt their authority. Using their power and their enthusiastic Irish bishops, they extended the faith into these territories to the south that had seen no Christians since the British-Celts had been overrun or enslaved there in the fifth and sixth centuries. The Irish mission that had, in the space of a short generation, established Christianity in the north was now about to do

181

the same over a swathe of central and southern Britain. Just how they did so is again a reminder of how conversion in Dark Age tribal societies differed from conversion in modern times.

Among the most important of the southern converts was one Peada. Bede, an historian of the early English Church, describes how a Midland prince of this name came north with his warriors not in war, but to ask for the hand of the daughter of Oswiu, king of all the Northumbrians. Oswiu explained that it was unthinkable that Peada marry his daughter without being of the faith, and so Peada had Christianity explained to him. In our medieval sources we learn that Christian missionaries were able to impress pagans with details of eternal life. Missionaries would also assault the validity of the pagan gods by asking how a god could live in wood or stone statues, or by taking the potential Christian through a bewildering array of logical arguments that would have tangled up a modern philosophy graduate, never mind an illiterate Anglo-Saxon king.

These strategies would have been rehearsed hundreds of times by anxious missionaries in pagan regions in Dark Age Europe, missionaries who were aware that the conse-quences of judging their subject wrongly might be martyrdom. But Peada was not able to do away with the missionaries. He was a guest. The quality of such arguments, not to mention the looming presence of the Northumbrian king, his host, soon convinced Peada of what he must do. The pagan prince confessed that, even were he now refused the hand of the king's daughter, he would still wish to become a Christian. And, at this decision, his bodyguards and aristocratic courtiers also converted to the new religion. We are, after all, in a tribal society where loyalty to a chief in battle or diplomacy or religion, as we see here, was what defined a man. And so it was that Finan baptised them all at a royal estate in the north, perhaps Walbottle (to the west of Newcastle-upon-Tyne). Unlike Aidan, almost twenty years before, Finan will have been able to communicate with the catechumens in Anglo-Saxon. But whether they understood the subtleties of the Trinity or remembered the stories he must have told them from the Gospels is another question.

Peada returned to the south with his new wife, his newly converted warband and four clergymen: three Englishmen and one, Diuma, a Celt. The Irish were already training competent priests from among the Northumbrians, another sign that the mission would make it beyond any misfortunes or civil wars. And now it fell to these four to begin the long work of converting the Anglo-Saxons of the English Midlands. Diuma was eventually made bishop there by Finan and was followed in the bishopric by a second Irish clergyman, Ceollach. Then, as Peada was helping to Christianise the central part of England, king Sigeberht of Essex also received the cross on the persuasion of Oswiu of Northumbria. He too was baptised with his followers on a visit north. And he too returned with priests, including one Chad who would become bishop of the king's lands.

Chad was Anglo-Saxon, but his Christianity was Irish. Indeed, one of his few recorded acts was a very Irish-sounding cursing of Sigeberht after the king had disobeyed the holy man's orders. Nor was Chad alone. Irish and Irish-trained clergy passed over much of southern England at this date. We know, for example, of an Irish hermit, Fursa (who we previously met swallowing a lizard, p. 118), who went with his brothers to Burgh Castle near Great Yarmouth in Norfolk in search of a 'desert'. One Mael Dub, established himself at Malmesbury on the other side of the country, where he became a teacher to Anglo-Saxon converts. And we have other clues of the exiles' presence. Sometimes they are as simple as a placename, so Malmesbury (Maeldub's Burh) originated from that same Irish name, Mael Dub. At other times they are still more indirect. For example, Irish influence on the handwriting and spelling used in English manuscripts at this date, or Irish traditions appearing in Anglo-Saxon sermons.

The achievement of the Irish in seventh-century Britain had been remarkable. Priests, for the most part from a tiny Hebridean island, had converted large swathes of Anglo-Saxon England. Colum Cille's spiritual empire had grown from the north-east coast down, through central England, to Essex and the banks of the Thames outside the wreck of Roman London. But with Finan Irish influence in Britain had reached its zenith. And the difficulty for the Irish, as the century progressed, would be their unusual Christian practices, practices that were disliked by continental missionaries operating in southern England.

I have already mentioned the refusal of Irish bishops to ride on horses, but as we saw with Columbanus this was just one of several divergences from Continental Christian practice. To a reader today the temptation is to shrug. So what if Celtic monks and continental monks had different hair-cuts? So what if they celebrated Easter on different days? Surely what mattered is that they all believed in the Trinity and the fundamentals of the Christian faith. But to Dark-Age Christians these divergences mattered *terribly*, for in their segmented and divided world with hundreds of kingdoms, Christianity was the common denominator. Christianity was the only thing that could put together that jigsaw existence. If Christian practice was different, then unity was but a mockery.

As the years had gone by, Continental missionaries became better established in Britain, especially in the south east and East Anglia where Italian and Frankish monks had been responsible for converting the locals. They bridled at what they interpreted as bizarre Irish behaviour. The Irish, on the other hand, defended their own customs with verve and confidence. They were not interested in compromise with what they believed to be corrupt traditions—it is sometimes forgotten by historians that the Irish hated Continental Christian practices as much as theirs were, in turn, hated. These theological battles among the pews and before the altar had consequences in the Anglo-Saxon kingdoms.

If you as an Anglo-Saxon king have a Celtic monk on your right who tells you that his way of doing things is correct, and a Frankish monk on the left who asserts that his way is right, you will start to worry—especially when it is insinuated that your entrance to heaven might depend on whose advice you follow. It was in Northumbria itself, where the Irish mission had started, that these royal preoccupations came to a head. In 664, at Whitby on the eastern coast of Northumbria, a special council was called to resolve the issue once and for all. Many questions had caused aggravation between the two religious traditions, but it was the question of the dating of Easter, one that Columbanus had made famous in the first years of the seventh century, that became decisive.

The meeting was held in a nunnery at Whitby. And to this nunnery came both Oswiu, who had been the king supporting Finan's missions to the south, and his son Alhfrith. They would act as judges over the Irish and

Continental traditions. The Irish party was represented by bishop Colman, an Irishman who had replaced Finan on Finan's death three years before. What might be called the Roman party was represented by a Frankish bishop Agilbert and a priest, Wilfrid, an Anglo-Saxon trained in the Continental tradition.

The Irish began the meeting by claiming that their method of dating Easter came from the apostle John, taking Oswiu and his court back to the time of Jesus. Wilfred, however, who spoke for the opposition, was scathing of Celtic traditions, claiming that his tradition, the Roman one, was of equal antiquity and that it had been handed down from Peter, first among the apostles and the first bishop of Rome. It is doubtful whether either party was correct in their claims. But what mattered was what John and Peter represented or could be made to represent. Certainly, Wilfrid—a smug and difficult-to-like individual whose vanities would plague the English church for the next generation—deployed Peter against the Irish as if he was a secret weapon.

'But even if your saints were holy, how can you possibly believe that a handful of the faithful in one corner of the furthest islands are to be preferred to the universal Church of Christ in all the world? And even if your Colum Cille—and, yes, ours too if he was of Christ—were a saint with great powers how can we prefer him to the holy head of the apostles to whom the Lord said: 'You are Peter and upon this rock I will build my church and the gates of Hell will not prevail against it and I will give to you the keys of the kingdom of Heaven.'

This Biblical passage became decisive.

When Wilfrid had finished, the king asked, 'Is it true, Colman, that our Lord said these words to Peter?' Colman answered, 'Yes, it is true, your majesty!' Then the king said, 'Can you, Colman, show any such power given to your Colum Cille?' Colman answered, 'None.' Then the king asked once more, 'Now do you two agree here, without any controversy, that these words were said to Peter, and that the keys of the kingdom of Heaven were given to him by our Lord?' And they both replied, 'Yes.' Then the king stated, 'And I, therefore, say to you, that he is the door-keeper [of heaven], and that I will not disagree with him. Rather, I wish... in all things to obey his laws in case, when I come before the heavenly gates, there is no one to open them up for me, Peter the key-holder having become my enemy.' Once the king had said this, all those there, seating and standing, great and small, agreed and renounced the less perfect custom and hurried to conform to that which was better.

It is depressing to think that the most important Church Council in English history ended with such a shallow argument. But, whatever the quality of that argument, Oswiu's judgement was not to be contradicted. Wilfrid and his party were ecstatic, of course. Wilfrid's victory would make most of Britain 'Catholic' and Britain would remain so for almost a thousand years, until in the early sixteenth century, the English king, Henry VIII fell passionately in love with the wrong woman, Anne Boleyn. From there, following the pope's refusal to annul Henry's first marriage, the Reformation would drag England, kicking and screaming, from the Catholic fold.

Even today English Protestantism—Anglicanism—is often Catholic in form and tone, and the Anglicans are the spiritual descendants of Wilfrid not Colman. However we look at those arguments at Whitby, they marked a watershed in English Church history. Nothing would be the same again. Whitby would also have an effect, curiously enough, on Irish Christianity. In the generations following what we called above 'Roman' practices would spread across Ireland itself. In 664 they were already established in parts of the south and in surprisingly little time displaced many of the practices that Colum Cille, Columbanus and Aidan had taken for granted: a special Easter and a special tonsure among them. Irish Christians would continue to have a reputation for peculiarities, but what differences there were with mainstream Christianity were increasingly seen as bizarre hangovers or eccentric Irish bluster, not heresy.

The human cost of Oswiu's decision was nonetheless heavy. While Wilfrid was jubilant, Colman and his allies were, of course, bitterly disappointed. The Council marked after all the end of their sojourn in Britain. Indeed, it would mark the beginning of the end of Irish influence throughout almost all the island. Refusing to surrender to traditions that they continued to despise, Colman with a group of disciples—Celts and not a few Anglo-Saxons—left for Ireland shortly afterwards. On his departure, the bishop was given only one favour by King Oswiu, namely that a certain Eata who had been among Aidan's English converts should be made abbot at Lindisfarne over those monks who had been convinced by Wilfrid's arguments. It was a sign that the victors would not be able to wipe out the past, and that there would be some continuity with that small mission that had been sent out of Iona thirty years before.

The last act of the united Lindisfarne community was to divide the bones of their founder Aidan. Some were left there, others were carried by the defeated Colman back across the Irish Sea. Colman travelled on with his exiles from exile to the far west of Ireland. They settled, true to their vocation and the tastes of Colum Cille, on another island, 'the Island of the White Cow' Inishboffin off Galway, today one of the last strongholds of the Irish language. It is a place where history echoes. Not only did it host those despised Irish monks in the seventh century who had sacrificed power in England for fealty to their fathers' traditions. In the seventeenth century, it became a penal colony for Romish clergy during Cromwell's ravages in Ireland.

16

DID THE CELTS
SAVE DARK AGE CHRISTIANITY?

he Irish contribution to Anglo-Saxon history—the conversion of half of a nation— had ended at Whitby in 664 as abruptly as it began thirty years before, when Oswald had sent messages north to Iona. But if the time of the Irish exiles in Northumbria had finished, the Irish contribution to the religious history of Europe most certainly did not end with Colman. There was a period of a half-century while Irish orthodoxy was questioned and the Irish were treated with suspicion. Then, as the Irish conformed with the more important points that had separated them from mainstream Christianity, fresh exiles started again to leave their homelands in force and were, once more, welcomed abroad.

Indeed, it would be possible to write a further five or six chapters on their adventures up until the millennium. In the next centuries, hundreds of Irish exiles would come to the continent and to Britain. With a talent for getting noticed and their pronounced eccentricities, they give us some rare colour in the bleak monotony of the Dark Ages. We have already come across an Irish bishop preaching about lunar fairies, a Celtic monk from Ireland writing begging songs for beer and to these we could add the two Irish monks who arrived in Frankia in the ninth century and began to sell wisdom in a fish market as if precious cod.

But if we look past the wonder, excitement and sometimes censure that these Irish visitors excited especially in the seventh century, the central question is: how did these visitors change Christendom in the years 500-1000? One claim is the idea that they changed the customs of Christian Europe, which is clearly not true. As we saw with Columbanus, the only important custom that the Irish exiles might have introduced was private confession with penance—an institution that has of course survived in the Catholic Church. Another claim that is more convincing is that the exiles revolutionised European learning both before and after Whitby.

According to this argument, the Irish had preserved in Ireland manuscripts lost elsewhere in the apocalypse at the end of the Roman Empire. In their packs they then brought back gems of learning to ornament intellectual life on the continent as the quest for knowledge, forgotten while the Roman Empire collapsed, began again. Irish scholars also—goes this argument—knew Greek and Hebrew, languages unknown elsewhere in the west, and so increased the breadth of learning at a time when many Frankish and German monks could not even write Latin. It was the Irish, then, that saved Christendom from ignorance and that put Europe back on track to learning, a track that would conclude in the fifteenth century with the Renaissance.

Unfortunately the idea of Irish Ivy-League MENSA monks with manuscripts tucked under their arms saving continental Europe from ignorance has to be rejected. The Irish may have had some manuscripts that had been lost elsewhere in Christendom, but they had in turn lost or never had some manuscripts that were widely available in France, say. In the Dark Ages there was a scrabble by the monastic librarians of all countries to fill yawning gaps in their collections. And while the Irish had a floundering knowledge of the Hebrew alphabet and also some Greek, they were not fluent in these two languages. Their translations from Greek included howlers.

This is not to doubt the intellectual quality of the Irish exiles from 500 to 1000, especially as compared to their continental and English peers. Some of the Irish exiles were men of exceptional intellectual ability. John Eriugena (Irish John) in the ninth century, was perhaps the greatest European thinker in the period from the collapse of the Roman Empire, in the fifth century, to the opening of Europe's first significant universities, in the twelfth century. But most of the exiles were workaday scholars who had a reputation for strange speculations and for their Biblical learning.

The Celtic exiles' great achievement was not in altering, but in the greater task of helping to preserve Christendom. Christianity experienced disaster after disaster from the fifth to the eleventh centuries when the exiles were most active. Christian civilisation partially caved in after the collapse of the Roman Empire. By 664 the first major Arab victories against the Christian world were taking place and would eventually destroy the oldest and most populated part of Christendom: the Levant, Egypt and North Africa. When these victories are added to those of other enemies of Christianity in the next centuries, including the Vikings and the Hungarians, it can be seen that the whole map of the Christian world had changed.

Indeed, it was a close run thing. If Abdul Rahman Al

Ghafiqi, the leader of the Arab army that penetrated into France in 732, had been wilier or if the Viking raids of the ninth century had included another two hundred dragon boats, we might be living in a very different world today. One where Christianity would be a religious curiosity, a forgotten monotheism, as obscure in fact as the Celts are to us today. As it was, a religion that had once stretched down the caravan routes to India, China and Ethiopia became an essentially European affair.

Nor was this all. Surrounded and assaulted, Dark-Age European Christianity seemed also to be decaying from within. This was as true after as before the Irish and their enemies sat down at Whitby. In many parts of pagan Europe the Church lacked the will to send out missionaries to convert. If missionaries were persuaded to go, the relatively rapid conversions of Roman times became long drawn out epics, often depending on violence and threats as much as a Christian belief in the unity of humankind. The death of a king could change the religion of hundreds of thousands of people as had happened with the Northumbrians. Continental clergy, too, lost their independence to local lords and, over much of Europe, were frightened to criticise abuses; bishops and priests were chosen by barons and counts, who preferred loyal allies to holy men. Finally and most tragically, Christianity, once a dynamic, intellectual religion, had become a sclerotic and unquestioning tradition where originality and verve were neither appreciated nor encouraged. What mattered to the continental church in writing a 'scholarly' work was bringing the authority of the Bible and the Church Fathers to bear on any problem, not individual inquiry.

Columbanus, Aidan, Finan and their post-Whitby successors, of whom there were many, brought with them

193

their passion and flair, and energised this flagging religion on a flagging continent. Irish priests, bishops and abbots came to England, to France and Germany and Italy and became missionaries, scholars and church administrators in an era when well-educated, capable churchmen were in short supply. As outsiders, owing their loyalty to no one, they spoke up with unusual courage on a range of issues that local clergy would not dare touch—like Columbanus's fearlessness in the face of local monarchs.

These Irish emigrants have been referred to as a blood transfusion for the Dark Age continent. But perhaps a more effective image would be of reanimation after cardiac arrest for a faith that was on the verge of terminal decline or of losing its identity in the pagan beliefs and superstitions that continued to govern the life of many of its adherents. What these Celtic monks really changed then was change itself: helping to conserve a religion that, for four or five hundred years, risked melting away.

Say, have you thought what manner of man it is
Of who men say 'He could strike giants down'?
Or what strong memories over time's abyss
Bore up the pomp of Camelot and the crown.
And why one banner all the background fills,
Beyond the pageants of so many spears,
And by what witchery in the western hills
A throne stands empty for a thousand years?

The Myth of Arthur, G.K.Chesterton

III

Creating the
Modern Mind

829/30	*Arthur's earliest certain appearance in Welsh literature*
1066	*The Norman invasion of Britain*
c. 1110-1130	*The Modena Vault*
1113	*French canons visit Cornwall and learn of Arthur's fame there*
1125	*William of Malmesbury writes about Arthur*
1129	*Henry of Huntingdon writes about Arthur*
1133-1189	*Henry II of England*
1136-7	*Gaimar writes that Arthur will conquer Britain for the British Celts*
c. 1138	*Geoffrey of Monmouth writes his* History of the Kings of Britain
1155	*Wace translates Geoffrey's* History *into Norman French*
1167	*Étienne writes his* Norman Battle Standard
c. 1170-1190	*Chrétien of Troyes composes his Arthurian poems*
1189-1199	*Richard I of England*
1191	*Arthur discovered at Glastonbury*
c. 1200	*Arthur discovered under Mount Etna*
c. 1210	*Gottfried von Strassburg dies leaving his* Tristan *incomplete*
1223	*Arthurian-themed tournament on Cyprus*

16

THE CELTS AND THEIR LEGENDS

here were two Celtic-speaking peoples by the early twelfth century: the British Celts (the Cornish, Bretons, Strathclyders and the Welsh) and the Gaels (the Irish, the Manx and the Gaelic-speaking inhabitants of north Britain, the first Scots). And, within these two peoples, there was a sense of kinship—the Welsh, for example, in the twelfth century, still considered the Bretons and the Cornish brothers; the Irish essentially spoke the same language as that spoken by their cousins in the Hebrides. And, as if to underline this, the Latin word for a Scot or an Irishman was the same, as was the Latin word for a Breton or for a Cornish man, respectively *Scottus* and *Britto*. Between these two families, however, there was little more community than might come about through a shared geography and, by 1100, there was no single Celtic nation. But, like a residual tail bone, the two families carried in their laws, their customs and, crucially, in their legends the evidence of a shared Iron Age past.

Take Raven, the Iron Age Celtic Hercules (whom we met before the walls of Rome and later again at Delphi). He was no longer an Italian or Balkan warleader, but had

199

Map 10 The Celtic World c. 1200

Irish-Celtic speaking

SCOTLAND

IRELAND

MAN

WALES

British-Celtic speaking

CORNWALL

BRITTANY

instead been cast as an ancient king of Britain. Then there was the medieval Welsh bogey man, Gwyn ap Nudd, lord of the other world, who enjoyed a similar antiquity. His father, Nudd, had been worshipped at a temple on the Severn in Roman times as Nodons, while Gwyn was known at early Celtic shrines on the continent. Then, of course, there was the most famous hero of the British Celts, Arthur of Round-Table fame. There are two possibilities with Arthur. One, that he is an entirely mythic figure who never existed, a Celtic deity like Raven; the second, that he was a historical figure who was, after his death, entirely absorbed and transformed by ancient Celtic myths. As we shall see, history cannot help us understand the mythical Arthur of our stories—though the question of historical origins are an enticing riddle (see the second Appendix).

The British Celts told stories about these figures in Wales, Brittany and Cornwall as they had for hundreds of years. But those concerning Arthur and his legendary associates began to be also told in England, in France, in Germany. And soon they were being recounted in Sicily, on the edge of the Christian world, in Iceland, on that world's northern marches, and even in the exotic setting of the near East in the crusader kingdoms. In fact, these British-Celtic legends became, for the Middle Ages, what Rock and Roll was to the later twentieth century: a contagious, cultural virus.

In the first part of the present book, the heroes were Celtic warriors. In the second, they were, instead, Irish monks passing into life-long exile abroad. But with these spreading legends there were no material protagonists, unless we think of the bards and their musical instruments, the singers who transported these same stories in their songs. The real heroes were the legendary figures that they described and who travelled in the bard's chords: Celtic heroes brought from out of the west to the fireplaces and bowers of England, France and Germany. We tend to think of these heroes today, the heroes of Arthurian legend in particular, as He-Men in shining armour, superheroes with metal costumes instead of lycra. But this is only a *faux* medieval version of legends that stretched back into the distant past and that were originally more bizarre and uncomfortable than those sanitised stories would have us believe. Back in their Celtic homelands these heroes were giants and god-like creatures who ran around the wilds of the west with their spectral pets and shape-shifting magic. And the rivals of these heroes were as surreal as they were evil: demon cats, drunk dragons, a flying church altar, a fortress of glass in the ocean…

How is it that these bizarre heroes had such success in a world that saw the twelfth-century British Celts as provincial barbarians? The key was the relation between these figures and Christianity. For these heroes were, to use a word applied to some of them by Welsh story-tellers, *bendigaid* or, as we would say 'blessed'. Of course, there were other heroes in other countries, too. But, in most regions of Europe, their legends had had a hard time of it in the shadow of the cross. Take the example of Anglo-Saxon England, a pagan country in 500 that by 800 had been entirely Christianised. In 500, there had been fantastic stories of gods and warriors—tales of which we get glimpses in fragments of surviving lore, monkish complaints about them, and even placenames. But by 800, these stories had been exorcised or driven underground. It is only very occasionally in tales like *Beowulf,* a grim Anglo-Saxon story of warbands and monsters, that we have heavily-censored insights into the pagan world of Odin and his wolves. And it is only very rarely in medieval folklore—for example, elf darts, which were said to be shot by supernatural creatures at nocturnally grazing cows—that we feel the sting of older pre-Christian beliefs. In England and elsewhere in Europe the Church had emphatically won.

The Irish and British Celts had been happier to compromise with the pagan past because ultimately they did not see that past as being offensive to Christianity. In other countries legends died the death of a thousand clerical cuts: sermons, polemic, penitence. What has Christ to do with Ingeld (a Germanic hero of legend), asked one Anglo-Saxon saint with stern eyes on his fellow monks? But, in the Celtic-speaking world, these ancient legends managed, instead, to cohabit with the new Christian myths. So monks there would often write down stories of pre-Christian times and name heroes that their great, great, great grandfathers had worshipped as gods. We gather from their writings that these monks saw such native stories as no more of a threat to their Christian traditions than Christians in other countries saw the revelations of the Old Testament as a threat to the message of the Gospels.

Take for example Wales. In medieval stories from the principality, we have characters from the Iron Age Celtic pantheons—Raven, for example. We have pious anecdotes where holy men are made to vanquish monsters borrowed from legends so old that they had stalactites hanging off them. While, in one late but striking case, a saint has a conversation with the character we established before as the Welsh lord of the dead, Gwyn ap Nudd. Then, most memorably perhaps, we have a fragment in a twelfth-century Welsh tale that contains the only trace we have of the Celtic story of creation, a story where woman is made not from rib-bone or mud but from flowers.

Again, none of this is to say that the Welsh were pagan. The Welsh and other British Celts were emphatically Christian and had been for the best part of seven hundred years by the twelfth century. The constant references to God and Christ in Welsh manuscripts recall this, as do the substantial sites of many early medieval Welsh churches. But most Welsh Christian leaders did not think of these old myths as a threat. And, as these legends were told again and again through the generations, they began to pick up Christian themes. We have just seen how one Welsh saint discussed salvation with Gwyn ap Nudd. And Christian figures and motifs crop up frequently in the world of Welsh legend. So when, in the sixteenth century, a Welsh soldier based at Calais took it upon himself to write down certain legends recalling a British-Celtic hero, Taliesin, he included, along with myths of ancient Celtic origin, Christian and even classical references. Indeed, in this work, we have not only the hero's very pagan union with the elements—motifs as old as humanity—but his knowledge of the Father, the Son and the Holy Ghost, and his boasts that he had been present on earth at the time of Noah and his Ark.

If the British Celts had reworked ancient legends to include Christian features, and this was all, they would today primarily be of interest to scholars. Modern readers would not know the names of Arthur, Gawain and others. But instead their legends spread in the Middle Ages, and the question, of course, is why? After all, these legends had been around for many centuries and had never previously interested the neighbours of the Welsh, the Bretons or the Cornish. What new event in Europe suddenly made them irresistible to alien peoples? It was, in fact, the overwhelming, destructive success of Christianity that made the tales so popular. Christianity had, by then, wiped out the antique legends of other European countries or tainted them. The merits of this extermination were self-evident to the Church. But, by the twelfth century, it had left many Europeans with only the Gospels and saints' lives as a source of entertainment and escapism. There were no longer the tales of the ancient peoples of the continent.

A bishop might lose himself entirely in the Christian faith, but for a knight or a peasant or merchant—the merchant class was gently rising in Europe in the twelfth century—these Christian stories offered only limited solace. It was under these circumstances that British-Celtic legends started to enjoy success. For here was a body of stories that had that frisson of significance familiar from myths—they were magnetic and magnetising. And yet these same legends had Christian details, for, having cohabited with Christianity for so long, they had naturally attracted Christian characters and Christian sympathies: saints, crosses, even Biblical characters. Unlike, say, Viking legends, these British-Celtic legends felt orthodox, they had the *imprimatur* of faith upon them. Here were legends that could be told by good Christians, from Breton to Frank, from Frank to Italian, from Italian to Greek.

And so it began. The heroes of the British Celts broke out of the homelands—Wales, Cornwall and Brittany—and, with their magic swords and magic steeds, they cantered over the continent. Their victories would be many and famous. This was a Christian age, a time when the Church controlled the life of thought. But the legendary heroes described below fought for a new space in which those who wished to could step away from

205

Christian certainties and look out of new windows into new worlds. And, in the course of the twelfth century, Arthur and his British-Celtic comrades would, in a revolution all of their own, help to set Europe free, anticipating a Europe beyond the Middle Ages. In fact, these phantoms, so antique that the Celts had told their stories in the Alps and the Balkans two thousand years before, would be an important agent in creating a secular or 'modern' mindset.

18

THE ORIGINS OF ARTHURIAN LEGEND

he Celtic myths that changed Europe in the Middle Ages, including those concerning Arthur, are, to say the least, difficult to get at. There was no Bible of Celtic beliefs, there was no Celtic litany and we do not even have a decent first-hand description of Celtic religious beliefs as they were practised in the pagan centuries. Our evidence, in fact, might be imagined as an enormous mosaic where two thirds of the pieces have been removed and the remaining third have been ripped up and muddled or, more often than not, have lost their original tints and colours. This sorry state of affairs is partly a result of the local nature of Celtic paganism. What we might call 'Celticism' was, like modern Hinduism, really a thousand different micro-religions that had coalesced together. It is partly a result of early Celtic worshippers lacking the interest to write their traditions down. And it is partly a result of these traditions surviving in only a few manuscripts in Wales, Ireland and Brittany. For all that the medieval Celts were more tolerant of their pagan pasts than their neighbours, they did not go about recording their native traditions with any particular gusto, trusting, instead, in the oral traditions that had kept their legends alive that far.

But, if we cannot speak with authority about the details of pagan Celtic religion, we sometimes see traditions that were mimicked in several times and places. So one corner of the mosaic of ancient Celtic religion that we can tentatively reconstruct, and one that is fundamental for understanding Arthur, is a Celtic mythological character, who has been called 'the Protector' and who was played, as we will see, by a number of different Celtic heroes.

Raven starred as Protector in ancient Celtic Europe, but we have too few of his ancient legends to come to any useful conclusions about his role. However, when we turn to medieval Celtic Ireland, we have a clear view of such a figure. So clear, indeed, that the tales concerning this hero—Fionn Mac Cumaill—might almost pass as a career description of what the Celtic Protector was expected to do. Fionn was said to live in the wilderness with his followers, the Fenians, and these spent their time having fun at their neighbours' expense and chasing boars. To this very day, out-of-the-way spots in Ireland are associated with Fionn. The Giant's Causeway in Ulster, for example, was said to be a series of steps that Fionn built to reach Scotland. Yet this wilderness outlaw was, for all his shenanigans, a patriot. If invaders from across the sea should attack Ireland, woe betide them, for Fionn and his companions would rally out to man the defences. And Fionn is described in Irish lore as fighting the Vikings, the one serious invasion that the Irish had to endure before the coming of the English.

There are several indications that—in the same way that Fionn was Protector of Ireland—the Arthur of British-Celtic legend became Protector of Britain. The role of Arthur as a benign outlaw is strange to the twenty-first-century reader. Modern audiences want their Arthur in beautiful castles and shining armour, where Walt Disney and Malory have taught us that he should be. But in the earliest British-Celtic legends available to us, Arthur is described in a surprisingly Fionn-like fashion. So Arthur, like Fionn, is associated not with towns or strongholds or kingdoms, but with the wilderness. In the earliest British-Celtic legends Arthur does not live at Camelot, but rather in a wood glade called Celli Wic in Cornwall. He is also associated with the boar hunt and prominent rocks and prehistoric sites out in the countryside. Indeed, up and down Britain, several prehistoric tombs are, to this day, known as Arthur's Oven—where a giant-sized Arthur was said to cook his meals; while the Quoits of Dartmoor, huge stones stranded among the heather, are said to be discs that Arthur threw in competitions with his companions. And in the earliest legends, Arthur is never described as a king, but only as a 'battle-leader', coming from out of the wilds to defend his people from invaders.

Of course, if this had been all, Arthur as Protector would have had the same success that Fionn had outside his homeland. That is, little to none. Poor Fionn was celebrated for centuries in Ireland. But the only time that he left his native shores was when he crossed the Irish Sea to the Gaelic colonies in the Hebrides—where stories of the hero are still told. Then, later, in the early modern period, Fionn was brought from Ireland and the Hebrides through 'the mists and wastes of seas' to Gaelic colonies on the eastern coast of Canada.

But Arthur did not have to wait for emigrants to take his story elsewhere. Tales concerning him and other British-Celtic heroes spread like a forest fire after a long dry summer, to corners of Europe where no one had ever spoken a Celtic language. If it had been possible to poll medieval Europeans who had heard stories of either Fionn or Arthur, then Arthur would likely have scored well over ninety percent by 1200—he was, in his day, a figure as well known as Santa Claus is today. Fionn would, however, have languished at two or three percent: a hero in the Gaelic lands, an anonymity elsewhere. So what was it that led to the different destinies of the two Celtic protectors and the transformation, in the case of Arthur, from guardian of Britain to European action hero?

Disastrous Invasions

The disastrous invasions that the British Celts suffered throughout the Dark Ages were the first ingredient in Arthur's success story. In the fifth century, the Anglo-Saxons had invaded Britain, overturning the old Romanised Celtic culture of the island. And in the sixth, the seventh and the eighth centuries these invaders continued to move further in, a fire 'licking the western ocean with its fierce red tongue', defeating the native British Celts. At the Battle of Chester in 616, the Anglo-Saxons of Yorkshire fought their way to the Irish Sea. In the south, similar battles near the Severn had also led Anglo-Saxon warriors to the land around what is today Bristol, breaking the Celtic fringe by reaching the far coast of Britain. Another two centuries went by and the Anglo-Saxons had conquered Cornwall and were raiding deep into Wales. At the same time, the Vikings had destroyed British-Celtic civilisation on the Isle of Man; and the surviving British Celts of the north had been forcibly annexed by Alba, the Gaelic-speaking kingdom that was to become Scotland. By the year 1000 it must have been clear to any outside observer that the British Celts were a doomed people. And, within three centuries, the last independent British-Celtic realm, Gwynedd in north-west Wales, would be overrun by the English.

In Ireland, Fionn and his wildboys were not particularly tested by events. The Vikings were the only serious threat to Irish life in the Dark Ages, and never a threat that was going to compromise the indigenous culture of that island. The English invasion of Ireland, meanwhile, lay centuries in the future. The British Celts in Britain were, however, weighed down by history and, under the tension of these invasions, disasters started to break through into their mythic tales and songs, in the same way that preoccupations in our lives feature in our dreams.

At this point it should be remembered that, as we saw in part one, the early Celtic way of viewing the world was one in which time is divided not by centuries or dynasties, but by invasions. Nor were invasions necessarily seen as a bad thing. The Irish, for example, with their isolated existence away from the wars that plagued most of Europe through antiquity, still saw their history as full of such incursions, most of these involving the arrival of mythical beings. Invasions were the building blocks of Irish mythology (pagan and Christian). But the British Celts, with their more bitter experience, talked not only of invasions, but of (to use the Welsh word) *gormesoedd* or 'oppressions' that would come from across the sea and ravage their people.

Gormesoedd, in fact, became one of the obsessions of Welsh legend. One story, for example, recounts quite routinely how three of these *gormesoedd* came to the island of Britain: the first, the Coranieid, a magical people who knew everything; the second, a noise that caused miscarriages; and, the third, a pantry thief who stole the food of the British—the mythical version of the wars for Britain.

In these tales of oppression, the protection against

211

gormesoedd was magic. One legend tells us that Raven had his head buried at Tower Hill in London. While his talismanic head remained there, said the story, no *gormesoedd* would be able to make their way into the island—the origin of the modern legend of the ravens at the Tower that while ravens remain there England will not fall.

Prophecies

The British Celts had been split by these foreign invasions into different communities: the Welsh, the Cornish and— before the Vikings—the Manx, the Bretons and other smaller communities scattered around the seaboard of Western Europe. Despite these failures and divisions, we know from various works of poetry, and from the very way that they described themselves, that the British Celts had never forgotten that they had at one time been a single people, and that the birthright of this people was the island of Britain in its entirety. Strangers had, to continue this keening tale, come and stolen almost all their land until the British Celts had been humiliated and reduced to their present small and wild fiefdoms in the west or across the sea in Brittany.

Any outside observer would have concluded that the British Celts were doomed. They simply did not have the might to resist larger, belligerent neighbours such as the French and the English. But legend, of course, need pay no attention to political realities. Legend is not legend if it cannot right wrongs and produce justice where justice has been lacking: the good, younger daughter defeats her ugly elder sisters; the frog becomes again the prince he once was; the evil stepmother perishes in the burning house.

Britain would, the British Celts believed, become theirs again in a holy war of short, sharp duration declaimed by their poets and prophets. In this war the British Celts would reunite. The Bretons would return from Brittany to Britain, their true homeland. The Welsh would rush out of the moors and mountains into which they had been boxed. And the Cornish, too, would raise their war standards. Together they would destroy the Anglo-Saxons—the early English—driving every one of that people into the sea.

This prophecy, of course, was just within the bounds of possibility. It violated no rule of physics, though it stretched probability to its elastic limits. Such a rising could take place and—while it would be almost certainly destined to failure—it is easy to understand why the British Celts might believe it. Wishful thinking is a natural enough consolation in bad times. However, to this prophecy of an alliance of the divided British-Celtic peoples, was added a dose of fantasy. For it was said that, when the rising came, the British Celts would be led, not by their kings and their warleaders, but by the spirits of dead heroes and the saints buried in their national churches.

Spelt out like this the Great Prophecy—as the Welsh knew it—might seem to us singular. But there is nothing comic in this legend as described by the British Celts. If anything the tone and the hysteria are chilling. Take *Armes Prydein*—the Prophecy of Britain—a Welsh poem, composed in the tenth century, that predicts the coming apocalypse. The Welsh poet, after calling the English by every name that he can think of—'foreigners', 'shit-men', 'peasants', 'usurpers', 'beast food', 'white cheeks', 'foxes', 'incendiaries', 'dark hosts', 'slaves' and 'a swarm'—informs his audience that the end is nigh for the British Celts' neighbours. When the rising comes, he tells with glee, British-Celtic warriors—the Cornish, northern

213

Britons, the Welsh and the Bretons with some Viking allies—will drive the invaders into the sea, killing those who do not flee. So many of the English will perish in this genocidal war that there will be no room for their corpses to lie down: 'cadavers standing, holding each other up until the port of Sandwich—may it be blessed!'

> Poetic inspiration tells that the day will arrive when the English of the south together with those English assassins of the Midlands make council together: they will wish to shame our glorious armies. But, no, the English will move and go everyday into flight. The Englishman does not know where to travel, where to run and where he should stay. The British Celts will run into battle, mountain bears, determined to avenge their kin. There will be spears pouring down. No friend will pity the corpse of his foe. Heads split without brain, widowed women, horses without their riders, screaming with the warriors' charge, many wounded, before the armies leave off, death's messengers will meet...

After this ethnic cleansing, Britain would be retaken by its rightful owners, the British Celts, who will unite and live alone and secure in their Britain, the island given to them by God.

This legend is certainly not unique. Other nations have had tales similar to this one—tales where a hero waits in a place put aside and returns from the dead to liberate his people from injustice. The Germans had Frederick Barbarossa. Shi'ite Muslims have the lost Prophet. Some Russians believe that Stalin survived his death. Tales are told today in Romania concerning the Ceausescus.

However, the British Celts were unusual in one respect. Their legend not only characterised them for a century, but seems to have filled their imagination for the best part of a thousand years, almost, indeed, to the end of the Middle Ages. Already in the sixth century there are elements of this belief, and there were still mutterings about it in the fifteenth century, at the time of the last Welsh rebellions against the English. What other nations had as a passing fantasy—a case of wishful thinking in hard times—had turned, in the case of the British Celts, and, above all, the Welsh into a national psychosis.

Messiah

Which dead hero was to lead this legendary Revival? We have the names of several Breton and Welsh would-be messiahs. But then, sometime in the Dark Ages, Arthur takes the lead. The first hint we have that Arthur has been given this messianic role comes in the early twelfth century, when a party of French monks visited Cornwall. As well as noting that the land was connected with a certain Arthur, they also experienced the passion that Arthur was capable of arousing in the locals, who were by this date a subjugated people under the rule of the Anglo-Saxons. In a church in Bodmin, one of the visitors seems to have riled the locals by telling them that their hero would not come back from the dead. The Cornish were so outraged that they attacked the French tourists. They were angry because for the Cornish Arthur was evidently a hope for a Cornwall free of Anglo-Saxon rule. In denying Arthur's messianic return the French had denied them their future. Nor were the Cornish alone. The same author informs us that the Bretons became similarly passionate about Arthur. And, a half century later, we learn of a preacher who had gone to Brittany and, while

215

trying to tell the Bretons that Arthur would not return, was stoned for his troubles.

The fact is that shortly after 1100 (but perhaps for some time before) Arthur had been enlisted as British-Celtic messiah. In the mid twelfth century (1136-7), a Norman poet tells us how Arthur will come back from the dead to reconquer Britain: not an isolated belief, for in the hundred years after this first reference there are approximately twenty further references to Arthur as a returning hero in English and Continental works. Arthur was clearly by now British-Celtic messiah in chief. In a very real sense Arthur is still there today in the notion of the Once and Future King, the idea that Arthur will return in his country's hour of need. How typical though of the perversity of history that today we think of 'his' country as being England—the country that he was originally enlisted to destroy.

European Arthur

In looking at the past or even at our own times, we often try and draw a line between religion and superstition. The myths that the British Celts told each other at their feasts or around their fires in the evening were different, we would like to believe, from the 'myths' that they listened to every Sunday in church. And this may, as a rule, be so. But all the indications are that with Arthur the British Celts had elevated one of their heroes to a point where he was venerated as a second Jesus. Certainly the bemused neighbours of the British Celts thought so as they heard of Arthur for the first time.

Frequently, in fact, amazed foreign commentators noted—Arthur is now being written about in other European countries—the similarity between the British Celts and the Jews: both of whom believed that a messiah would come and whose messiah threatened to upstage Christ's second coming. This does not seem to have particularly worried the British Celts, who added blasphemy to blasphemy by having Arthur associate with the Virgin Mary in their legends. Their local messiah was waiting, waiting in a cave or under a mountain or on an island across the sea for the angel or divine message that would send him brushing cobwebs from his face and racing for his mount.

For the British Celts this religious fervour had an important consequence. We have referred before to the national psychosis that had gripped the British Celts for so many generations. It proved, in the case of the British Celts, especially the Welsh and Bretons, an unexpected instrument of survival, the shot of adrenalin that was to take them across some difficult centuries even though it marked them apart. The Welsh, in the midst of one of their fifteenth-century rebellions against English rule, wrote diplomatic letters to neighbouring peoples, quite routinely discussing the Great Prophecy and the return of a free British-Celtic people.

But seeming ridiculous to kings of other countries was a small price to pay for their victory. And victory of a sort there was. The Welsh and Bretons were conquered, but in their messianic legends there was the memory of their noble origins and forebears—a strong sense of identity that would help them survive occupation and foreign rule. It is very easy to make light of such beliefs. But the fact that the Breton and Welsh languages have scraped through to the present, and the fact that the Welsh and Bretons continue to think of themselves as a community apart, depended on the dream of a messiah in the Middle Ages, told from parent to child down through the generations.

Arthur's promotion from outlaw and Protector to Messiah had an important effect on British-Celtic legend, too, and how that legend was perceived abroad. While Arthur had been an important figure in myth in the ninth century, by the twelfth century he had expanded to such a size that he pulled other heroes and heroines into his orbit. Some of these figures had long been associated with Arthur. Kai, for example—the knight Kay in the versions of the legends known to us—was already Arthur's ally in the ninth century. Guinevere, too, seems to have always been Arthur's wife. Other heroes were though only gradually nudged into Arthur's retinue by story tellers. Gawain, for example—who later became famous for a decapitation game with the Green Knight—or Tristan and Isolde, had their own legends and traditions. Yet, irrespective, they were all coralled into the Arthurian parade.

It was this ballooning, all dominating Arthur that the neighbours of the British Celts increasingly took notice of. The excitement Arthur engendered among the British Celts was, at first, responsible for Arthur's growing prestige. But Arthur's new-found foreign fame was made still easier by changes to the myth of the British-Celts' favourite warrior-messiah. The old Arthur had dwelt in the wilderness. But his new prestige demanded more than hobo trappings and, for the first time, Arthur begins to be described as a king or even an emperor—a title that made more sense to non-Celtic audiences. Admittedly, his behaviour did not always improve. Arthur is spotted doing deeds in Welsh stories that one hopes legendary kings did not generally do and that were hangovers from his wild days: bad-mouth saints, recklessly hunt boar, play dice. But the transition was otherwise seamless and for the last thousand years it is necessary to speak of 'King

Arthur': 'Wilderness Arthur', 'Arthur of Wales' and 'Celtic Arthur' just do not work. Then, as a king, his old habitat was no longer suitable. In early legend Arthur had dwelt in Celli Wic, a woodland glade in Cornwall. But, a hero with royal pretensions needs a shave, a crown and a court. As the British-Celtic Arthur inched towards the more conventional life of a legendary monarch, more than just his name spread. His stories were now ready to galvanise the knightly culture of the medieval kingdoms of non-Celtic Europe.

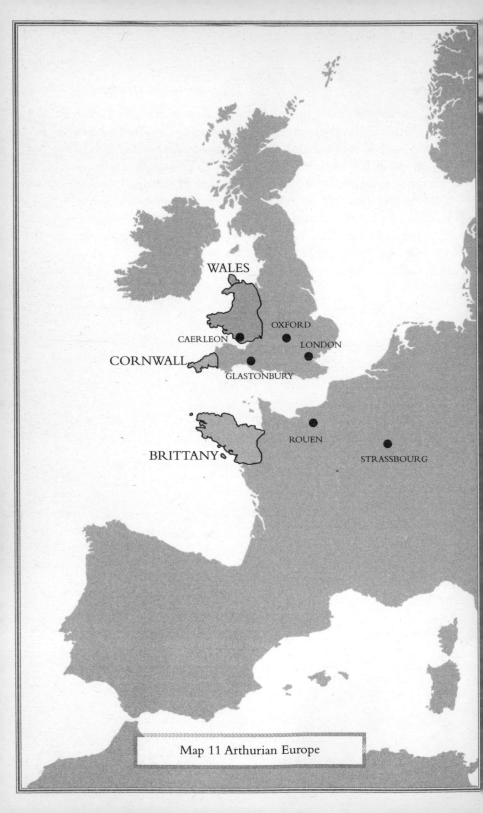

WALES

OXFORD

CAERLEON

LONDON

CORNWALL

GLASTONBURY

BRITTANY

ROUEN

STRASSBOURG

Map 11 Arthurian Europe

British-Celtic homelands

MAGDENBURG

MODENA

OTRANTO

ETNA

CYPRUS

19

ARTHUR LEAVES THE HOMELANDS

he twelfth century was not like the Dark Ages. Not two or three, but two or three thousand texts survive. But still, most of what was written has been lost to us. And we have no record of the sagas told in taverns in Europe in the 1100s, nor do we have any record of the poems sung in court unless, by some great and rare fortune, someone troubled to write one down and that copy survived. All that we have are the occasional chance mentions of Arthur bobbing up above the waterline, before they sink back into the black depths again.

Rare though these mentions are, they are enough to convince us that Arthur had crossed the threshold and that from 1100 he began to enjoy modest success among peoples that were not his own. Our first reference to Arthur abroad comes in 1113 when one Belgian author describes how the French and the Bretons argue 'concerning Arthur': the legend had evidently crossed the Breton borders or been carried back across them by irritated French visitors. At approximately this time—the date is usually given as 'the 1110s or 1120s'—a cathedral was built at Modena in northern Italy incorporating sculptures that include characters from Arthurian legend: the sculptures can be seen, to this day, on the arch above the northern door.

Arthur's entry into respectable history came instead in 1125 in England, when one William of Malmesbury gave some details of Arthur's supposed achievements in his *Deeds of the Kings*. William stands as the first modern Arthurian in his attempt to separate history from legend: an almost certainly futile task. In 1129 the English scholar Henry of Huntingdon wrote a similar passage, also weighing Arthur's suitability as a historical subject. Then, some ten years later, Ailred, a monk based in Yorkshire, shows us another aspect of the interest in Arthur, noting that one of his novices was never moved by pious tales, but wept openly over common stories about Arthur. Stories concerning Arthur were, evidently, being told in England in the early twelfth century.

At first, this list, slight as it is, might not appear to justify talk of 'Arthur fever'. But it should be remembered that, from 600-1100, there are no references to Arthur outside the British-Celtic homelands; and there are no certain references within the British-Celtic homelands before c. 830. These few nods then must stand as evidence of change. At times, we know where these authors and artists had heard of Arthur. But, in other cases, we can only guess. How was it, for example, that the legend of Arthur had arrived in Yorkshire by the early twelfth century, an area that was stolidly English? Are we to imagine British-Celtic bards travelling into these territories and selling their songs to northern barons? Or did the stories just seep across Britain, carried from mouth to mouth? Or had, perhaps, the Celtic legend of Arthur survived from when the Anglo-Saxons had occupied these once Celtic areas in the centuries after the fall of Rome? It is unlikely that we will ever know. All we can say is that these few, brief mentions are the first intimations of the runaway success that Arthur would enjoy in the 1140s and thereafter.

That runaway success may not have ever come if it had not been for one man and his quill. C. 1138, at Oxford, a certain Geoffrey of Monmouth put the finishing touches to his work, *The History of the Kings of Britain*. It was an ambitious book, one that described the British past from the time of human settlement in the island (an event that Geoffrey dated to about 500 BC) through to the times of the Welsh king Cadwallon in the seventh century AD—a long British millennium with Arthur prominently included. Geoffrey was by no means the first to attempt such a feat. Others had given themselves up to descriptions of British antiquity: not least Henry of Huntingdon and William of Malmesbury, both noted above for their brief mentions of Arthur in the 1120s. But they had faced an insuperable problem, the same problem, in fact, that historians face today. They had been able to find almost no written records from this period and no historical mention of Arthur.

Geoffrey, however, did not let such a lame excuse get in his way. Trailing through manuscripts, he noted—as had other historians before him—extracts relating to Britain. But, when he came to gaps, and gaps there were many, he turned to the one resource that historians had not employed: British-Celtic legend. The result is three hundred pages in modern type of glorious, ripping yarns. Tellingly, the most tedious parts of Geoffrey's epic are those based on historical sources.

In fact, in his quest for a page-turner, not only did the author pass off legend as history. He also manipulated or made up legends to ensure a riveting read for his public.

The problem today is that, when we look through his book, we cannot be sure what was his own invention and what is genuinely British-Celtic. For example, Geoffrey tells us of one pre-Roman king of Britain named Leir and his three daughters Goneril, Regan and Cordelia. Leir is, of course, King Lear, and Geoffrey's story is essentially the same as that of Shakespeare. But what we do not know is where Geoffrey got his story from. Did he just invent it? Did he take a pre-existing story and bend it to his purposes? Or did he faithfully record a British-Celtic tradition about an early mythical monarch of the island? There is no way to satisfactorily answer this question. No surviving British-Celtic source mentions Leir, though Leir may be the Welsh Llyr, a sea god who is said, in Welsh tradition, to have been Raven's father.

We have similar problems with the tales that Geoffrey recounts concerning Arthur. That he had some kind of source is, in this case, self-evident. After all, Arthur was known in Britain before Geoffrey. But to what extent Geoffrey embroidered or invented, and where he embroidered and invented, we cannot say.

In what is among the great red herrings of literature, Geoffrey claims that he was lent an ancient book in Welsh by a friend at Oxford, one Walter 'the archdeacon'. This book is an unbearably tempting morsel, lying just beyond the margins of the work. If modern scholars interested in the British Celts were asked what missing manuscript they could conjure back, a sizeable majority would certainly pick this one. (Just to put this in context, we have no Welsh-language manuscripts older than the thirteenth century, though there are fragments of Welsh written in Latin manuscripts from before that date.) What it would be to turn through its pages for even ten minutes. But the truth is that, knowing Geoffrey's mischievous ways, this ancient book may have been an invention, as many of his stories were. Or perhaps it did exist, but it was a fairly unremarkable work that spurred Geoffrey on to write his own *opus*. In fact, the inspiration for Geoffrey's knowledge is far easier to identify than this missing and perhaps never-existing manuscript. It is to be found in the author's Norman childhood.

The Normans had arrived in Britain in 1066 in an invasion that famously started and ended at the Battle of Hastings. They had rapidly taken control of Anglo-Saxon England and then moved into Wales, Scotland, and would break the back of independent Ireland a little after Geoffrey finished his work. Geoffrey's family had come to Britain as part of this invasion. But the Monmouths were not Norman. They were, instead, almost certainly Bretons—the continental British Celts. Bretons had been an important contingent in the Norman army that conquered England in 1066, being under William's control at that date. At Hastings, indeed, their knights rode on the left flank as the invaders chased up the hill at the Anglo-Saxon shield walls. Then, after the Norman victory, they were posted all over Britain as Norman enforcers—barely an English county was without these Bretons. And it seems that Geoffrey's family had been sent to Monmouth on the Welsh borders where Geoffrey (if his surname is to be believed) grew up.

This means that the young Geoffrey had access to three different traditions. His family will have told him Breton British-Celtic legends, his nursemaid and family servants will have given them their Welsh British-Celtic legends and the Norman friends of his parents and grandparents will have brought him their own versions of their Norman past. And it was this unusual triple-faceted childhood that was likely his most important resource in writing the *History* rather than a mystery book. It would have been the last of these influences, his contact with the Normans, that allowed him to describe Arthur in a way that non-Celtic Europe could appreciate.

It is a matter of record that non-Celtic Europe not only appreciated but *loved* Geoffrey's work. In fact, Geoffrey's book was that rarest of things—a medieval publishing phenomenon. Manuscripts of his *History* were copied with speed—the medieval equivalent of a bestseller—and sent to different libraries, fanning rapidly out over the continent. There are over two hundred copies in existence today and there must originally have been a thousand or more copies of the *History* in circulation, an extraordinary achievement when you think of how few copies of many pre-modern works have come down to us—twenty, ten, in too many cases one or none. Within a decade, this popular work was being translated from its clunky Latin into Norman-French, within two decades it was being translated into English and, by 1200, it had even been translated into Norse so that Icelanders and other descendants of the Vikings could read about Arthur or listen to his stories being declaimed.

Questions of veracity barely came up. Yes, in the late twelfth century a crusty old scholar, mercilessly took the hatchet to Geoffrey: 'only one without knowledge of the history of ancient times would doubt with what shame and impudence [Geoffrey] lies about everything'. One other critic told the story of a man possessed by demons: when the Gospel of John was placed on this man's chest the demons were driven out, but when *History* was placed there the demons multiplied. But these were isolated voices, drowned out in the chatter as Europeans read and discoursed on Geoffrey's book. Until 1138 the spread of

Arthur and his legends through non-Celtic Europe had been haphazard. It had depended on word of mouth and on visitors to and from the British-Celtic lands. But now Arthur travelled in luxury in packs and on mule backs, protected in a leather manuscript. Only a fifth of the *History* touched on Arthur's story, but the passages that did were considered the most interesting—especially his description of Arthur's court and Arthur's final battle. Geoffrey's Arthur was a towering hero, a palladin that the audience could hardly fail to remember; other characters in Geoffrey's *History* did not manage to escape his pages in the same way—until Shakespeare revived him, King Lear was all but forgotten. Geoffrey's writings became so popular in even the British-Celtic homelands that his version of events often overlaid the older, indigenous ones.

And the result of this success was dramatic and can be traced in those few monastic and court libraries that made it through the Middle Ages. By 1138, when Geoffrey lay down his pen, Europeans outside the British-Celtic homelands—especially in England and France—had already heard of Arthur, particularly in connection with the strange, messianic beliefs of their Breton and Welsh neighbours. But, by the time that Geoffrey's work had run its course, being copied and translated as far as Scandinavia and Sicily, Arthur was a commonplace—the 'A' in a new legendary alphabet that Europeans were beginning to employ. After Geoffrey's *History* had arrived references to him mushroom and it is no longer practical to set them out. Some of these references include accounts of the passion that Arthur excited. Others are sober and historical, treating Geoffrey as a reliable (or, in a few cases, an unreliable) source. There are also some grudging comments about the British Celts' own strange beliefs in an immortal Arthur: beliefs that Geoffrey had tried to play down.

By 1170, we have a new development. Records show French writers, from both north and south, composing works on Arthur in their own tongue, elaborating stories to their own ends, much as Geoffrey had elaborated British-Celtic traditions. Marie de France, a French poetess living in Britain, may have been the first to touch on Arthur in her gentle *lais*, short, lyrical poems. Then, her near contemporary, Chrétien de Troyes built his entire career on poetic renditions of Arthurian tales and became one of the most celebrated authors of his day, feeding details from British-Celtic singers to wider and ever more eager European audiences. Before the twelfth century was out the stories, translations, or adaptations of already adapted works, were also being told in other languages following the same route as the *History*. And all this Geoffrey had made possible. In Western history, we take the birth of Christ as being the beginning of our era: the gap between the ancient and the modern. In Arthurian studies scholars speak as naturally about BG (before Geoffrey) and AG (after Geoffrey). Once the *History* had been written nothing concerning Arthur would ever be the same again.

20

THE BATTLE BETWEEN THE OLD AND
THE NEW ARTHUR

y the mid twelfth century the legendary Arthur suddenly found himself in a peculiar position. He was, thanks to Geoffrey, the new European hero, a flower of chivalry and a Christian knight. Or at least he was in France, Germany and England. Walk a few hundred miles to the west and the marches of the British-Celtic homelands, Brittany or Cornwall or Wales, and Arthur was something else. Here he was still the tribal chieftain who would return and restore the British Celts to their greatness. Mythical heroes often have multiple personalities, but they do not have personalities so obviously at odds, and these contrasting Arthurs were bound sooner or later to come to blows. As, in fact, they did in two episodes: one in Brittany on the continent and the other at Glastonbury in England.

The Breton punch-up is recorded in only one place, a poem by the name of the *Norman Battle Standard*. The author of this poem, written in 1167, was one Étienne, a native of Rouen in Normandy. Through his verse Étienne described the recent successes of the Norman dynasty that controlled England and—above all—its then king, Henry II. Henry was the most successful descendant of

William the Conqueror. And, as many twelfth-century monarchs, he was a keen Arthurian, emulating Arthur in his conquests, ambitions and knightly excellence. Given Henry's interests it was only natural that Étienne inserted an episode concerning Arthur in his poem. But what is strange is the character of that episode.

In the previous year Henry had campaigned in Brittany, for Brittany had by this date become a frontline state in the wars between the king of France and the king of England. Henry, in fact, as much as any other ruler, bears the responsibility for ending Breton independence, which was one of the first casualties of the long drawn-out wars between England and France that span the Middle Ages. It was in the midst of these Breton battles that Henry received—and we can do no more than quote what Étienne says—'a letter from Arthur to Henry', *epistola Arturi ad Henericum.*

Arthur, according to the poet, had written to Henry to explain that he had been resting in the *antipodes*—not a medieval Australia as we will see—awaiting the hour of his return. Arthur goes on to tell Henry that he now rules these *antipodes.* Then, explanations and niceties out of the way, Arthur blusters and threatens. He has been angered, he writes, by a message from a Breton partisan fighting Henry, and so has sailed back from the *antipodes* to the woods of Cornwall. Here Arthur is preparing his warriors—nothing is said as to who these warriors are, but we are left to imagine such names as Kay and Gawain—and he will soon attack Henry, unless the English king treats the Bretons better. On this note the unlikely letter ends, with Étienne describing Henry's reaction. The English king laughs and 'not at all scared' states that he will conquer Brittany whatever Arthur might do. But Henry does pay one small tribute to his

231

hero. He concedes that he would hold conquered Brittany on Arthur's behalf.

This is, by any measure, an extraordinary passage and yet it is one that most historians of the Arthurian legend pass over, considering it an unfunny Norman joke. Some of the detail suggests, though, authentic British-Celtic traditions. First we have the *antipodes*, a medieval nod to unknown, mysterious islands out in the ocean such as those that thronged early maps. And even a glance at the stories of the British Celts and the Irish will show that these peoples both had traditions that their fairy worlds or even a Christian heaven were to be found on islands deep in the ocean (islands such as those that we saw Saint Brendan scouting out from Celtic Ireland). *Antipodes*, then, was an elegant, Latinate way of referring to such mythic Celtic realms. By decamping to the *antipodes* Étienne's Arthur had, in fact, done the same thing as the Arthur of British-Celtic tradition when, after the Battle of Camlann, he is taken away to a better place by fairies on a boat, a place in which he will cure his mortal wounds and await his country's hour of need. To these British-Celtic touches should be added, too, the detail that Arthur was basing his operations out of certain woods in Cornwall. These words echo the court of Celli Wic, the glade in that region where British-Celtic bards had said that Arthur resided.

But where did Étienne get these details and why did he risk angering Henry with such an unfamiliar Celtic Arthur? The king, after all, was used to the chivalrous, knightly hero. As mentioned above, historians are inclined to write off this part of Étienne's poem as a joke. But, bizarre as this may seem, it may have been a real life event. It is quite possible, given the strong British-Celtic traditions, that a Breton leader had openly called upon

Arthur to come to Brittany's aid 'from the islands of the ocean', or that some imaginative Breton nationalists, knowing Henry's Arthurian predilections, had sent a letter purporting to be from Arthur to court. Stranger things happened in the Middle Ages.

What is certain is that in Étienne's poem, or in the episode that hides behind it, Henry—the great fan of a chivalric Arthur—was brought face to face with a very different hero. And how curious it is to see, in this thousand-year-old poem, the enthusiastic Arthurian confronted not by a paragon of knightly virtue, the Arthur of the King's imagination, but an island-hopping, forest-dwelling figure from out of earlier lore. How fitting as well that this battle between the Arthur of the British Celts and the English king's favourite, the new chivalric Arthur, may have triggered another notable encounter between the two Arthurs at the end of Henry's reign and after his death—an encounter that was to take place in England at the monastery of Glastonbury.

The abbey of Glastonbury is among the most famous of Britain. By the twelfth century, when it became embroiled in the battle over Arthur, it was perhaps six centuries old, and it would continue to prosper until the Reformation when its last abbot was taken out and hung on Glastonbury Tor. Glastonbury is known today, above all, for that Tor, reckoned by New Agers to be a blessed hub, a place where leylines meet (the modern 'science' of leylines was born at Glastonbury). However, even back in the twelfth century Glastonbury had a reputation as a special corner of England. British-Celtic storytellers described the area as being that of Avalon, the Isle of Apples, an earthly paradise. It is possibly to the British Celts that we owe the legend that Joseph of Arimathea, the man who according to the Gospels buried Jesus, came

233

to Britain and resided at Glastonbury. The poet William Blake famously refers to this story in his 'And did those feet in ancient times...' And an antique thorn tree in the general environs of the abbey—said to be the very tree that Joseph planted—survived until the English civil war in the seventeenth century, when a puritan soldier decided to bring an axe to what had become an object of common piety.

Given this heightened mystical atmosphere it was perhaps inevitable that Arthur would turn up at Glastonbury. It has been suggested that the abbot and monks of the monastery were inspired in their Arthurian adventures by ancient Celtic Latin works in their library— the monastery may date back to Celtic times. Or perhaps they were set off, instead, by stories coming across the borders from Wales, one of the British-Celtic homelands, or Cornwall where Glastonbury held land. It is even hinted that Henry II personally had a hand in encouraging the house of Glastonbury to take an active interest in Arthur.

But, if we cannot understand the origins of the following peculiar episode, an equal, in its way, to Étienne's letter, its consequences, at least, were clear. In 1191, twenty four years after Étienne's poem was written, picks were put in the hands of the monks and the order was sent out to excavate parts of the grounds of the abbey. The earliest recorded archaeological campaign in Britain had begun and a discovery was made that, in an age of tabloids, would have pushed every other news story off the front page—Arthur's tomb.

The results of this dig were set down by several writers. But the most lively description is that of Gerald, a Welsh author who on a visit to Glastonbury had been told by the monks how Arthur's grave had been found in the earth there.

Arthur's body… in our own days was discovered at Glastonbury between two ancient stone pyramids erected in the holy cemetery, hidden deep in the ground in a hollow oak and revealed by wonderful signs and marvels: it was afterwards moved into the church with honour and committed properly to a marble tomb. In the grave there was a leaden cross, under the stone and not above, as is typical today, with the words on it…: 'Here lies buried King Arthur with Guinevere, his second wife, on the Isle of Avalon'…

Arthur had two wives, the second buried with him there and her bones were in the tomb with his. But they were separated from them so that the two thirds of the grave, at the head naturally, were given over to Arthur's bones, while the bottom third, at the feet, held the woman's bones apart. There was a blonde lock of the woman's hair found still coloured. But when a monk snatched greedily at this lock and lifted it up, the lock crumbled straight-away into dust.

Now Arthur's shinbone when measured against the shin of the tallest there by being fixed in the ground… went more than three inches over that one's knee. The skull, meanwhile, was spacious and so large that it seemed to be of a freak or prodigy, with a hand's breadth for the eye-socket alone. And there were ten or more wounds there, all of which had scarred over, except for one greater wound which had left a substantial hole.

How did the monks know where to dig? Gerald tells us

235

that they were led by various clues ranging from letters on 'the pyramids', visions, and books in their library. But Gerald is also emphatic that Henry had been the key, telling the monks that he had heard from a British-Celtic bard that Arthur would be buried sixteen feet beneath the earth in an oak trunk.

If we could get rid of that medieval touch about the visions, we would have a modern conspiracy thriller: pyramids and ancient traditions. The story is, in truth, no more believable. In fact, another account gives us the tell-tale detail that the abbot had curtains placed around the excavations as diggings proceeded. The bodies were presumably transferred from a real grave elsewhere—the 'giants' are not impossibly large—and the detail of a hollow trunk is reminiscent of some kinds of Bronze Age burials. Perhaps 'Arthur and his wife' were found in the nearby countryside and then quickly moved to the abbey and the 'stone pyramids'.

This was an age when monasteries and churches, in order to protect or expand their lands, did not hesitate to manipulate past records and, indeed, blithely faked entire manuscripts. Glastonbury had a particularly bad reputation for this. It had rewritten its history in the twelfth century, managing to convince the Irish that St Patrick had once been abbot there. As a result, Irish pilgrims, with their gifts and donations, were a common sight at the abbey. It had also, in the years before, earned some notoriety for stealing saints' relics from other churches. And by 1191, the monastery was living through difficult times that demanded special remedies: the abbey had suffered from a disastrous fire ten years before and a decade of costly litigation with the local bishop.

The discovery and the confirmation that this was Arthur's resting place would win it fame and perhaps a little money. And, who would be happier with the monastery than the English monarch, Richard the Lionheart, Henry's successor? The Cornish, the Welsh and the Bretons (who Richard had to govern as well) were believers in the myth of Arthur's return. If the body had been found, then surely the legend of Arthur's return would die with it and, so, an English ruler might think, rebellion against English overlords. That this strategy failed—the Welsh at least continued to rebel—does not mean that the idea did not have a certain crude logic.

In Étienne's poem Henry had ridiculed the notion that Arthur could come back from the dead to fight him. A score of writers in the late twelfth century decried heretical British-Celtic beliefs in an undead hero king. Glastonbury had discovered the body of Arthur and so shown, through the unlikely medium of archaeology, that he had not survived death after all. But the fact is that the British Celts were simply not listening. The time had come for more drastic measures.

In Geoffrey's *History* Arthur's survival is alluded to but played down. In the French-Arthurian legends of Chrétien de Troyes it is mentioned, but passed over quickly, almost with embarrassment. However, at the end of the twelfth century, we begin to see something new. The return of the immortal Arthur becomes central again, with actual sightings. But these sightings—and here was the change—were from outside the British-Celtic homelands. So, in 1200, the story reaches us that a groom (of a bishop) had been walking at the base of Mount Etna in Sicily when he had come to a cave entrance. The groom walked in and there he had found a land of plenty in which Arthur and his knights were awaiting their call to duty.

The tale is in itself telling. After all, we have here

evidence that the story of Arthur's court had not only arrived in Sicily, on the southern marches of the Christian world. Sicily had been ruled by the Arabs until two generations previously and had been conquered by Norman cousins of William the Conqueror only shortly before. The story had also been fully-absorbed into local tradition.

We do not know why the groom (or his bishop) thought that Arthur would return. Perhaps they believed that he would come back to defend the recently established Christian kingdom there. What matters is that, from 1200 onwards, when we have legends concerning Arthur's resting place, they are not restricted to the British-Celtic world anymore. And, as if admitting as much, the British Celts slowly surrendered their Arthur. He continued, of course, to appear in their story-books, if only in stories borrowed from Continental writers: and the Welsh and Bretons were doubtless proud of the fame that he had earned abroad. But it was no longer Arthur who would be the Once and Future King: that role—at least in Wales—fell to other more obscure Britons of the past.

21

LOST IN TRANSLATION

efore the year 1150 it is necessary to search for references to the Once and Future King. Between 1150 and 1200 these references start to appear everywhere, running up and down the street, as it were; and then, from 1200 onwards, notices press uncomfortably in on us, as Arthur and his court become a Europe-wide obsession.

We hear of a special Arthurian pageant in the German city of Magdeburg with, among other entertainments, a poetry competition for best Arthurian poem. Richard I of England gives a sword with the name Excalibur to the King of Sicily. In Cyprus an Arthurian themed tournament is organised by crusading knights: northern warriors charging at each other with lances, pretending to be Lancelot and Gawain. A fabulous golden mosaic of Arthur was included in the works of the new cathedral at Otranto, a few score miles from where Arthur had been spotted sleeping under fuming Mount Etna. 'Arthur' starts to be used everywhere and in every class as a name for boys, a name that a hundred years before would have been dismissed as uncouth and barbaric. And, at the end of the thirteenth century, while in the east the Greeks were writing their first Arthurian tales, Vikings pattered on in their language, Norse, about Tristan and Isolde, the most popular Arthurian story in the Arctic Circle. Indeed, so great had Arthur's popularity become that by 1300 two things tied Europe together: Europe's Christian faith and its fascination with Arthur and his stories.

And what stories... Within a century the myths of Arthur and his court were fully established. There was the sword in the stone, of course, there was Excalibur coming out of the lake, there was a goodly circle of knights, there were the love affairs of Tristan and Isolde and Lancelot and Guinevere, there was the enchantment of Merlin and his seduction by the fey Morgan, there was the quest for the Holy Grail and the sad, final battle with which Arthur's reign ended, Camlann.

But what would the British Celts who had first told these stories have made of Arthur's extraordinary triumph? One thing that they certainly would have understood was the passion. True, the new listeners to Arthurian tales did not get excited for the same reasons as the British Celts had—there was no land or people about to be liberated. But Arthur continued to make people sit up. One French prior tells us how, while preaching, if he mentioned the Son of God the monks would stare ahead vacantly. But if he mentioned Arthur all his congregation would become wide-eyed with curiosity. The passion had transmuted, altered its form, but it was still there, pulsing beneath the surface of the legends and this, surely, the British Celts would have appreciated.

However, what a British Celt might not have recognised were, strangely enough, the legends. Take the modest list we have given here, which is a fair summary of what was later known as 'the Arthurian Cycle'. One can almost see the British Celts shaking their heads. There was no sword in the stone back where they had heard the stories in Cornwall or Wales or Brittany. There was a sword Caledfwlch, but not Excalibur: had someone perhaps spelt it very, very badly? The Round Table? Nothing doing. Yes, there was a magician called Myrdin— not Merlin. And, as for the Holy Grail, they would not have had the least idea. Arthur had started his life among the British Celts, but the neighbours who had borrowed Arthurian stories had changed them. What we do not know is how much they had changed them. The Arthurian spring broke the earth in the Celtic lands, afterwards becoming a stream and afterwards a mighty river. But how much of the water that reached the sea was 'Celtic'?

The most straightforward clues are names. Many of those that are used in the legends that were recounted on the continent are British-Celtic and so must be, it is sometimes reasoned, names that came from the homelands in pre-prepared, oven-ready British-Celtic legends. There is Arthur, for example, a British-Celtic or Celticised Latin name, as is in origin Kay, and Guinevere and Gawain. Then, on other occasions, we have not only names, but also nicknames that forced their way across the linguistic divide. In, for instance, one French poem of the late twelfth century, we hear of a certain Carados Briebras. Carados is a mispronounced version of a Welsh hero, Caradawc, nothing unusual there. But interestingly Caradawc has travelled together with a mispelt Welsh word Brecbras 'strong-arm'. This was the hero's nickname in Wales. At other times, we cannot be sure of a word's British-Celtic origins, but there are suspicions. One hero of French Arthurian romance was the lover Eric. It has been argued, and persuasively, that Eric is, in fact, a Dark Age Breton tribal leader, Weroc. And Eric (Weroc)

241

eventually settles down with his love Enid, who is likely a Breton placename transformed, through misunderstanding, into a woman.

At times Germanic or Romance-speakers slurred British-Celtic names out of recognition, especially if they were difficult to pronounce or sounded silly. British-Celtic Myrdin, for instance, was uncomfortably close to the French word for 'shit', hence the more polite-sounding Merlin. And some of the names above would have been difficult for a British Celt to recognise in their new form. Guinevere, for example, was Gwenefar in Wales; even Arthur was sometimes Latinised into Artorius or perverted into the strange Arcturus, while Gawain may have been Gwalchmei back home. And this process often made British-Celtic names all but impossible to find in the confusion of mangled syllables. So, on the Modena Cathedral arch in northern Italy where the tableaux mentioned earlier shows various Arthurian heroes, we do not have Guinevere, Arthur and Gawain, but Winlogee, Artus and Galvagin. Then, in still other instances, we have names that were not borrowed from the British Celts at all, but still found their way into Arthurian legend. One famous knight in the early French versions of Arthurian legend was Cliges, possibly a Turkish name. The name 'Galahad' was possibly invented. And 'Lancelot' might be British-Celtic, or French, or, it has been suggested, Iranian. Perhaps another way of saying that we have not the least idea where it came from.

But even if these names were British-Celtic, so what? It was not only the name or the label given to people and things that could change, but also their nature. Take Camelot, the capital of Arthur's kingdom. Camelot, that, for many children, is the first thing they learn about Arthur's world, is never even mentioned in a British-Celtic work though it is, indubitably, a British-Celtic name. In fact, it is not until Geoffrey of Monmouth in the twelfth century that we have our first description when his Arthur is crowned king. 'Situated as it is in Glamorganshire, on the River Usk, not far from the Severn Sea, in a most pleasant position, and being richer in material wealth than other townships, this city was eminently suitable for such a ceremony. The river which I have named flowed by it on one side, and up this the kings and princes who were to come from across the sea [to the coronation] could be carried in a fleet of ships. On the other side, which was flanked by meadows and wooded groves, they had adorned the city with royal palaces and, with the gold-painted gables of its roofs, it was a match for Rome.' Geoffrey goes on to regale us for pages with names of visitors, most of which he will have invented: 'there remained no prince of any distinction who did not come when he received his invitation. There was nothing remarkable in this: for Arthur's generosity was known throughout the whole world and this made all men love him.'

One thousand men in waiting, including chief seneschal Kay, brought in the food at the coronation and a thousand chalice bearers brought in the drinks. This was, then, the most extraordinary of medieval courts. And, after a few paragraphs of such excitement, Geoffrey sensibly calls a halt. 'If I were to describe everything, I should make this story far too long. Indeed, by this time, Britain had reached such a standard of sophistication that it excelled all other kingdoms in its general affluence, the richness of its decorations and the courteous behaviour of its inhabitants.' And then, in his excitement, he lets himself go again describing the games played, as knights jousted, their women on the city walls urging them on with flirtatious acts, and others still, who could not ride, enjoyed archery, dice and shot putting (with stones). So this was the glory that was Camelot…

This was, however, not the first description of Camelot. Rather, it was the description that inspired Camelot. For Geoffrey is describing Caerleon, once a Roman legionary base and today a lovely but modest Welsh village. We know of its Roman origins from excavations of an amphitheatre there, not to mention baths and barracks. But there is no archeological trace of the phantom palaces that Geoffrey described, though there were—and this may have been a factor in Caerleon being chosen by Geoffrey—Roman ruins still protruding above the ground when he sat down to write in the twelfth century.

And what is clear is that the court Geoffrey was describing conformed to a knightly Norman model, not a British-Celtic folkloric one. It was this knightly court that would give birth, a generation later, to Camelot. The first recorded mention of Camelot comes about thirty years after Geoffrey had written the *History*, in the works of a French poet who states that Arthur held a great court at Camelot on Ascension Day. Arthur, however, had left Caerleon to go to Camelot: so Camelot had not yet got the upper hand in the battle of the courts—Carlisle and London and eventually Winchester were sometimes also mentioned as Arthur's capital. And it would be another two hundred years before Camelot, finally stamped Caerleon, Carlisle, London and other rivals, back into the subsoil of legend.

What is unusual about 'Camelot' is that it is a recognisably Celtic word—in some form or other it did originate among the British-Celts. But how it vaulted half a continent to tumble into the verse of a French poet is at this date unknowable. The commonest explanation is that a Breton bard brought the name with him on one of his tours: by the twelfth century, such Breton bards were travelling with their songs in continental lands. But another explanation would cut out middle men altogether. As any educated, Latin-reading French scholar would know, the first city of pre-Roman Celtic Britain, where the Roman Emperor Claudius himself had campaigned, was Camulodunum, modern Colchester. And Camulodunum is a credible origin for the French Camelot. How easy it would have been to fish this Celtic-sounding name out of a library, the ancient capital of Britain no less, and appropriate it for an Arthurian romance.

Other Arthurian staples also have dubious origins. The Round Table, for example, first appears not in any record in the Celtic homelands, but in a foreign poem. The writer in question was one Wace, a native of the Channel Islands, who, in his translation of Geoffrey of Monmouth's *History* into Norman French, adds the detail that at Arthur's court (that Wace names as Caerleon) there was a certain 'Roonde Table'. Like a snowball rolling down a snow-covered hill-side the legend concerning this marvellous piece of furniture just keeps growing. Afterwards we hear that it seated fifty, then one hundred and fifty, then comes the detail that it could seat sixteen hundred, but could also be carried easily on the back of a donkey. That Merlin had the table made is a detail only introduced in the thirteenth century: though before that it had been said that Merlin chose the knights who would sit there. And, likewise, the story that one seat will be left empty for the man who is equal to the quest for the Holy Grail comes afterwards, as did the idea that no knight could be replaced unless one was found that was better than he. That all the knights who sit at the table are to be treated equally is an idea already in Wace and one suggested by the table's shape. That all those who sit there should never take arms against the other, 'except in sport', is also reported early on.

Wace claims that the tale was taken from British-Celtic tradition: but such claims are common in later Arthurian works and are not to be taken very seriously—we previously saw how Geoffrey's 'ancient book' may not have existed. In fact, the Round Table is not only absent from British-Celtic legend, but conspicuous by its absence. In the eleventh century the Welsh tale *Culhwch and Olwen* includes a list of Arthur's paraphernalia, but there is no table in the list of objects owned by Arthur. And a later Welsh account actually describes the Round Table being reintroduced into Wales, as the tradition of the Round Table had been 'forgotten' there.

In the sixteenth century the antiquarian Leland talks of a Round Table out in the countryside of Denbeighshire in Wales 'in the Side of a stony Hille, a Place wher there be 24 Holes or Places in a Roundel for Men to sitte in, but sum lesse, and sum bigger, cutte oute of the mayne Rok by Mannes Hand; and there Children and Young Men cumming to seke their Catelle use to sitte and play. Sum caulle it the Rounde Table.' But, by this date, the legend of the Round Table had become one of the mainstays of European story and such wilderness sites can be found in other lands—it is no proof of the origin of the legend, only of where it had become popular.

The Round Table is, in fact, more likely to have been inspired by Christian imagery than Celtic mythology. Christ is often shown seated at a circular table with the apostles and Arthurian legend marches hand-in-hand with Christianity. Its inspiration may also owe something to the knightly fraternity of Wace's time, a fraternity that Wace would have found at the court of Henry II where Wace lived for over a decade. Wace was, in fact, writing for Henry and would be expected to reflect the values of Henry's knights. There is no good reason for thinking that it had its origins in the west in Breton or Cornish or Welsh tradition. There is not really any reason at all other than that throwaway comment of Wace's. For someone who has grown up on 'Celtic' Arthurian legends these can be shocking and unwelcome revelations. But, for the lover of a Celtic Arthur, it is even worse than this. The truth is that not only names and objects originated outside the Celtic homelands. In some cases, the stories themselves were new creations, including perhaps the most famous of all, the Quest for the Holy Grail

The story of the Grail has been retold and re-elaborated so many times that the novelty of the earliest surviving version can almost smart the reader's eyes. Percival, the hero of the Grail Quest, was, according to the poet Chrétien de Troyes, out riding one day when he came to a wide river. There was no bridge or ford that would allow him to cross and so a fisherman invited him to spend the night in his house. From this point on the experience of Percival is—as sometimes happens in Arthurian legend—a descent into a dream world where the normal rules of cause and effect appear no longer to work. Percival discovers, to his surprise, that the fisherman's house is not a shack, but a substantial mansion. Percival is, then, taken to the hall where the host of the house lies in a bed, injured. The crippled lord presents Percival with a sword and Percival draws the sword to admire it in the brightly lit hall: 'and no house lit by candles could ever provide a brighter light than there was in that hall'. At this point things begin to get even stranger.

While they were talking of one thing and another, a boy came from a chamber clutching a white lance by the middle of the shaft, and he passed between the fire and the two who were sitting on the bed. Everyone in the hall saw the white lance with its white head; and a drop of blood issued from the tip of the lance's head, and right down to the boy's hand this red drop ran. The lord's guest gazed at this marvel that had appeared that night, but restrained himself from asking how it came to be, because he remembered the advice of the nobleman who had made him a knight, who had taught him to beware of talking too much; he feared it would be considered base of him if he asked—so he did not. Then the two other boys appeared, and in their hands they held candlesticks of the finest gold, inlaid with black enamel and in each burned ten candles at the very least. A girl who came in with the boys fair and comely and beautifully attired, was holding a vessel [*grail*] between her hands. And when she entered holding the vessel, so brilliant a light appeared that the candles lost their brightness like the stars or the moon when the sun rises. The vessel was made of fine, pure gold; and in it were set precious jewels of many kinds, the richest and most precious in the earth or the sea. The procession passed before the bed and disappeared into another chamber.

Percival says nothing. But he is curious: what is this wonderful *grail* (*grail* means simply 'vessel' in French)? Percival, then, goes to bed, but on waking in the morning, more curious than ever, he finds no one in the hall. He

248

takes his horse and rides out onto the drawbridge that lies across the moat, still looking for a servant or resident who can tell him of the *grail* and its purpose. But then Percival's horse jumps and Percival is shocked to find, now on the wrong side of the moat, that the drawbridge has been closed behind him. He shouts to be readmitted 'but he was wasting his time calling out like this, for nobody would answer him'. The dream-like quality of this episode burns away. Percival sets off on his adventures again. Afterwards he is told by a woman he meets that the crippled lord, the Fisher King as he is known, continues to lie ill because Percival failed to ask the purpose of the *grail* and the bleeding lance. If only Percival had asked, then, the Fisher King would have been restored to health and the land and Percival would have been spared much suffering.

Chrétien never tells us what the Grail is because—after setting such a puzzle—he died without finishing the poem c. 1190. However, in a later part of the work we do at least learn that the Grail is a 'holy thing', from which ultimately we get our 'Holy Grail'. On some levels, of course, that answers Percival's question as to the Grail's purpose. But, in the style of the best mystery novels, it answers one question only to open another even bigger one. What was the Grail and why was it so holy? If Chrétien had survived, then, he would have answered that question for us. But he did not and his discontinued poem piques not only our curiosity, but also piqued that of his immediate twelfth- and thirteenth-century successors. Indeed, it has sometimes been said that the key to the success of the Grail legend was Chrétien's death that left all these maddening loose endings needing answers.

Certainly, Chrétien's successors wrote continuations, further adventures concerning the quest for the Grail.

And in these new legends Percival was sometimes in competition with other heroes and sometimes eliminated altogether. But such changes were far less important than the new traditions about the Grail's origins. For, within ten years of Chrétien's death, one author had made the suggestion, which would afterwards define it, that this was the cup that Christ had used at the Last Supper. The connection with Christ may have been a simple way to explain the Grail's holiness, and perhaps the solution that Chrétien himself had in mind. What is clear is that the solution gave satisfaction to Europe's avid Arthurian fanbase, and over the next century and a half many, many more stories detailing the Grail's early history or the quest for its home would be composed in several languages. In a very real sense these legends continue to be written to this day. The Grail, in fact, arouses more modern interest than any other part of the Arthurian legend.

But, as with the Round Table, we have the question of where this legend came from. Was it simply invented by Chrétien, was it borrowed, as perhaps the Round Table was, from Christian lore—its Christian associations are very strong, or was this borrowed instead from Celtic legend and then altered on the continent? There is much uncertainty, but we can point to one coincidence that might suggest the Grail has at least something Celtic in its alloy. The name of the Fisher King was, it is revealed, Bron. 'Bron' is a very strange name. It is not Germanic or Latin and is most easily explained as a careless adaptation of the Celtic name Bran, a British-Celtic word meaning 'raven'. In which case, we have come full circle, for Bron here seems to be the same Raven, the mythic hero who all these years before led the Senones to the gates of Rome. And from our one extensive Welsh legend concerning Raven we know that the hero was given a zombie-producing cauldron of regeneration, where dead bodies came to life again. Is this perhaps then a Celtic Grail that only later was converted to more Christian purposes? That Bron is Bran is probable. That a cauldron became the jewelled Grail is far less certain. We might even say that it is unlikely.

22

DID THE CELTS CREATE THE
MODERN MIND?

If you lend a book to a friend then the book will come back unchanged bar perhaps some creases. But lend a legend and those borrowing the tale will bend it to suit their own purposes and soon the legend will, as we saw with Geoffrey of Monmouth, have little in common with the legend that was lent. Perhaps the legend with slurred names, changed plots and the inventiveness of the borrower will have even become incomprehensible to the lender. This, certainly, is what happened to Arthurian legend in the course of the twelfth and, above all, the thirteenth century. And it was the very flexibility of the stories that led to their success. Like a magic glove, the sort that could have appeared in one of the tales told of Arthur, and, for all we know, perhaps somewhere did, Arthurian legend shrank or expanded to fit whoever wished to wear it. And, if, in the British-Celtic homelands, that glove had been a woodcutter's mitten or a bowman's brace, in France and Germany and England it became a metal, mail fist such as a knight might wear. The new Arthur was a true medieval king who lived and eventually died according to the laws of knightly society and was most passionately followed by the rulers and aristocracy of Europe. And not surprisingly Arthur's world quickly came to resemble theirs.

We suggested above that the name 'Camelot' *might* have originated in the pre-Roman name for Colchester. But what is certain is that, whatever name we give Arthur's court—Camelot, Caerleon, Carlisle, London… his capital was emphatically not a historic attempt to reconstruct a British-Celtic fort of the Saxon wars. It was a feudal capital, an idealised version of the homes of kings like Henry II, Richard I and those other Arthurians we have mentioned in earlier pages. And the description of Arthur in Camelot is of a generous feudal lord, not a Welsh folklore hero. The Round Table likewise was an object that was particularly well-suited to knights in a feudal society. This, after all, was the age of the Orders of Knights: the Knights Templars, the Knights of St John and the Hospitaler Knights, to name only the most famous, for whom Arthurian legend became an ideal. The Round Table with its overtones of brotherly love and sacrifice made perfect sense to them, explaining why from Wace's score of words about it the Round Table spread so quickly through hundreds of tales. Even the Grail and the idea of a Quest undertaken by Christian warriors to save the land was a legend that, whether or not it had Celtic origins, was quickly given a feudal stamp. To read the Grail legend today is to read a quintessential medieval story, a story that better represents medieval society than any other. It will give no such insights into Celtic mythology.

There are two ways to measure this knightly interest in Arthur. The first, and the most entertaining, is to see how it intruded itself physically into the lives of kings and courts. I mentioned earlier, for example, an Arthurian jousting competition in Cyprus in the early twelfth century. Jousting competitions had already long existed, of course, by 1223, when the event on that island took place. But from then on more and more meetings were held along Arthurian lines with participants taking Arthurian names in jest or ritual. By the mid thirteenth century an English magnate, possibly Edward I, had a special Round Table built, for one of these Arthurian Tournaments. And, these Arthurian themed events had become so common that in English 'roundtable' took on the meaning of 'knightly tournament'.

Nor did the craze die. Edward's grandson Edward III was also an Arthurian. As a young man he went incognito to joust at one of these tournaments. Then, as king, he went one step further and pronounced an actual order of Knights of the Round Table: archaeologists have found the massive circular palace that he started building for his Arthurian order at Windsor, before an expensive war in France meant that it had to be called off. Edward never again had the money to send artisans back to work on the palace and he eventually settled for the more modest Knights of the Garter. It is an order that survives to this day within the British honours system and whose members include two past British prime-ministers, Lady Thatcher, Sir John Major and another score of latter-day Arthurians.

A second and more difficult way to measure the impact of Arthurian legend, but also a more important one, is to measure how Arthur changed the balance of power within Europe. There had been, since the fall of the Roman Empire an aristocratic class that had ruled the continent together with the Church. In the Dark Ages, this aristocratic class and the Church had ruled in something approaching harmony: the secular class had dominated in might, the Church in learning. But, by 1100, this harmony had come to an end and the two classes were fighting each other for the continent, straying into each other's traditional spheres. As we have noted the great resource of the Church was that it controlled intellectual life and written culture. In the twelfth century many knights will not have known how to read. And even if they could, it was difficult for a knight to articulate any feelings of rage or discontent with the Church because those feelings could only be expressed in the language of learning, medieval Latin, the language of the Church Fathers, a language that naturally favoured the Church.

The Arthurian legends represented a new chapter in the war, not least because they were often written in living languages rather than Latin. Here was a body of myths that the Church sometimes grumbled about, but accepted: lulled into a false sense of security by the constant references in the tales to saints, monks, hermits, grails and the like. Here also was a body of legends that Europe's aristocratic rulers could call their own and employ to articulate their own view of the world and become more confident in their powers. Of course, it is not possible to chart this growing confidence in numbers of Arthurian tournaments or roundtables. But it is there and, in the cult of Courtly Love, we have an example of how this confidence manifested itself.

Courtly Love had not originated in the Celtic homelands. It was a feudal creation, the almost religious veneration that a noble man might feel for a noble woman: and it was also an area of medieval life where aristocracy and church came close to violent disagreement. Courtly Love suffuses later Arthurian legend. Indeed, it is difficult to find an account of Arthurian knights that does not involve the hero becoming hopelessly enamoured of some maiden. If, today, a modern reader wants to understand the idea of Courtly Love, he or she could do no better than read the Arthurian poems of Chrétien de Troyes—the primers and textbooks of this cult. In its purest form—in some practitioners would say its correct form—Courtly Love was a noble calling quite compatible with the office of marriage and quite incompatible with some of the torrid affairs that Arthurian heroes stray into. The knight held his love as a form of devotion, sometimes secret devotion: the woman might be married, she might be queen. But there was no question of that love actually being consummated physically. It remained a delicate and spiritual thing. That was the theory in any case. The practice was rather more difficult, and courtly devotion in twelfth- and thirteenth-century Europe naturally led to love affairs, divorce and disgrace. And these dangerous loves are mirrored in the retellings of Arthurian legend, especially in the case of two parallel Arthurian love stories, those of Lancelot and Guinevere; and Tristan and Isolde.

The love story of Lancelot and Guinevere is today the most famous of these two, perhaps because it transfers so easily to the cinema screen. Guinevere—'White Shadow' her name had meant in British Celtic—was, of course, married to King Arthur. But, after several years of Arthur's rule, a new knight, a certain Lancelot came to sit at the Round Table. Lancelot was an extraordinary warrior and a good man. But his idealism had one weakness—it would perhaps be truer to say that his idealism was his weakness: his capacity to love was immense. Guinevere, at first, playfully repelled his advances and then provoked them until they became lovers and broke the unity of the kingdom.

The story of Tristan and Isolde—her name means

simply 'Worth Looking At'—is more fantastical but similarly tragic. Tristan was a Breton aristocrat and Isolde an Irish princess. They met when Tristan was sent to Ireland to bring Isolde back to marry Tristan's master, King Mark of Cornwall, one of Arthur's subject kings. But, unfortunately for them, on their way home, they accidentally drank a fairy potion that made them fall hopelessly in love with one another. Their love survived Isolde's marriage to Mark—Tristan managed to trick the king into sleeping with Isolde's maid instead of Isolde on his wedding night—and would end only with their deaths.

We will not examine the possible Celtic origins of these legends. Suffice to say that if there are British-Celtic traditions here, and there almost certainly are, then a good deal was misunderstood or altered. What is, instead, of interest is how Courtly Love penetrated so deeply into the stories and took them over. Sometimes Courtly Love is there in the details: the methods Lancelot uses to get Guinevere's attention or confirm his adoration for her. But sometimes we see how the plot itself cedes to feudal pressures. The potion in the story of Tristan and Isolde, for example—very likely a British-Celtic tradition—is increasingly played down in German and French retellings because it gets in the way of Tristan and Isolde's free will and their ability to sacrifice everything for love. In some retellings it seems to be no more than a stimulus to bring out a love that was already there. Celtic love stories tend to be, in contrast, big on magic and short on psychology.

But what matters is not what the legends were, but what they became, and with these tales of love we see just how far the Chivalric class and its hangers on were earning their independence from the Church. In twelfth-century France, one middle-aged woman, writing to the darling of her youth, noted that she would go to Hell for her love—a shocking and even dangerous statement in a narrowly Christian world. In medieval Europe this sort of sentiment would never survive. Sooner or later it would come up hard against the tenets of the Christian faith; and denying those might lead to the stake. But, in the hot house of the new Arthurian myths, a world set apart, these revolutionary tendencies could be explored. After all, with Isolde or Guinevere we have not only the love between knights and ladies, we have two of the greatest love stories in Western literature. And, not surprisingly, these tales became the very centre of the revolt in favour of love. We have quoted above the superannuated lover who announces that she would be prepared to go to Hell for her love. In the very early thirteenth century the German poet, Gottfried von Strasbourg, perhaps the greatest of all Arthurian authors, conveys in his epic *Tristan* the same idea. Tristan, in a moment of great passion says that he will woo 'everlasting death' if only he can continue to love his Isolde.

To a medieval priest, of course, Tristan was already well on his way to the flames. And even the more respectable Lancelot and Guinevere did not have a particularly holy reputation. Stories about them were criticised in the Middle Ages as corrupters of youth, much as video nasties or violent computer games are today. So Dante, the master Italian poet of the Middle Ages, in the *Inferno*, his poetic description of Hell, has a young man and woman, Paolo and Francesca suffering damnation for becoming lovers, after reading of Lancelot and Guinevere kissing. Of course, not all Arthurian legend played with Christian morality in this way. When Chrétien de Troyes, the early Arthurian poet from France, described the adulterous love of Lancelot and Guinevere, he did so with a distaste that he could barely hide. And, in another of his poems, the heroine, embroiled in her own love difficulties, compares herself favourably to Isolde, a woman who shared her body with two men and her heart only with one. But, whether illicit or commendable, the popularity of these early classics in the households and palaces of Europe are a reminder of the subversive power and appeal of legends outside the Gospels, the saints' lives and fragments of apocrypha.

Compared with the creation of the Roman Empire, described in the first part of this book or the survival of Christianity in the second, the arrival of mythical figures can seem—with all respect to these figures—a rather unreal affair. There were no warriors as such, no monks, no druids, no tribesmen getting off boats or crossing frontiers. There were story-tale heroes and magical objects and a series of memorable villains: but nothing that you could see or touch or feel. If you had been in the area when a party of Irish exiles had turned up in the seventh century, or when, back in antiquity, a Senones warband had arrived outside your city, you would have been acutely aware of the presence of these visitors from the Celtic homelands: the noise and the pageant of it all. But, if you had been in a court in France or Italy when these legendary heroes got there, it is unlikely that you would have noticed a thing. At best you would have seen a squire with a manuscript under his arm, or one of the travelling singers who went down the road selling his verses being called over by the provost and being asked for an evening's performance.

And yet these ethereal figures helped bring about changes that were in their way as dramatic as any of those wrought by the Iron Age invasions or the monkly migrations of the Dark Ages. Courtly Love was only the most visible part of a long conflict being fought

259

throughout the continent, the conflict between Europe's Church and Europe's aristocracy, a conflict that for a time was played out in Arthurian costume. As in an arm-wrestle, the Church and the ruling aristocracy struggled for dominance. And the Middle Ages—at least from the twelfth century onwards—is the story of the ruling aristocracy slowly triumphing over the Church and with the generations, and ever more force, pressing down its advantage to the table. The victory of State (for want of a better word) over Church was a civilisation-defining moment. What we today call the West can be, in part, characterised by the division of roles between the various successors of the medieval European Church and the feudal aristocracy. Modern notions of democracy and, indeed, freedom depend on the conviction, almost universal in the Americas, Australasia and Europe, so universal that it is too easily taken for granted, that religion is a private not a public matter.

That the crisis happened is a simple fact that no one would dispute. That the crisis was resolved in the favour of 'the State' is also a matter of record. A much more difficult question, and one where there is inevitably disagreement, is when and how this victory came about. Scholars usually associate the moment of victory—the moment when the back of the Church's hand touches the table—with the Renaissance and the fifteenth century. And certainly the final victory did come in Florence, Venice and Bruges with the rise of a new class of merchants, bankers, professionals and independent farmers, the ancestors of our present-day middle classes. But the Renaissance was only the end point of long and painful divorce proceedings between the mother and father of medieval civilisation: the Church and the medieval aristocracy. Disputes between these two can already be traced back to the tenth and above all the eleventh century, when Popes declared themselves higher than all the kings of Europe. Some of the resulting battles, really did involve warfare. Blood was spilt and armies sent charging at each other. But, for the most part, the struggle was a tussle for power played out in books and words: in libraries and in courts, through the confessional grill and across palace dining tables.

It is here, as we have seen, that Arthurian legend was important. For those legends were, already in the twelfth century, helping to create the most important prerequisite for that later and decisive push: an articulate, self confident, secular mindset. That the victory of the European aristocracy had many causes is hardly surprising. But just how much credit should Arthur and his court take for this victory? Arthur and his knights and his monsters and his ladies certainly did their bit: they became a language of ideas that the secular classes began to speak, a language that was, as we suggested, blessedly free of Augustine or Aquinas and other mystifiers of the world. Perhaps they were a vital contribution, but hardly a fundamental one. Or perhaps we should see the moment that these Celtic heroes were unleashed on Continental Europe as the moment that the aristocratic rulers got the upper hand in the generations-long struggle: the beginning of the end for theocratic Europe.

The question is one that is more easily answered in Camelot than in the heavy, material world in which we find ourselves: the connections between legend and history are made of web-like strands of fairy gauze that no one can hope today to measure or weigh. But this posthumous contribution of the ancient Celts—Celtic civilisation, as we understand it, had ceased to exist by the time of Geoffrey of Monmouth and Chrétien de

Troyes—nevertheless served its purpose. Yes, its heroes, heroes in some cases as old as the Iron Age, had been changed and manipulated. But, in the strange alchemy of symbol and myth, they had become a potion every bit as powerful as that of which Tristan and Isolde drank.

DISCOVERING AMERICA?

THE IRISH EXILES
IN THE NORTHERN ATLANTGIC

Today when we think of explorers we think of Marco Polo, Magellan, Columbus and other figures from the later Middle Ages and from the Renaissance. But the truth is that explorers have existed right through western history pushing out from the literate, map-making Mediterranean heartlands. So even Ireland and Britain were 'discovered': they certainly were not always on the map known to Mediterranean peoples. Indeed, it fell, perhaps eight hundred years before the first Irish exiles, to an inhabitant of Marseilles, one Pytheas to circumnavigate the island of Britain: a task the Romans, who did not know whether to trust Pytheas, would repeat four centuries later; some Romans had believed that Britain was a peninsula.

But, if Britain and Ireland fell to the cartographers in antiquity, then other lands, further to the north, were rumours before the Irish exiles began their voyages. Learned men claimed, for example, that there was an island to the north of Britain called Ultima Thule: Last Thule. But we have no idea which island or island chain this was: Iceland, Greenland, Orkney, Shetlands, Faeroes or even Scandinavia have all been suggested. When these northern islands do appear in our records they do so as legends: a place where a peculiar god lives; a place where a caste of priests go; a place where the sea congeals; a place where 'the sea breathed'... We are speaking about the misted edges of the world: a region where ignorance far outweighed knowledge. Nor was there any overriding motive to explore these places. The Romans had found in Britain that the further north you went the more difficult things became: crops were given up for pasture, daylight hours became shorter and when the sun did show its face it was weaker.

The inhabitants of Britain and Ireland might likewise have been reluctant to explore the northern seas. But with the Irish exiles a strange new chapter in the history of exploration was opened. The exiles, after all, were looking for deserted islands. Their motivation was completely different from other explorers. They also had another thing going for them. They were numerous and suicidally keen. Most explorers leave home and make their way into the unknown with carefully-husbanded supplies. But, as the Irish exiles were letting the wind and currents decide their destination, elements that they understood as the instruments of God, then they did not take this kind of care. This was kamikaze exploration, a completely different method of exploration from the normal trial and error: go a bit north, go a bit west, if the water is running out head for home... Most must have died in waves many times higher than their boats in the open seas. But, as perhaps hundreds of Irish exiles undertook this unusual form of exploration, at least in some cases, they came to land and found new worlds.

The list is impressive. Cormac arrived on Orkney that was already known to the Irish. But other Irish exiles start to turn up further to the north in Shetlands, in Faeroes and in Iceland. Indeed, the first account in history of the Midnight Sun comes from two Irish monks who remarked how, sitting in a hermitage, probably on Iceland, they were able to pick lice off each other's backs, even deep into the night. And when, several centuries later, the Vikings arrived in Iceland they found the place without a native population save for some curious men dressed in white with books and bells—a Viking description of monks, for the monks had continued to make the journey in the intervening centuries. That this was new knowledge is proved by the works of a geographer, Dicuil who wrote in France in the ninth century. Dicuil, for the most part, slavishly copied ancient geographies. But every so often he added new facts: in his section on France and Germany, for example, he discussed an elephant that had been brought to the royal court. And, when he described the northern Atlantic, he wrote of the voyages of Irish monks there as no Classical sources had any information. Dicuil was, in fact, Irish—he was an exile himself—and he had lived for a time in the Hebrides or Orkney. As such he was an excellent channel to bring the news of these journeys to a wider world.

Irish monks certainly sailed then deep into the northern Atlantic, uncovering the mysteries of that ocean. And, in their legends, but also in more sober works, such as Dicuil's, they catalogued their discoveries. No one today would question that the exiles made it as far as Iceland in their boats. But what remains controversial is whether the exiles made it any further to the north or to the west. Scholars—some desperados, some worthy of the greatest respect—have suggested that they did and crosses have been put on maps. The Irish, according to these claims, made it to Greenland and as far, in steeply descending order of likelihood, as Canada, New England, the Caribbean and even Central America. And the most extraordinary range of evidence has been used to justify these claims including a peculiar Native American Temple in New Hampshire and statues of bearded men among the Aztecs.

One Irish explorer, Tim Severin even reconstructed an Irish vessel using illustrations from a (late) manuscript and then, in 1976, successfully sailed from Ireland to Newfoundland to show that such an accomplishment was feasible. And those who claim that the exiles themselves made such a voyage point to the example of the Vikings. For many years it was thought that the Vikings had visited North America on the basis of comments in Viking histories about a land to the west of their settlements in Greenland. Sceptics disagreed. But the debate ended when, in 1960, a Viking village in Nova Scotia (Canada) was identified.

So did the Irish discover the Americas about a thousand years before Columbus? To assess this question it is useful to concentrate on that word 'discover'. Discovery involves three things. First, the explorer must arrive in the new land. Second, he must return home: it is not discovery if he never gets to share his secret with anyone. And, third, he must manage to convince those at home to include his discovery on a map or in a history. It is important to break down discovery into these three parts because the probability that the Irish made it to Greenland or even North America is actually quite good. Yes, they had fragile boats. Yes, they were unprepared. Yes, these lands are a long way away. But what is extraordinary about the Irish method was that it was done with perhaps scores of potential explorers all giving themselves up to the wind. Throw one message in a bottle in the sea in Kerry with the wind blowing west and it is extremely unlikely that it will ever arrive in North America. But if you throw a thousand in the water the chances that at least one will land there are high...

As we have noted though we must not confuse arriving with discovery. If tomorrow some archaeologists in Conneticut find the remains of an Irish *curragh* miraculously preserved in mud with three Caucasian skeletons and a sentence scratched in Gaelic on a rock nearby this does not mean that the Irish discovered America. It means that one boatload struggled that far and then failed to get back. We have two instances, one from the ancient world and one from the Renaissance, where records suggest that Native Americans may have washed up on the coast of Europe, after having been blown across hundreds of miles of sea, probably lost after a storm. In both cases, the foreign crew in strange boats were brought to a local king and then quickly died. There are likewise legends from the Hebrides and Orkney of 'Eskimos' turning up on the coast there. These kinds of accidental voyages are credible. But they are curiosities: wonderful, interesting, yes, but colourfully and magnificently irrelevant. They are the insignificant meetings of early North American and European culture. And, if the Irish had made it to North America or Greenland alive then it is likely that they would have ended as the same kind of freaks as these early Americans, carted around to the good and great in cages or chains.

The only way that discovery would work is if the Irish had brought back news of this other continent across the ocean to the native scholars working in monasteries like Glendalough and Armagh: as Viking voyagers included references to North America in their sagas. But, while descriptions of sea journeys to a marvellous land in the west are extensive in Irish lore, they are described in terms that make us think of legend. For the Irish believed that this marvellous land was to be found somewhere in the ocean—just as the early Desert monks had believed that a heavenly garden was to be found deep in the desert. And sometimes descriptions of this vast land have been confused with descriptions of America. The fact, however, that this paradise is said to be just off the shore of Ireland should probably be taken as a warning that we are speaking here about a symbol of spiritual perfection rather than a physical entity. Likewise descriptions of a crystal sea where it was possible to see to many metres of depth and the animals that swum there is far more likely to be a traveller's tale from the Red Sea than a record of an early Irish visit to Jamaica!

Perhaps the only thing in the Irish legends of islands that gives serious food for thought are the accounts of pygmies that were said to live out in the ocean. These pygmies could be mythological creatures. But it has been suggested that they are, instead, a confused early Irish description of the Native Americans of the north: the Inuit or their ancestors. If these tales really are stories about the Inuit then the Irish perhaps had travelled to North America proper: as Greenland in the fifth through to the eighth century was, it seems, uninhabited by Native Americans—a result of plunging temperatures. But even our Irish pygmies do not give us any certainty. For if the pygmies are based ultimately on Native Americans, it is always possible that the Irish learnt of these people, not personally, but from later Viking contacts or 'Eskimos' washed up in British and Irish waters. The Irish discovery of Iceland and other northern isles is secure, but the discovery of North America remains unproven.

WILL THE REAL KING ARTHUR
PLEASE STAND UP

In the last twenty years the 'true' king Arthur has been spotted by avid fans in almost every corner of the world. So fragments of his grave-stone were, for example, noticed in the wall of a church in Croatia. Enthusiasts found his sword in America, hinting at a pre-Columbian visit to the United States. There were rumours about a visit to a fairy land in the Pacific—in 2003 it was 'proved' that the Celts had colonised New Zealand. A group of Slavic nationalists determined that Arthur was really a Russian Tsar and that all his subsequent history had been faked by the dastardly English. Then there were, of course, insular sightings. Two British historians, who met in the library at Newcastle-upon-Tyne, dug up Arthur's grave in Glamorgan. A chiropodist from Hull offered ten thousand pounds to anyone who could prove that Arthur was not Irish—the challenge, to the best of our knowledge, still stands. Some archaeologists at Tintagel thought that they had come across Arthur's name on an inscription only to discover that the name was Artognov—not even a close relation. Then there has been the Mr Arthur Pendragon who has stood at Winchester in recent General Elections and, as a druid, has found by far the most sensible modern solution to the Arthurian problem: he has announced that he is the great man's reincarnation.

However, this collection of misunderstanding, wishful thinking and exuberant neo-paganism cloaks (or perhaps compliments) the progress made in serious studies into the origins of Arthurian legend over the same period. If we today asked one hundred Dark Age historians, archaeologists and Celticists who the historical Arthur really was we would get a lot of mumbling and evasions—scholars of the Dark Ages are necessarily a chary bunch. But if we held a hundred guns to the hundred heads of this century of Arthurian professionals and insisted that they give us their best guess it is likely that three solid and respectable candidates would race ahead of the pack of circus freaks mentioned above. And these three might be reduced to simple monikers: Artur the Gael, Artorius the Roman, and Arthur the Warlord.

The most popular of these three, if not among our hundred scholars then certainly among the general public, is Arthur the Warlord and his story is quickly told. In Britain c. 410 the Romans abandoned the island. There followed the two darkest centuries in British history. But, in those obscure years, we know that the Anglo-Saxons arrived and made much of south and eastern Britain their own pushing out/slaughtering/assimilating (opinions differ) the native British-Celtic population. Arthur the Warlord would be the leader or a leader of the native British Celts against these invaders sometime between 450-550 AD. Supporters of the Warlord point out that later British-Celtic documents situate Arthur in this period. And they also remind us that our ignorance about these hundred years is so vast that there is ample room for a great man to govern an island, win battles and woo the

British-Celtic imagination while not being noticed in our very few contemporary works—all Arthurian references come in later centuries. As to where this warlord lived different partisans push for Wales, Cornwall, the Scottish Lowlands, the Pennines and almost every other part of what was, in the sixth-century, British-Celtic Britain and, across the waters, Brittany.

With the second candidate, Artorius the Roman, we do not have to worry about disputed locations because we are speaking about a concrete, well-situated historical personality. In the late second century Lucius Artorius Castus was a Roman officer based at Ribchester in what is today northern England in charge of a large contingent of Sarmatian cavalry, Iranian-speaking warriors who had been sucked into the Roman army as mercenaries. (Lest this sound overly exotic we should remember that this was a time when 'Ethiopians' served on Hadrian's Wall.) We gather from contemporary accounts that Artorius was a well-regarded commander who led his warriors on several campaigns including one in Britain and one in Gaul. He later retired and was buried in Roman Dalmatia: the Croatian grave referred to above belongs to him. What Artorius has in his favour is his name. In fact, of the thousand plus names we know from Roman Britain Artorius is the only one to be so called: and as the Latin name Artorius is very probably the basis of the familiar British-Celtic 'Arthur' this is suggestive. Supporters of the Roman Artorius claim that there is also additional evidence. The Sarmatian cavalry, they argue, were Arthur's knights. And there have even been attempts to find Sarmatian material in early Arthurian legend.

The third candidate, Artur the Gael, also had the right name. In the sixth century there were a series of Gaelic or Irish settlements on the western coast of what is today

271

Scotland, especially in the inner Hebrides and Argyll. And one of the sons of sixth-century Aidan mac Gabrain, the most famous of all the early kings of the Gaelic settlements there and a contemporary of Colum Cille, was a certain Artur. Supporters of the Gaelic Artur point out that this Hebridean prince is the only well-attested individual in Dark Age Britain with a name like Arthur's. And, as a Gael warlord, he may have fought in battles that earned him a place in later legend. These same supporters are not worried by the fact that this Artur is Gaelic rather than British-Celtic. Heroes from one culture are easily adopted into another, they argue, and there are also features of Arthurian legend that could be said to be Gaelic in origin. That the same parts of Arthurian legend are said to be Sarmatian in origin is maybe a warning about the unreliability of these kinds of deductions...

What is perhaps most striking about these three candidates is just how varied they are. In the late 1960s, in the wake of inspired and inspiring digs at the hill-fort of South Cadbury in southern Britain ('that was Camelot' according to early modern legend), the Warlord Arthur was very much in the ascendant. These excavations under the archaeologist Leslie Alcock allowed us, for the first time, to peer into the years 450-550 at a British-Celtic stronghold such as one that a Warlord Arthur might have used. But forty years later we have two contenders who lived as many as two hundred years before or after the Warlord (respectively Artorius and Artur). Given this it is reasonable to ask whether we have made any progress at all. Are we not confessing our total and embarrassing ignorance of who the historical Arthur was to admit three so very different figures to the canon of Arthurian possibilities?

In fact, we do know more today, though that

knowledge—and this is admittedly paradoxical—is about how very little we know. The single greatest step in Arthurian studies, a step that has opened the way to these three so very different candidates, is the understanding of how unreliable our earliest Arthurian sources are. In the 1960s, it was believed that the earliest references to Arthur appeared in certain British-Celtic poems that dated to c. 600, chiefly one called the *Gododdin* that waxed lyrical about a British-Celtic battle with the English and the fate of the British-Celtic heroes who fought there. It is now accepted though that while, these poems might be early, they might equally be from 700 or 800 or 900 or perhaps even later. That means that our earliest certain source is the *History of the British Celts* written in 829 or 830 in northern Wales, the most intriguing of all British-Celtic works to survive the Middle Ages. This 'history' (the inverted commas will soon be justified) used to be the jewel in the crown of Arthuriana, the gold under the mountain. But, in truth, the Arthur found there is, above all, a folklore figure; a western-dwelling Puck who is associated with giant-sized objects in the wilderness including a shape-shifting tomb.

In fact, we understand better now than a generation ago that the *History of the British Celts* does not transmit history but myth, or, at best, history churned through the sausage machine of British-Celtic legend. Take, for instance, the fate in the *History* of a fifth-century probably southern British-Celtic warleader, named Ambrosius Aurelianus. We know about Ambrosius from a five-star reliable, near-contemporary source, where he is said to have been related to an Emperor and to have been 'the last of the Romans' in Britain. Yet, by the time Ambrosius appears in the *History of the British Celts*, he has become the son of a demon who is taken to a mountain lake to be sacrificed by magicians, but who manages to avoid being killed by digging up two dragons, dragons that proceed to fight each other on a piece of cloth... If the *History of the British Celts* is gold then it is fool's gold. And the dating offered by the *History of the British Celts* and the associated *Welsh Annals* for Arthur have all the characteristics of an attempt to situate a legendary figure in history: something that, as we shall see, can be paralleled elsewhere in early medieval Irish and British-Celtic writing. For example, the all too legendary Irish divine hero Fionn is wheeled out by medieval Irish story-tellers to fight the all too historical Vikings...

Still not convinced of the Arthurian historical vacuum? So fascinated has the modern world become with the historical Arthur: that we cannot easily come to terms with this shredding of evidence concerning the 'real' Arthur. But consider, now, the most historical-sounding extract from the *History of the British Celts* that describes Arthur's battles with the Anglo-Saxon invaders and that is much used, especially by those supporters of Arthur the Warlord.

'At that time Arthur fought against the Anglo-Saxons with the kings of the British Celts, for he was leader of battles. The first battle was in the east at the mouth of the river that is called Glein. The second, the third, the fourth, and the fifth, were on another river called Dubglas. The sixth battle was by the river that is named Bassas. The seventh battle was in the wood of Caledonia, that is Cat Coit Celidon [in Welsh the 'Battle of the Wood of Caledonia']. The eighth battle was in the stronghold of Guinnion, in which Arthur carried the image of Holy Mary, the eternal virgin upon his shoulders and the pagans were turned around into a rout, and there was a great slaughter of them through the might of our Lord

Jesus Christ and through the might of Holy Mary, the virgin and His Mother. The ninth battle was fought at the City of the Legion. Arthur fought the tenth battle on the bank of the river which is called Tribruit. The eleventh battle was made on the mount that is called Agned. The twelfth battle was on Mount Badon, in which nine hundred and sixty men fell from one rally of Arthur's; and no one brought them low except he. And he showed himself victor in all his battles.

At first glance this list might seem a war diary: a digest of a real-life campaign in which thousands died; an impression that is helped along by it appearing in a work known as a 'history'. But as we have seen the *History of the British Celts* scores low on fact and this passage gives off all the danger signals of being, instead, fiction. After all, Arthur here resembles not so much a general as a god: nine hundred and sixty men killed in a single charge is a tall order for a mere mortal. And this is an impression added to by the fact that Arthur elsewhere in *The History of the British Celts* is shown to knock around with such magical objects as a dog called horse that leaves footprints in rock and a flying stone! Then, to problems of legend, we must add problems of accuracy. Unfortunately for those who like their Arthur historical these battles have been filched from others, the rightful owners. So the Battle of Chester ('City of the Legion') took place in the late seventh century when a fifth-century Arthur would no longer have been alive. The Battle of Badon was a battle that an early British-Celtic writer tells us was presided over by Ambrosius Aurelianus. But why play the magpie and steal battles in this fashion? The writer, in this passage, wants to convey not 'history', or, at least, not history as we understand it: he wants to add to Arthur's prestige as a protector of his people.

What this brief poison-pen portrait of the *History of the British Celts* should have demonstrated is the blankness of the desert in which the search for the historical King Arthur takes place. And, in fact, the reason that we can pick three such divergent Arthurs (Warlord, Roman and Gael) is that, whereas a half century ago, historians seemed to have evidence about the original Arthur, that evidence has now been surrendered to experts on folklore and legend: and Arthur is no longer anchored to the years 450-550. This has freed interested parties to look further afield for the historical Arthur and, in plucking Gaels and Romans out of our meagre records, scholars are enjoying their new found freedom. But the truth is that even these three candidates are limiting. We have written so far as if the search for the historical Arthur approximates to a murder mystery. There is a body in the library and we have to choose which of three members of a dinner party 'did it'. But early medieval history is emphatically not a murder mystery with a limited number of suspects, where the butler conveniently locks the doors before the killing.

If we had access to a digest of what had happened in every year in the Roman centuries and the Dark Ages we would find that actually there are fifty or sixty or, for that matter, two hundred credible candidates. It is a product of our execrably poor records that we can name only two individuals and a generality (a warlord from c. 450-550). Take occurrences of 'Artorius', likely the name from which the British-Celtic 'Arthur' derives. Now Artorius is a rare, but not an ultra rare Latin name. It is found in most provinces of the Empire. If the population of Roman Britain was, say, a million strong: in any generation there were probably a hundred British-based Artoriuses. And in each of those hundred Artoriuses we would doubtless find details that could be construed as being 'Arthurian'.

276

So if Artorius the Roman is reckoned to be Arthur because his Sarmatian cavalry were 'knights', what is to stop us saying, when archaeologists tomorrow dig up the gravestone of an obscure Cornish Artorius who happened to have a wife with the British-Celtic name Gwenhwyfar (Guinevere), that he was not the true Arthur?

The 'sensible' answer would be that the Arthur of British-Celtic legend, and later of European legend was such an enormous figure that he must have been a great man, he must have done something that was outstanding. But in legend—and it is tempting to write *especially* in Irish and British-Celtic legend—historical figures take on a life of their own, independent of their original deeds. An individual is remembered and is then celebrated on the basis of how important his children become or how important the tribe or monastery he is associated with make themselves in later generations. So, to give an ecclesiastical example, saints in Ireland and Britain often are spoken of not because they were particularly well-known, but because their foundations became famous after their deaths and history was changed to take this into account. In fact, a good rule for the Irish and the British-Celts is that their medieval antiquarianism tells the present not the past: it embodies contemporary aspirations; it is not the study of years gone by.

Reality and legend in British-Celtic culture often then have nothing to do with each other. And so while Arthur could have been a mighty fifth-century warlord who turned the tide in the battles for Britain. He could equally have been, say, a third-century cross-dressing gladiator who scandalised a provincial British town, but who was then elevated from memory ('do you remember when Arthur…') to myth ('once upon a time, Arthur…')

277

because his sons and grandchildren became important magnates in the region. Would we not though then have details about gladiatorial fights in his legend? Would something of his life not survive? Parallel examples suggest otherwise. We have already seen how general Ambrosius Aurelianus from southern Britain became a demon's bastard and a dragon hunter in Wales. If we had only the legendary ninth-century *History of the British Celts* to recreate his historical fifth-century acts we would fail miserably.

Given this extraordinary lack of good historical material for Arthur it is not surprising that a fourth candidate has emerged in recent years, pushing Artur, Artorius and the Warlord to the side: a mythological Arthur, an Arthur that never existed outside of the British-Celtic imagination. Proponents of the Mythic Arthur point out that everything that that hero does in British-Celtic writings can be paralleled in the works and lives of other mythological heroes from the British-Celtic and closely-related Irish pantheons—and this is, as we have argued in the present volume, true. Arthur like Raven and Gwyn ap Nudd is, Mythic Arthurians insist, a figure passed down from the Celtic Iron Age, when he and his supernatural colleagues stood as the guardians and gods of their people.

Now, yes, Arthur *might as well not have existed*. There is no reason at all for thinking that his personality or achievements have survived in the accounts we have: and good reasons, as we shall see, for thinking that they do not. But nor is there any need to submit Arthur to the final indignity of non-existence, ripping off the last fig-leaf of history. For there is one suggestive proof that he did once walk and breathe. And that proof is his name that, as we have seen, probably derives from the Latin

'Artorius'. *If* 'Arthur' derives from that Latin word then something hard and real must be shining at the bottom of the well because the British Celts would not have created a hero or a god from a Latin name without a historical original. The legendary Arthur would have grown out of someone who lived in Britain between the Roman conquest in 43 AD when Latin arrived and the time of better historical records, c. 700 AD: though save a miracle—a tomb, a forgotten Byzantine manuscript, an inscription...—we will never know the whos or hows or whens of forgotten Arthur's life.

FURTHER READING

There are now some excellent reference books for the Celts. We have Bernhard Maier's *Dictionary of Celtic Religion and Culture* (translated from German into English) and an impressive if expensive five-volume encyclopaedia *Celtic Culture*, edited and largely written by John Koch. On the Celtic languages (ancient, medieval and modern) there are a good collection of essays in Bell, *The Celtic Languages*. A reader for the antiquè and medieval sources is Koch and Carey, *The Celtic Heroic Age*. Then two worthwhile atlases are Koch, *An Atlas* and Haywood and Cunliffe, *The Historical Atlas*: the first more expensive and specialist, the second more popular in format and more widely available.

On the Celtic Iron Age Bernard Maier's *The Celts* is to be recommended as is any of Barry Cunliffe's popular writing. An important corrective and a challenge to the idea of the Celts and their Iron Age is given by Collis, *The Celts*. Miranda Green's *Exploring the World of the Druids* is a useful introduction to ancient Celtic religion and the most 'popular' of the several tomes that that author has published. Peter Berresford Ellis has written a host of books on the ancient Celts that are occasionally unreliable, but give a useful framework for early Celtic history.

On the Christian Celts Nora Chadwick's, *The Age of Saints in the Celtic Church* still makes, forty years after it was written, for pleasant light reading. On the medieval Irish Church see also Kathleen Hughes, *The Church in Early Irish Society*, Ó Cróinín, *Early Medieval Ireland* and anything by Liam de Paor in this area. With the early Christian Celts we have too Latin and Irish works that are surprisingly accessible to the twenty-first century student: among these Richard Sharpe's translation of the *Life of Columba* by Adomnán (with its outstanding introduction) and the *Voyage of St Brendan*, a work that is also easily read in the original for anyone with even basic Latin.

For the rise of the Arthurian Legend E.K. Chambers, *Arthur of Britain*, is almost a century old but comprehensive. Significant (relatively) recent work on Arthur by Jones, Dumville, Bromwich and Padel is largely out of reach in academic journals. Richard Barber has published numerous books on the legendary Arthur for the general reader and now we also have Thomas Green's more demanding but very important *Concepts of Arthur*. Jon Coe and Simon Young, edited, as undergraduates, *The Celtic Sources for the Arthurian Legend*: any of the numerous mistakes therein being, of course, the second author's fault. And, of the many non-Celtic Arthurian works, Nigel Bryant's collection and translation of medieval grail stories, *The Legend of the Holy Grail*, would make an excellent starter, whereas Chrétien de Troyes's other poems and Gottfried's *Tristan* might be served up as a main course.

NOTES

Preface

For the early medieval British-Celtic colony in Galicia see this author's *Britonia*; for the Galician interest in Celts Armada Pita, 'Unha revisión' and for the Galician nationalist Celtic fringe Berresford Ellis, *Celtic Dawn*, 19-27. Two of the most stimulating examples of Celtic-scepticism are James, *Atlantic Celts* and Collis, *Celts*. The new 'early evidence for this apparently phantom people' is, largely linguistic, and is to be found in a series of books published in the last years. Celtic Placename evidence from ancient sources, a useful, though limited index of the ancient Celtic-speaking world, was studied systematically in the Ptolemy project, some of whose papers have been published: Parsons and Sims-Williams, *Ptolemy* and de Hoz, Luján and Sims-Williams, *New Approaches*. An overview is given in Sims-Williams, *Ancient Celtic Place-Names*. Another still more problematic index of Celtic speakers is Raybould and Sims-Williams, *Geography of Celtic Personal Names*. These linguistic works have moved in parallel with dissatisfaction at the theoretical basis of Celto-scepticism: Sims-Williams, 'Celtomania', the same author's 'Le post-celtoscepticisme' and the introduction to Koch, *An Atlas*, 7-17. There have also been works of synthesis that have attempted to marry the archaeological and linguistic and historical evidence together: Koch, *An Atlas*, is the most ambitious to date. One of the main supports of Celto-scepticism was the lack of expressed identity among ancient Celtic-speakers (an inevitability given that little ancient Celtic writing survives): essentially archaeology, the discipline that is least able to judge identity among ancient peoples, exported its doubts. But there are, and this is not noted enough, several clues for what we term a 'sense of oneness among the tribes' at a regional level. We have proof in some cases and hints in others for agglomerates of tribes or Celtic nations, see p. 95 in the present work. The question of whether these Celtic 'nations' felt a oneness among themselves is unanswerable, though they would certainly have spoken similar languages and had similar or overlapping religious traditions. The death of a common sense of Celtic identity may have begun in the Roman period, but if the traditional date for the end of mutual comprehensibility between the Brittonic and the Gaelic tongues is correctly dated then it will have been stretched to breaking point in the fifth century AD; perhaps to be fortified though in the sixth century by a distinctive and contested version of Christianity as described in part two of this book. The question is a very difficult because the last Celtic-speakers were neighbours and geography as well as a shared past linked them together. On that memory having entirely vanished by the twelfth century see Bonfante, 'A Contribution', 17-21 on a notable passage in Gerald of Wales. The discovery that the Welsh, Bretons, Cornish and Gaelic speakers were the descendants of the ancient Celts came in the eighteenth century: see Morse, *How the Celts*, 19-33. On terms of 'convenience' an excellent collection examining modern reworkings of the Celts is to be found in Brown (ed.), *Celticism*.

1   The Iron Age Celts

On a general introductions to the Iron Age Celts see our Futher Reading section. On names for the Celts it is possible that the words 'Celt', 'Gaul' and 'Galatian' all come ultimately from an early Celtic word meaning 'the Hidden Ones', Sims-Williams, 'Celtomania', 22. Hyperboreans is Greek and means, instead, 'People from beyond the North Wind'. On trouser-wearing most memorable is Cicero, *Pro Fonteio*, 33: for other quotations see Sherwin-White, *Racial Prejudice*, 59. On different names for the Celts see Collis, *Celts*, 98-103 to be read together with Sims-Williams, 'Celtomania', 22. On the ecology of clans a recent important study, using early medieval material to fill in gaps in the ancient record is Woolf 'Romancing' and for numismatic evidence suggesting an ancient system of clans in Britain see Allen, 'The Coins', 14-15. For a description of Celtic feasts and an early Celtic poet see Athenaeus, *The Deipnosophists*, 4, 37. For the druids and rebirth see Caesar, *Gaulish War* 6, 14, on the Gaulish love of Mars see Caesar, *Gaulish War* 6, 17 and more generally, Green, *The Gods of the Celts*, 100-101 and on Celtic names, warlike and otherwise, see Evans, *Gaulish Personal Names*. On our (very generalised) view of Mediterranean war see Raaflaub, 'Introduction', 13-25 and essays 8 through 15 in the same volume. Of the quotations for war madness ascribed to the Celts see Diodorus, *Library*, 32 and Strabo, *Geography*, 4, 4, 6. On the Pharaoh and the island Pausanias, *Description*, 1, 7, 2; on the Asian ruler settling and then exterminating Celts Polybius, *Histories*, 5, 111. On the contrast between the Mediterranean and Celtic armies a good, though inevitably Roman-centred, overview is Goldsworthy, *Roman Army*, especially

53-60, for the Gauls and the Romans at war: for nudity see among many other ancient sources, Appian, *Gallic Wars*, frag. 6 (which survives in the *Suda*). On Celtic cavalry generally Ritchie and Ritchie, 'The Army, Weapons and Fighting', 44-46. Superior Norican Celtic metalwork is referred to by Pliny, *Natural History* 34, 145, though he places Chinese and Parthian metalwork ahead of these Alpine efforts. On Celtic invasion myths see Carey, *Irish National Origin Legend* that might stand as an introduction to the *Lebor Gabála* (*Book of the Takings*). On ceaseless wars see Ammianus Marcellinus, *History*, 15, 9, 4. The movements of the Helvetti are described (and were in part witnessed) by Caesar, *Gaulish War*, 1, 1-29. The Helvetii gave their name to the Latin word for the Alpine regions, Helvetia and the word appears later in other guises. In the sixteenth century there was, for example, the Helvetian League – that would, of course, become Switzerland. On the division of various Celtic tribes: the Atrebates had been an important tribe in Gaul in Caesar's time and, by the Roman invasion of Britain, there was also an Atrebates tribe established there; a Brigantes tribe is included in Ireland (Leinster) in Ptolemy, De Bernardo Stempel, 'Ptolemy's Celtic Italy and Ireland', 101; the two Parisi appear to have shared similar 'Arras' burial customs. On the taste for wine and gold see Plutarch, *Parallel Lives, Camillus*, 15, on coral there is a striking Celtic-style helmet inlaid with coral at the Staatliche Museen Antikensammlung in Berlin (find site, Canosa di Puglia in Italy).

2   The Invasion of Italy

Livy's reference to the invasion of Ambigatus's nephews appears in *History*, 5, 34. This text is sometimes taken as quasi-factual by historians, e.g. Haywood, *Celts*, 20, but it has, instead, all the signs of being a Celtic origin legend – possibly taken from a Greek source? – see Dobesch, 'Zur Einwanderung'. The alleged Celtic interest in wine and olive oil depended, in part, on horrified southern reactions to beer and butter so Dionysius, *Roman Antiquities*, 11: 'The Celts in those time did not know of grape wine or of oils such as those made from our olive trees. Instead, they consumed a form of stinking alcohol made of barley left to fester in water and, in the place of oil, rancid animal fat, foul-smelling and disgusting to taste.' Note that another (Etruscan?) origin legend for the Celts is given, Livy, *History*, 5, 33 and Plutarch, *Lives, Camillus*, 15. Population pressure is commonly offered as a reason for barbarian movements: Junianus Justinus *Epitome* 24, 4, Strabo, *Geography* 4, 1, 13… – classical *topos* or tribal fact of life? On Italy in the prehistoric centuries see Pallottino, *Italy*: the comment on the Etruscans is of Dionysius of Halicarnassus, *Roman Antiquities*, 1, 30. For a useful summary of Celtic activity in Italy Frey, 'The Celts in Italy', and of these Celtic names De Bernardo Stempel, 'Ptolemy's Celtic Italy and Ireland', 89-91; for an alternative view that sees the Celts as non-invaders see Williams, *Beyond the Rubicon*, 100-139, while for an answer to such invasion scepticism Koch, *An Atlas*, 14-15. The ancient Celtic for throwing spear has been reconstructed as *gabalaccos* that made its way through the Latin and the Romance languages to become 'javelin' in English. *Carpento*, meanwhile, was a Celtic word that would become *carpentum* (chariot) in Latin; a related Latin word *carrum* (also with a Celtic origin) gives us our 'car' see Piggott, *The Earliest Wheeled*, 229-38. The material culture of the Celts in Italy is sketched out in Frey, 'The Celts in Italy', 520-530. References are given to Raven in the notes to chapter X. For the Celts and the Ligurians, Avienus, *Ora Maritima*, 138-142: for the attack on Melpum Pliny *Natural History*, 3, 17. The idea that the Celts had not mastered town life is reported in Polybius, *Histories*, 2, 17 and commented upon by Williams, *Beyond the Rubicon*, 80-81. The 'new war' comes in Livy, *History*, 5, 35. The Senones' Celtic weapons are to be found Kruta, 'Les Sénons' – for an overview of Celtic helmets Ritchie and Ritchie, 'The Army', 43-44. The Senones attack on Chiusi and later on Rome appears in four sources in book five of Diodorus, *Library*, 14, 113-117, Livy, *History*, 5, 34-49, Plutarch, *Lives, Camillus* 15-30, Polybius, *Histories*, 2, 18 and Dionysius, *Roman Antiquities*, 13, 6-12. The date is approximate see Williams, *Beyond the Rubicon*, 78. For their numbers see particularly Diodorus, *Library*, 113. For the Senones suffering in the heat see Diodorus, *Library*, 113. For the Etruscans this author owes a great deal to Haynes, *Etruscan Civilization*: for Curzio Inghirami see Rowland, *The Scarith*, and for Lawrence, *Sketches of Etruscan places*. The reference to after dinner sex comes in Theopompus, *Histories*, 43. Note also for the Etruscan language Richardson 'Archaeological Introduction to the Etruscan Language' with appended 'grammar', an account we used here. On Porsena's tomb at Chiusi see Pliny, *Natural History*, 36, 19. For the Celtic war with the Chiusians see Livy, *History*, 5, 35 and for the descriptions of Celtic noise, Polybius, *Histories*, 2, 29, 6 – see also Ritchie and Ritchie 'The Army', 53-54 and for the Celtic justification 5, 38 'in our swords' to be compared with Plutarch's rhetoric in *Lives, Camillus*, 17 on the same point. The fact that this was the earliest meeting between the Celts and the Romans is suggested in Rome Livy, *History*, 5.36. The encounter between the Roman ambassadors and the Senones warriors (as quoted) is found in Plutarch, *Lives, Camillus*, 17, 5-6: the reminiscence of Alexander is found instead in Strabo, *Geography*, 7, 3, 8 and Arrian, *Anabasis*, 1, 4, 6.

3   The March on Rome

The number of the warband on its way to Rome is reported on by Diodorus, *Library*, 114: the quotation concerning the noise of the invaders, appears in Livy, *History*, 5, 37. For Roman numbers see Diodorus, *Library*, 114 who says that there were 24,000 good soldiers, compare with Plutarch, *Lives, Camillus,*

18, 4 (who claims that the Romans were not inferior in numbers). The place of the battle is said by all authors save Diodorus, (14, 114) to have been on the far side of the river (from Rome): Livy, *History*, gives an 'exact' description, 5, 37. On Celtic tactics see Livy, *History*, 5, 38 and 'whether by fortune or design' Diodorus, *Library*, 114. For Celtic swords bending on impact see Polybius, *Histories*, 2, 33 and Manning 'Ironworking', 312 and for their limits in close combat Polybius, *Histories*, 2, 30 (compare with Tacitus, *Agricola*, 36) the Celtic war-charge see Polybius, *Histories*, 2, 33. The collapse of the Roman line is found in Diodorus, *Library*, 114 and Livy, *History*, 5, 38. 'The Friday 13th' is shown by later rituals to ward off the memory of the defeat: see especially Plutarch, *Lives, Camillus*, 19. The Celts delay is recorded by both Plutarch, *Lives, Camillus*, 20, Livy, *History*, 5, 39 and Diodorus, *Library*, 115 though different reasons and different times are given: we have followed Diodorus. Weapons being piled up is found in Livy, *History*, 5, 39 were regularly thrown into rivers and lakes in northern Europe by both Celtic-speaking and Germanic-speaking peoples. Heads being collected is found in Diodorus, *Library*, 115; see also Green, *Dying for the Gods*, 95-110, though note that head-hunting was by no means restricted to the Celts; we even have examples of Roman head-hunting. Celtic-era skulls have turned up in various rivers including the Thames. Embalmed heads depends on a reference in Posidonius that survives in slightly different versions in Strabo, *Geography*, 4, 4, 5 and Diodorus, *Library*, 5, 29; while wine beakers depends on a reference in Livy, *History*, 23, 24. The defence of Rome is described by Plutarch, *Lives, Camillus*, 22-29, Livy, *History*, 5, 40-49 and Diodorus, *Library*, 116. There are difficulties with the historical accuracy of this war, but the legends concerning Rome are particularly problematic – for an example concentrating on one small episode, the geese, Horsfall, 'From History to Legend'. Heraclides Ponticus's record of the attack appears in Plutarch, *Lives, Camillus*, 22. Raven or Brennos (a Celtic hero of this name is recorded as attacking both Rome and Delphi) has been judged by a series of scholars – for example, De Vries, *Keltische Religion*, 83-4 – and most recently and most convincingly by Benozzo, 'Stratigrafie' [available online at the time of writing] and, by the same author, *La Tradizione*, 129-56 as the Bran (Raven) of later Welsh legend: the parallel is not just in the name but also in some details of the legends. For an alternative view that nevertheless connects the historical raid on Delphi and later Welsh legend see Koch, 'Bran, Brennos'. The Roman charge down on the Celts is recorded in Livy, *History*, 5, 43. The description of the angry geese is a quotation taken from Livy: as other episodes in this war appear to have come from Celtic legend the geese episode should be read together with Breeze, 'Ptolemy's Gangani'. Livy's scepticism, meanwhile, relates to an Etruscan episode: 5, 21. Of the later Roman-Celtic wars Polybius is our best ancient source: the most accessible narrative in English is to be found in Berresford Ellis, *The Celtic Empire*, 23-42. The gold being paid to the Celts can be read in Livy, *History*, 5, 48 – all the ancient authors include the detail that Brennos (Raven) threw his sword onto the balance when the Romans complained. The Romans ambush the Celts Livy, *History*, 5, 49 though compare with Diodorus, *Library*, 117. Of the infamous sacrifice of Gaulish and Greek prisoners in 228 BC see Plutarch, *Lives, Marcellus*, 3 who links the rite to the terror of the Celts and Várhelyi, 'The Specters of Roman Imperialism'. It is tempting to take this as an Etruscan solution because of hints of similar Etruscan customs; and it is interesting that the Emperor Claudius, a passionate Etruscanophile, reinstated the custom of burying enemies of Rome alive, possibly Britons, see Syme, *Tacitus*, vol II, 456-459. Celtic gold serving to steady Roman nerves is found in Polybius, *Histories*, 2, 27. Polybius's reference to athletes appears, meanwhile, in 2, 20 and should be read together with a similar though less vivid passage in 1, 6.

4 Down the Danube

A good general description of the Celts move down the Danube is to be found in Cunliffe, *The Celts*, 78-80. The story of Alexander's meetings with the Celts is found in Strabo, *Geography*, 7, 3 ('the Celts around the Adriatic') and Arrian, *Anabasis*, (talks of Celts from 'the Gulf of Iona') 1, 4, 6 and the laxative story Athenaeus, *Deipnosophistae*, 10. The fate of the Senones comes in Polybius, *Histories*, 2, 18. For Celtic movements into modern Romania see the linguistic evidence now gathered together by Falileyev, *Celtic Dacia* that will perhaps one day be spliced together with the archaeological record. The evidence, above all, the linguistic evidence for Tylis is discussed in Falileyev, 'In Search of Celtic Tylis', see especially 107-116 and Polybius, *Histories*, 4, 46. The grave in the Ukraine refers to the La Tène finds near Pripyat (Zalesye). For Kazakhstan see Sims-Williams, *Ancient Celtic Place-names*, 298-299. On Celtic mercenaries in the Mediterranean see the various references gathered together in Griffith, *The Mercenaries*, (in the index under Gaulish): some of the evidence for Celtic mercenaries in Egypt is especially vivid. So four Galatians warriors (the Celts of Asia Minor) chased a jackal, 'a fox' they called it, into a Nile tomb and left some graffiti there (in Greek) celebrating its capture, Rankin, *Celts and the Classical World*, 34. The Celtic cavalry is described in Ritchie and Ritchie 'The Army', 44-46 see especially Strabo, *Geography*, 4, 4, 2 (notes the Roman recruit Celtic cavalry), Pausanias, *Description*, 10, 9 (on the three horse system) and Arrian *Ars Tactica*, 33 on Roman use of Celtic exercises. The best modern synthesis of the Celtic invasions into Macedonia (and the necessary background on Macedonia) is Rankin, *Celts and the Classical World*, 86-89: another modern account drawn upon here with relation to Thrace is Theodossiev, 'Celtic Settlement'.

Cambaules or Cimbaules appears in Pausanias, *Description*, 10, 19 as does the reference to his veterans: note this name may not be Celtic, a reminder of the complexity of barbarian identity in the north and southern confusion concerning that identity. The quotation concerning the invasion of 280 comes in Junianus Justinus, *Epitome* 24, 4. The Macedonians being defeated is found in the same work 24, 5.

5   Into Greece

Among the ancient accounts touching on this invasion the most important are Junianus Justinus, *Epitome* 24, 4-6 and Pausanias, *Description*, 10, 19-23 in the Greek author's description of Delphi. Still the best modern study is Nachtergael, *Les Galates*, though see also Rankin, *Celts and the Classical World*, 86-102. On the Celts not being interested in Empire building Pausanias, *Description*, 10, 20, 8, and 10, 20, 6 on the Celtic general being 'not entirely stupid'; on killing civilians in the field, 10, 20, 9; on the uselessness of the cavalry 10, 20, 2 and on the slaughter of the Celts and their refusal to parley for the bodies the successive chapters 10, 20, 2-7, on making the Celts angry generally see Livy, *History*, 5, 37 and on the need to make them angry before destroying them see Polybius, *Histories*, 2, 35, 4 and Williams, *Beyond*, 84-86, on the massacre at Aeolia, Pausanias, *Description*, 10, 22, 3-4. The druids and mist we found in Rankin, *Celts and the Classical World*, 93. References to Raven are to be found instead in the notes for chapter 3. For gravestones from the battle at Thermopylae see Pausanias, *Description*, 10, 21, 5. Details on the history of Delphi are taken from Pausanias, *Description*, 10, 9, 5-14, Sourvinou-Inwood, 'The Myth', Lloyd-Jones, 'Delphic Oracles', 63 as well as more generally from Roux, *Delphes*. Junianus Justinus, *Epitome*, 24, 6, 5 for the description of echoing. The idea that gods should share with man Junianus Justinus *Epitome*, 24, 6, 5. The line on Delphi in *The Iliad*, the most ancient that survives, is 9, 405. Drunk tribesmen are described in Junianus Justinus, *Epitome*, 24, 7: the snow meanwhile is hinted at in 22, 9 ('white maidens'). The description of the battle and divine participation is also found in the *Epitome* 24, 8. The hymn is Callimachus' paean of praise to Delos, 170-76. I have used the edition of Gigante Lanzara, *Inno a Delo*: the hymn is dated to 274 in Mineur *Callimachus*, 16-18: these words are placed into the mouth of prophetic Apollo (while still in his mother's womb). On the suffering of the retreating army Junianus Justinus, *Epitome*, 24, 8, 13-14. On the Welsh folktale see Koch, 'Bran'. The story of Caepio and lakes being auctioned off is found in Strabo, *Geography*, 4, 1, 13. The Greeks had seriously inconvenienced the Romans with the Pyrrhic Invasion that was contemporary with the Celts' invasion of Greece. But, thereafter, the only serious conflicts between Romans and Greek-speakers were the one-sided Macedonian wars of a hundred and a hundred fifty years later when Rome cemented its grip on the eastern Mediterranean.

6 Into Asia Minor

Studies on the Galatians include Rankin, *Celts and the Classical World*, 188-207; and Mitchell *Anatolia*, 1-51. Cicero's comment appears in *De Imperio Cn. Pompei*, 14: many details in our paragraph are taken from Dalby's *Empire of Pleasure*, and his section on Anatolia, 161-168. The reference to the Statue of Liberty is not found there and the author's claim about the size of the Colossus does not take into account either statue's base. Nicomedes inviting the Galatians into the region is described in Livy, *History*, 38, 16, in what sounds, again very much like an origin legend, we learn that their one of their leaders had already made their way across the straits when Nicomedes hired them: in this passage we are also given the numbers of these Galatians though 'only 10,000 were carrying arms'. The references to Hannibal in disguise, 22, 1; for Celtic mercenaries in general Ritchie and Ritchie, 'The Army', 55-56 and for an example of self interest Griffith, *The Mercenaries*, 253: '[S]ome Gauls [i.e. Celts]... appear as the garrison of the independent Epirote city of Phoenice. Their history is so varied, and perhaps so typical, that it is worth telling. In the beginning they had been expelled from their own land by their compatriots. Having entered the service of Carthage they were sent to Sicily, where they quarrelled with their general about pay, and attempted to sack the city of Acragas which they were supposed to be guarding (at this time they were about 3000 strong). In the same way at Eryx they first tried to betray the city and its garrison to the Romans, and, foiled in this, they deserted to the Romans themselves. Next they sacked a temple and made themselves so unpopular with their new masters that, when the war was over, they were at once disarmed, put on board ship, and forbidden to set foot in Italy. It was then that they sailed to Epirus, where they were entrusted with the garrision of Phoenice. By now they were reduced to 800. The last that we hear of them is that they betrayed Phoenice to the Illyrian raiders of Queen Teuta.' For Bithynia we have used Vitucci, *Il regno di Bitinia*. For sheep or cattle dung being burnt Livy, *History*, 38, 18 and Briscoe, *A Commentary*, 82. On 'Celtic' hill forts in the area see Darbyshire, Mitchell and Vardar 'Galatian Settlement', 88-93. For suicide Rankin, *Celts*, 189. For digs at Gordium Sams, 'Gordion archaeological activities', 436-437. For the quotation relating to Galatian terror see Livy, *History*, 38, 16 and note that in the Middle East, Northern Africa and India armies were, of course, used to having elephants deployed against them and had found ways to cope, not least herds of oil-coated burning swine – an ancient equivalent of the fire ship, Aelian, *On Animals*, 16, 36. But the Celts were reportedly stunned at seeing an animal that they had never even imagined, one that they could only have assimilated to an enormous diabolical cow. The Dying Celt or the

Dying Gaul does not survive in the original. But a Roman copy is housed today in the Capitoline Museum in Rome. It has been seen in Rome by many thousands of visitors over the years including Napoleon who stole it and Lord Byron who praised it in *Childe Harold's Pilgrimage* 4, 140-142 at a time when it was generally thought to be the statue of a gladiator. On the three Celtic tribes and their origins see Strabo, *Geography*, 4, 1. For an analysis of the name Tectosages see Garzonio, 'Tectosages' and Sims-Williams, *Ancient Celtic Place-names*, 295-298: it is possible that the name was for a function (raiders) rather than a tribal grouping. For the tribal constitution see Strabo, *Geography*, 12, 5, 2, on ancient Celtic social structure generally Champion 'Power', on clientship Caesar, *The Gaulish War*, 6, 15: for clientship see also Polybius, *Histories*, 2, 17. The feasting points are described in Athenaeus, *Deipnosophistae*, 4, 150: for eating like a Galatian Mitchell, *Anatolia*, 44. (Another example of Celtic feasting and hospitality comes in Athenaeus, *The Deipnosophists*, 4, 37 where we learn that one Gaulish king, Lovernius, filled two square kilometres with food and drink for guests.) For Drunemeton Mitchell, *Anatolia*, 49: several British placenames contain Nemetum (in a modern form) including the river Nymet in north Devon and associated settlements George Nympton and Kings Nympton, Nymet Rowland and Nymet Tracey as well as Nympsfield in Gloucestershire. For further discussion and examples see Dowden, *European Paganism*, 135-136. On Gaulish assemblies and rowdiness see Livy, *History*, 21, 20, on calming music see Pseudo-Scymnus, *Periplus*, 186 and the dishonour of having your weapon cut from you Strabo, *Geography*, 4, 4, 3. The 10,000 clients came in the train of Orgetorix Caesar, *Gaulish War*, 1, 4. On the central meeting place see Koch, 'A Welsh Window', 47-49. Acorns being eaten by druids are recorded in an early medieval text, the Berne Scholia on Lucan 451. For background to this text, Shirley Werner, 'On the History of the *Commenta Bernensia*'. Note that acorns have no hallucinogenic qualities and there is the suspicion that this is either a false etymology based on druid = *drus* (oak in Greek), going back perhaps to the time of Pliny (*Natural History*, 16, 24) or that we have a memory here of the (Celtic?) myth known in Ireland of the hazelnut of wisdom. The Latin, however, is unambiguous: 'an quoniam *glandibus* comestis diuinare fuerant consueti'. For Galatian Celtic gods there is no certain evidence but Onomaris is a candidate (even if presented by a Latin author in historical terms): Gera, *Anonymous*, 219-224 as are the two Celtic-sounding names produced by Anderson, 'A Celtic Cult' in 1910.

7 The Galatians and the Romans

The Galatian war is narrated by Polybius (21) and, above all, as here, Livy, *History*: Galatian dismissal of the Romans (38, 16), the speech (38, 17), an initial surrender (38, 18), the attack on Olympus and the quotation (38, 21), the numbers of prisoners (38, 23), the raped Galatian who has her captor decapitated (38, 24), the trick and its consequences (38, 28). On the Galatians being favoured by the Romans, Mitchell, *Anatolia*, 27-34. On Galatian placenames see now Luján, 'Galatian Place Names', on Pessinous see Stephanus Byzantinus, 519, 10, on the lack of archaeological material Darbyshire, Mitchell and Vardar, 'Galatian Settlement', on intermarriage and assimilation, Mitchell, *Anatolia*, 48-50, for a take on Paul's letter to the Galatians Ellis, *Celt and Greek*, 250-253. This is not, incidentally, the only appearance of the Celts in the Bible. The Celts also crop up in *Macabees* I, 8, 2 where Roman fortunes against the Celts are discussed (perhaps the Celts of Italy, Williams, *Beyond the Rubicon*, 94). The Jewish historian Josephus, *Antiquities*, 1, 6 gives an interesting take on the Galatians alleging that they should be identified with the sons of Gomer (*Ezekiel* 38, 6), a titan race – the giant Celt again. The Indo-European clan are the Tocharians of north-western China; for (the very doubtful theory of) a Roman legion in China Harris *Black Horse*, for the last Vikings of Greenland Seaver *Frozen Echo*, 113-158, for crusaders in a Georgian clan see Halliburton, *Seven League Boots* at 162-170. For the Galatian language see Freeman, *The Galatian Language* and Koch, *Celtic Culture*, 788: other nouns are also offered but are not certainly Galatian. Leaving aside placenames and personal names we have only four nouns that survive from Cumbric: the words for circuit (*kelchyn*), lad (*gwas*), blood fine (*galnes*) and dowry (*mercheta*), and the last of these may not be Celtic – for references Brooke, *Galloway*, 74 and Minard, 'Mercheta'. The evidence for late Galatian is collected together in Luján, 'The Galatian Place Names', 263-264: evidence from Jerome may be anecdotal and, in the writings of Cyril of Scythopolis, there is the problem of the meaning of 'Galatian'.

9   The Dark Age Christian Celts

On the British-Celtic conversion of Ireland Mytum, *The origins*. 'Celtic Christianity', a problematic term, has been discussed by many authors, however, Gougaud, *Christianity in Celtic Lands* is still perhaps the most global. Self harm: freezing water, Ireland 'Penance and Prayer'; sleeping naked with comely young women Gougaud, '*Mulierum consortia*'; human faeces eaten to shatter the pride, Davies, 'Kings', 45-6. The legend concerning the lizard of Fursa is convoluted but worth reporting in full, Stokes, *Martyrology*, 45-47 (translation of Stokes): 'Fursa once happened to visit Maignenn of Kilmainham, and they make their union and exchange their troubles in token of their union, to wit, the headache or piles from which Fursa suffered to be on Maignenn and the reptile that was in Maignenn to enter Fursa. So that it became Fursa's practice every morning to eat three bits of bacon that he might abate the reptile's violence. It came to pass that Fursa crossed the sea and came to a certain city. Therein he practices his usual custom and he is brought before the bishop (of that city) to be censured. 'Not devoutly dost thou spend thy life,' says the bishop. 'Thou hast permission, O cleric,' says Fursa, 'to prove that which inflicts this on me.' Forthwith then the reptile leaps into the bishop's throat. So when everyone knew that, Fursa calls the reptile back to him; and God's name and Fursa's are magnified by that miracle, and the whole city... is conveyed to God and Fursa.' On Irish exile see Charles-Edwards, 'Peregrinatio'. In writing the final paragraph I had very much in mind a celebrated sculpture from the Shetland Museum, sometime said to show the arrival of Christianity in the islands, but more likely recalling a pilgrimage.

10 Colum Cille and Iona

On the Uí Néill see Charles Edwards, Early Christian Ireland, 441-468. On the wars with the Romans see Rance 'Magnus', 250-1 and especially 251 n. 56. The Irish story (the Tale of Mac Dathó's Pig) and its correspondence with Athenaeus, The Deiphnosophists, 4, 40 has been noted on many occasions: it is one of a number of striking parallels between Celtic Ireland and Celtic Gaul. On parallels between Iron Age continental Celts and medieval insular Celts Charles-Edwards, Early Christian Ireland, 189. Fionn is an Irish reflex of the Celtic divine figure Vindos see Oì hOìgaìin, Fionn, 1-50. In Admomnán's Life, the editor, Sharpe, 10 suggests that even Colum Cille's parents may have been pagans. On the druids in early Ireland see Oì hOìgaìin, Sacred Isle, 69-127 and Smyth 'The Earliest Written Evidence', 37 on the druid describing his belief in transmutation into a bird – note that the bird was a common Irish (and, indeed, European) symbol for the soul. On Cruithnechán see Admomnán, Life, 3, 2. On the civil war among the Uí Néill see Charles-Edwards, Early Christian, 294-5. As to the different traditions about Colum Cille in this war see Sharpe, Life, 12-14 and Annals of the Four Masters under the year 555. On the claim that he had fought in the battle see Smyth, Warlords, 98. On British-Celtic derision for Irish history see Historia Brittonum, 13. On Ireland's lack of deserts it should, of course, be remembered that Ireland had challenges to offer the hermit that an Egyptian or Syrian Christian might not have dreamed of. James Carney, an Irish scholar of the last century, wrote how eastern asceticism 'lost nothing of its severity by being practised in the Irish rather than in the Mediterranean climate. Indeed, this was brought home very forcibly to the present writer when, on a cold wet day in summer, he took a Coptic [Egyptian] priest on a tour of [the Irish monastery of] Glendalough, and out of pure compassion for his misery, spared him half the sights. In the patient enduring of climatic rigour and the heroic determination not to alleviate it, the Irish are surely without equal in the world', 'Sedulius Scottus', 232. For Lindisfarne see chapter 14, for Honau Gougaud,

Christianity, 149-50, for Skellig Michael see Moorhouse, *Sun Dancing*, 99-148 and the luscious but difficult to find Horn, *Skellig*. The sentence concerning 'the thin place' comes in Sheldrake, *Living*, 7. On Colum Cille being protected from onlookers Adomnán, *Life*, 1, 3. Colum Cille's name was brought to England with the mission detailed in chapters XX; for the continent see Gougaud, *Les Saints*, 66-70 and Picard, 'The Cult of Columba'. The poem is *Amra Choluimb Chille* and a full edition is to be found in Clancy and Markus, *Iona*, 96-128. On druidic origins see Sharpe, *Life*, 20. On the clairvoyant reading Adomnán, *Life*, 1, 23 and the weeping horse 3, 23. On Librán, Adomnán, *Life*, 2, 39, on Fiachnae 1, 30 and for the incestuous fratricide 1, 22.

11 Cormac and the Desert in the Ocean

On the visit to some coastal rocks *Navigatio*, 1, on Easter, 10 (and Bieler 'Casconius'), on Judas Iscariot, 25, on the smiths, 23, on the choir, 17. Cormac appears in three voyages in Adomnán, *Life of Columba*: on the first and the disobedient monk 1, 6; for the Orkney episode see 2, 42 that also describes the third voyage and that is quoted from here. The Loch Ness episode also appears in Adomnán. However, the beast in question, which appears in Loch Ness or Ness River and which Colum Cille frightens off, bears little resemblance to the pseudo-dinosaur of modern lore. It has been suggested that, instead, Colum Cille encountered a rogue sea lion! The *curragh* is described in Wooding, *Communication*, 10-12. The ancient Britons were said to use coracles by Pliny, *Natural History*, 4, 104. On modern recreations we are relying here on the figures given by Tim Severin, *Brendan Voyage*, 289-290, for his heroic trans-Atlantic voyage on a curragh in 1976/7. Severin's crew made an average of forty miles a day, but this included days where they did not move (because of a lack of wind) and days when they were blown backwards... On their best day they managed an impressive 120 miles. For the giant squid/woman with sixteen-foot plaits (tentacles?), *Annals of Inisfallen* for 906 AD. Interestingly the early medieval Koreans also recorded a giant woman/squid on their beaches – the *Samguk Yusa* under 661/667 AD; as did thirteenth-century continental Europeans – Jacobus van Maerlant in his *Der Naturen Bloeme*. Thomas Charles-Edwards discusses Colum Cille's apparently psychic gifts, *Christian Ireland*, 192-194. Portents in the annals include genocidal lightning storms under the year 961, ships in the heavens Woods, 'On Ships', flying moles (probably locusts) Thornton, 'Locusts' (896 AD recorded in Wales but regarding Ireland) and dragons (the *aurora borealis?*) in 746.

12 Columbanus's First Exile

On the collapse of the Empire, Ward Perkins, *The Fall*, 13-62. On

Columbanus's arrival see Jonas, *Vita*, 10: Gall and Libranus are deductions based on later occurrences of Irish names associated with Columbanus. On Libranus see Columbanus, *Epistola*, 4, 2: we do not know why Libranus (a Latinised Irish name) was left behind when the British Celts and other Gaels in Columbanus's community had been driven out. Gall is claimed by late lives to have been Irish; if this was the case then his Gaelic name was perhaps Callech, Clark, *The Abbey*, 21-22. On the first recorded conflicts see Smyth, 'The Húi Néill'. On Columbanus's birth date Bullough 'Career', 3: 'It is a reasonable inference from the scanty evidence that Columbanus was born shortly after or shortly before 550', though all this is complicated by the uncertainties surrounding 590 as the date of arrival on the continent. On Comgall and Columbanus Jonas, *Vita*, 9. On his discussion with the hermit Jonas, *Vita*, 8. On Christian Irish attitudes to women see Harrington, *Women*: on the brooch pin (Samthann) see 183-4, on women as counsellors see 170-3: note that there are many hagiographical examples of holy men going to women for advice including *Vita sancti Mochoemog, Vita Prima Sancti Brendani,* and the various Latin lives of Brigit. On claims being made for the warlessness of warlike Ireland see Jonas, *Vita*, 6 and on Columbanus's aims, see Jonas, *Vita*, 10. On the newly-collapsed Europe see Ward Perkins, *The Fall,* especially part two of that book. In his life Columbanus is offered land by the Frankish royal family in the Vosges, Jonas, *Vita*, 12. On the bear cave Jonas, *Vita*, 15: then on 'nature miralces' and saints see Stancliffe 'The Miracle Stories', other Columbanus animal legends are found Jonas, *Vita*, 15, 21, 30, 55. On the idea of Irish retreats see Young, 'Donatus', 20-21 and chapter 14 for the Farne Isles. On Columbanus's popularity among the nobles of the region Jonas, *Vita*, 17. Note that the accusation of a Jewish Easter was mud to be slung, not a factual description of the Irish system, Bede, *History*, 2, 19 and 3, 4. Scythians are found in Cummian, *De Controversia Paschali*, 94-95 and the husband and wife (Oswiu and Eanflaed) celebrating Easter at different times in Bede, *History*, 3, 25. The letter to Gregory is Columbanus, *Epistola* 1 see especially sections 4 and 11. On Columbanus's multiculturalism *Epistola* 2, 5. On Franks and human sacrifice see Procopius, *History*, 6, 25 and on hostages, Shanzer, 'Dating the baptism', 47-48. On the Franks' family violence see Gregory of Tours, *History*, 4, 20 (the burning hut) and Jonas, *Vita*, 58 (the grandmother). On Columbanus's arguments with the Frankish royal family see Jonas, *Vita*, 32; we have taken up, at the end of the chapter, the tone of James Campbell, *Essays*, 60-61. For vindictive Celtic saints Gerald of Wales, *Journey* II, 7: 'both the Irish and Welsh are more given to anger and revenge… than other people, and similarly their saints… seem much more vindictive'. One example from Columbanus's *Life* by Jonas must suffice, 20. Returning from a sojourn in the bear cave in the woods the saint finds that all his monks at Luxeuil had been lain low by a dangerous illness.

The saint immediately instructs the monks to get up and work. Some of the monks did so before quickly collapsing again. However, these were cured for their obedience – a key monastic ideal. But the others did not fare so well. 'Wonderful revenge! The disobedient remained so sick for one whole year that they only just escaped death!'

13 Columbanus's Second Exile

The Irish giving their escort the slip is found in Jonas, *Vita*, 47, and see also Columbanus *Epistola* 4, 7. On the break-out Jestice, *Wayward Monks*, 175 (a little known passage) and on the bodies of Columbanus's seventeen comrades see *Epistola*, 2, 5. On his time with Chlothar and Theudebert see, respectively, Jonas, *Vita*, 48 and 51. Columbanus's time in Brigantia is described in Jonas, *Vita*, 53. On duels between pagans and Christians see, for example, Adomnán, *Life of St Columba*, 2, 34. On Theudebert's death Jonas, *Vita*, 57. The vision of the angel in the Slav lands, Jonas, *Vita*, 56, though this appears out of sequence. (The present author does not confidently understand the angel's words: he has never found though a better explanation of what they mean.) On the Irish monk and the extraterrestrials see Carey, 'Ireland the Antipodes'. On Bobbio see Jonas, *Vita*, 60 and more generally now Richter, *Bobbio*. On Columbanus letter to the Pope Boniface, *Epistola*, 5, and to Chlothar see Jonas, *Vita*, 61 (that letter is described, it does not survive). On the question of private penance, Frantzen, *The Literature*, 19-60 and on Columbanus's influence, Charles-Edwards, 'The Penitential', 237-9. The image of the oak is borrowed from George Elliot who used it for Carlyle.

14 Aidan and England

The Battle of Heavenfield is described in Bede, *History*, 3, 2 and Adomnán, *Life*, 1, 1, while, for the England of the seventh-century, see Campbell, 'The First Christian Kings'. Cadwallon is described in Bede, *History*, 2, 20. Bromwich, *Trioedd*, 293-6 has collected Welsh traditions about Cadwallon, and the reference to the bloody Severn is found in Bromwich, *Trioedd*, 182 to be read together with Rowland, *Early Welsh Saga Poetry*, 446-447 and, now, Charles-Edwards 'Cadwallon'. On Aethelfrith see Bede, *History*, 1, 34 and Aethelfrith as twister (*flesaur*) (presumably meaning 'crafy one') see *Historia Brittonum*, 57, on Oswald more generally see Craig, 'Oswald' and Stancliffe 'Oswald'. On the queen and Irish martyrdom (Eigg), Sharpe, *Life*, 369-370. The early Irish failure and the subsequent meeting is found in Bede, *History*, 3, 5 – note that in the sixteenth century Hector Boece claimed that the name of the Irish missionary was Corman, but Boece is often unreliable and we have no reason for thinking that his work (here) was based on contemporary or near contemporary sources. On Anglo-Saxon pagan religion Wilson,

Anglo-Saxon Paganism. On the problems of the conversion of the barbarians see Wood, *Missionary*, 3-18. Aethelbert is found in Bede, *History*, 1, 25. Oswald is described as translating Aidan's sermons in Bede, *History*, 3, 3. On the earlier conversion of Northumbria see Bede, *History*, 2, 13. On Northumbria more generally Rollason, *Northumbria*, and the Irish reluctance to use horses see Gougaud, *Christianity*, 175-176 and for the angry archbishop of Canterbury (Theodore) Bede, *History*, 4, 3. For the wild fauna of northern England at this date Yalden, *British Mammals*, 130-163 and the king who guaranteed security of a sort Bede, *History*, 2, 16. For Lindisfarne Thacker 'Lindisfarne', 103-7. On Sedulius Scottus and his requests for drink see for example *carm.* 49: 'Nunc uiridant...'. On Mankinholes the first reference comes in the late thirteenth century, if this was not an Irish *peregrinus* then we could have a later Hiberno-Norse settler, *English Place-Names*, 396.

15 The Road to Whitby

The death of Oswald is found in Bede, *History*, 3, 9 (as is the dismemberment, 3,12): Thatcher, 'Membra Disjecta', 97. The battle probably took place at Oswestry (Shropshire): Stancliffe 'Where was Oswald Killed?' For the legend of the bird see Tudor, 'Reginald's Life of St Oswald', 190. Aidan dining moderately with Oswiu is found in Bede, *History*, 3, 5, the reference to carousing comes from *Beowulf* 2, 1232-33: note that Mayr-Harting, *The Coming of Christianity*, 98 already associated these two passages and we imitate him here. On Aidan's death and relics see Bede, *History*, 3, 17. Finan appears little in Bede, *History*, 3, 25 for his arguing ways and the building of the cathedral on Lindisfarne. On the missions to the south see Bede, *History*, 3, 21-22 and Mayr-Harting, *The Coming of Christianity*, 99-102. On the philosophy graduate see the eighth-century letter from Bishop Daniel to Boniface, an English clergyman working among the pagans on the continent, *The Letters*, (trans.) Emerton, 26-27. Chad's Irish cursing is found in Bede, *History*, 3, 22. For Fursa's time in Britain Bede, *History*, 3, 19. On Malmesbury see Dempsey, 'Aldhelm of Malmesbury'. Irish influence in manuscripts is found in Olive, 'Irish Influence'. Irish 'locutions' and other kinds of literary influence are studied extensively in Wright, *The Irish Tradition*. The Council of Whitby is described in Bede, *History*, 3, 25 and discussed in Abels, 'The Council'. On Eata's succession, the breaking of Aidan's bones and the journey to Inishboffin see Bede, *History*, 3, 26 and 4, 4.

16 Did the Celts Save Dark Age Christianity?

On the two Irish exiles selling wisdom Notker, *Gesta Karoli Magni*, 1,1. An exaggerated sense of Irish learning was typical of scholarship in the early and middle part of the century: for example, Le-Rops, *Miracle of Ireland* and was given popular coverage by Cahill, *How the Irish* at a time when most scholars had abandoned this stance. It is true that the Irish had an interest in Greek and Hebrew as two of the three sacred languages. The question is whether this interest translated into real knowledge of these two languages in the early Middle Ages. Certainly, some Irish *peregrini* mastered Greek but it is easiest to suppose that they learnt Greek on the continent: and there are no serious, sustained compositions in either Greek or Hebrew from early medieval Ireland. In recent years David Howlett has been more optimistic about the Irish achievement in these two languages, for example, in 'Supported Claims' and it may eventually be possible to make a stronger case for Greek. On the derivative nature of early medieval Christian writing see the fine introduction to Cantelli, *Angelomo*.

17 Warriors of the Fourth Invasion

Arthur we cover extensively in the following notes: on Bran see the notes for chapter 3, on Gwyn ap Nudd and his father Nudd (Nodons), Carey, 'Nodons'. On Arthur and his heroes in the homelands see now Green, *Concepts of Arthur*. On *bendigaid* see Goetinck, 'The Blessed Heroes', on elf shot see Bonser, 'Magical Practices', 353-4. What has Christ to do with Ingeld?, is a comment of Alcuin in *Epistola* 124. On saints vanquishing monsters see for example, Coe and Young, *Celtic Sources*, 36-43. A saint (Collen) talking to Gwyn ap Nudd can be found in Henken, *Traditions*, 221-25. The Celtic book of a genesis is a reference to Blodeuedd in Math uab Mathonwy and the interpretation of Carey, 'Myth of Origins?'. On the Calais writings concerning Taliesin see Ford, *Ystoria Taliesin*.

18 The Origins of the Arthurian Legend

On Celtic mythology the best general guide remains Mac Cana, *Celtic Mythology*. The words 'Protector' and 'Defender' have been borrowed from Green, *Arthur*, 93-130: it should be noted that Green's use is slightly different at some points. For the role of 'Protector' see Padel, 'Nature', 19-23 an article that permeates this chapter. Benozzo, 'Stratigrafie del romanzo arturiano', would effectively put Raven in this protecting role. On Fionn see Oì hOìgaìin, *Fionn* and Nagy, *The Wisdom of the Outlaw*. Arthur's wilderness role was placed centrally by Padel, 'Nature'. On ovens there are several examples but a well documented one is Steer, 'Arthur's O'on' (Stirlingshire). The presence of Fionn in north Britain and Canada is well established, note though that Fionn also latterly made an entrance into English literature MacKillop *Fionn*. Goetinck, 'Blessed Heroes', stresses the weight of invasions that the British Celts had to suffer. On *gormes* see Sims-Williams 'Some functions', 105-6. On the three *gormesoedd* mentioned here see the Welsh tale *Llud and Llefelys* (in most modern 'Mabinogion' editions). Raven's head is taken to the White Hill in London (Tower Hill) and buried there so as to prevent invaders coming to the land. The striking parallel between this legend and the popular modern belief that the ravens at the Tower will remain so long as there is an England has led some to speak of an ancient, surviving tradition. However, the ravens were actually a late Victorian creation, Dr. John Parnell, pers. comm. concerning an article to be published in *Newsletter of the London Topographical Society*. The ravens were introduced by the Scottish lord Edwin Richard Wyndham 1896-1903. Wyndham clearly knew the legend of Raven and wanted to celebrate it. On invasions being negative and the Bretons return (implied) see the *Historia Brittonum*, 27 and, again on the Bretons' return *Armes Prydein* a sentiment echoed in Geoffrey of Monmouth's *Vita Merlini*. On the invasion of Ireland see the Welsh tale Branwen. On Welsh messianic prophecy see Dumville, 'Armes Prydein' and *Armes Prydein*. The prophecy quoted here is the *Armes Prydein*, 106-127 for Sandwich see 187. On the Welsh 'national psychosis' (our own phrase) see Henken, *National Redeemer*, and Goetinck, 'Blessed Heroes', who wants to drag this 'psychosis' back into the Roman period. On the monks in Cornwall see, for discussion and date, Tatlock, 'The English Journey'. The idea that the Cornish were expecting to be liberated by Arthur is not stated. But it is surely not an unreasonable deduction based on what Arthur does elsewhere. On the Bretons stoning a French preacher see Alan of Lille, quoted in Chambers, *Arthur*, 265. On the Norman statement that Arthur will come back to conquer – the first explicit comment to this effect is Gaimar, *Lestoire*, 1, 287. For later comments see Sherman 'The Legend of Arthur's Survival' (many comments compare the British Celts to the Jews) to which should be added the reference in Cohn, *The Pursuit*, 93. Mary is associated with Arthur in several native texts: *Historia Brittonum, Vera historia de morte Arthuri, Darogan yr Olew Bendigaid...* This is a significant number given our small corpus – there must have been some bond between them in Welsh lore. The diplomatic references to the Great Prophecy came in the time of Glendower, Davies, *The Revolt*, 157-160. On Arthur dragging other heroes into his orbit a nice example comes in *Culhwch ac Olwen* where a traditional story seems to have lost its plot to the king's vanity. So, in that tale, Arthur eclipses Gwynn ap Nudd as boar hunter see *Culhwch*, 142-143 and 155: note that, as the Welsh cognate of the boar hunting Fionn, Gwynn was presumably the original boar hunter. On Arthur as bad-boy king, Henken, *Traditions*, 301-303. On Celli Wic see Padel, 'Some South Western Sites', 234-238.

19   Arthur Leaves the Homeland

For Arthur in 1113 and the reference to Bretons see Tatlock, 'The English Journey'; note that this throwaway sentence could date later to the time of redaction in 1145. On the Modena Archivolt Stokstad, 'Modena Archivolt',

William of Malmesbury, *Gesta Regum Anglorum*, 1, 8 and Henry of Huntingdon, *Historia Anglorum*, 2, 18 then finally Ailred of Rievaulx, Barber, *King Arthur*, 30-31. Note that Ailred's writing comes after Geoffrey's *History*, but is usually taken as being independent of Geoffrey and hence 'pre-Galfradian'. On Geoffrey of Monmouth and his history writing style see Leckie, *Passage*. On King Lear see Perrett, *The Story*, 1-28. On Walter the Archdeacon see Barber, *King Arthur*, 39-41: much has been made of Walter's book over the years, for example, Ashe 'A Certain'. A superficial glance at Geoffrey's biography would suggest that he was himself Norman. Certainly, 'Geoffrey' was a name used by the Normans. While Geoffrey grew up, if we are to believe his surname, in Monmouth in central Wales, where Norman barons were trying to tame the Welsh. But, confusingly, Geoffrey describes himself as a *Britto* or British Celt that should mean that he was either Welsh, Breton or Cornish, Padel, 'Geoffrey of Monmouth'. And we also know that he was sometimes described as 'Geoffrey Arthur' instead of Geoffrey of Monmouth: if normal medieval conventions were being followed then his father bore the British-Celtic name of Arthur – indeed, Geoffrey's fascination with Arthur may have stemmed from filial affection. The best explanation is that his family was Breton. Arthur was an established name in Brittany – so his father could easily have been so called, Brittany was a British-Celtic region and, crucially, Geoffrey lauds the Bretons in his writings. Barely an English county was without its Breton settlers, Keats-Rohan, 'Bretons and Normans'. On the spread of the manuscripts see Crick, *Historia*: she counts some 213. On the two attacks on Geoffrey see William of Newburgh ('crusty old scholar'), *Historia Rerum Anglicarum*, 1, 2 (quoted Chambers, *Arthur*, 274-276) and Gerald of Wales ('gospel'), *Journey through Wales*, 1, 5. For the Welsh reception of Geoffrey see now Wood, 'Where does Britain End?'

20 The Battle between the Old and New Arthur

The *Battle Standard* is the *Draco Normannicus*. For recent discussion on the rhetoric of this poem chronicle see Echard, *Arthurian Narrative*, 85-93. On Henry's campaign in Brittany see Everard, *Brittany*, 56-57. For 'antipodes' see Carey 'Ireland and the Antipodes'. *Antipodes* is literally 'Opposed Foot'. Contrary to modern assumptions, most of Greek and Roman and many medieval writers believed that the world was a globe, Russell, *Inventing the Flat Earth*, 13-26. There was also, in antiquity, the idea that there were islands on the other side of this round earth, the *antipodes*: this based not on early knowledge of America or Oceania but on the classical love of symmetry – there would have to be other lands to balance the known world: Europe, Africa and Asia. As the flat earth theory gained ground in later antiquity this notion was ridiculed, Lactantius, *The Divine Institutes*, 24: 'But how can there be those who think that there are feet opposite to our feet [i.e. in the *antipodes*]? Do they have any evidence? Or are there those who really think that there are men with feet above their heads and that the things that are the right way up here hang there upside down? Do the crops and trees grow down then? Does the snow and rain and hail fall upwards towards the earth? And no wonder that the Hanging Gardens [of Babylon] are included among the seven wonders of the world, when thinkers believe that there are hanging fields, seas, cities and mountains!' That Étienne's poem may have had a factual origins has, to the best of our knowledge, not been suggested before: clearly if there was a letter it was not though the poetic rendering of Étienne. Etienne claims that Roland (the leader of the rebellion against Henry) had sent a letter to Arthur, Etienne, *Norman Battle Standard*, 1161. An excellent introduction to Glastonbury is Carley, *Glastonbury*: for Glastonbury and Avalon 302-306, for Joseph, the thorn tree and its sad end, 181-184, and now Walsham, 'The Holy Thorn'. On Glastonbury's claims to antiquity see Crick, 'Marshalling Antiquity' and, for a sober look at the historical realities, Abrams, *Anglo-Saxon Glastonbury*, 1-8. On land in Cornwall, Padel, 'Glastonbury', 253-256. The dig for Arthur is recorded in several sources: we quote here from Gerald's *On the Instruction of Princes*, (note that the text was probably written about thirty years after the 'discovery'). On the question of the dig and its background see Barber, *King Arthur in Legend and in History*, 57-64 and 63 for the curtains – all medievalists accept that this was 'fixed' for some of the reasons we note afterwards, though Carley, *Glastonbury*, 148-152 is sympathetic towards the monastery. On Glastonbury manipulation of records and *furta sacra* see, for a beautiful example, Sharpe 'Eadmer's Letter'. For Irish pilgrims at Glastonbury Lapidge, 'Cult', 182. On the twelfth-century crises in the abbey see Carley, *Glastonbury*, 21-24. Richard Barber, *King Arthur: Legend and History*, 63, refers (quoting C.F.Hawkes) to 'tree trunk coffins' in Britain 'in the earlier northern Bronze Age'. On Geoffrey's attitude to the legends of Arthur's return Padel, 'The Nature of Arthur', 11-12: 'a very typical example of Geoffrey having his cake and eating it, yielding to sober and cultured Norman views of what should have happened, while simultaneously providing an escape clause for those who wished to take the Romantic view based upon Celtic legend'. On the Mount Etna incident Chambers, *Arthur*, 221-22 and Gardner, *Arthurian Legend*, 12-16, on the Welsh abandoning Arthur as messiah Henken, *National Redeemer*, 44-51.

21 Lost in Translation
On the festival in Magdeburg (1281) see Loomis 'Arthurian Influence', 555-56, on Richard I and Excalibur Gillingham, *Richard*, 141-2, on Cyprus see Crouch, *Tournament*, 117. The French abbot stunning his congregation with Arthur was Caesarius of Heisterbach in his *Dialogus Miraculorum*, 4, 36. On

Carados Briebras and Eric and Weroch and Enid see Bromwich, 'First Transmission', 278-9. On Arthur and Arcturus see Bromwich, *Trioedd*, 544. On the names of the Modena archivolt, note that perhaps Winlogee is not Guinevere. For Cliges, Sims-Williams 'Cliges'. On Lancelot Loomis, for example, believed that he originated from the (minor) Welsh hero Llwch Llenlleawg. For Geoffrey and Caerleon see, *History*, 9, and Roberts, 'Geoffrey', 98 – for twelfth-century Caerleon and Roman remains see Gerald, *Journey*, 1, 5. The legendary history of the Round Table is set out in Mott, 'Round Table', 231-233. On the Welsh Round Table 'near Denbeigh' in Leland, *Itinerary*, ch 5. Our biography on Wace is based on Foulon, 'Wace'. The question of the fate of Arthur's other Celtic paraphernalia is an interesting subject in its own right. Take Excalibur. Excalibur is the name we know the sword by today, but it is only the end point of a long tradition. Geoffrey of Monmouth had called Arthur's sword Caliburnus. And this was in turn a Latin version of Caledfwlch, the Welsh name, or Hard-lightening as we would say, that was the twin brother of a similarly named sword in ancient Irish myth – we probably have a very ancient mythic object here. It is forgivable that that name was transformed into Caliburnus in Latin: Geoffrey of Monmouth was a storyteller not a philologist. But quite how Caliburnus became Excalibur is a mystery. This is the same kind of accident of transmission that made Arthur's spear in Welsh legend, Rhongomyniad, into the endearingly proletariat Ron, the end being twisted off the word; while Pridwen, Arthur's boat, survives – it was evidently easy for a non-Celtic speaker to say – but faced the indignity of becoming a shield. On the Grail Quest see Barber, *The Holy Grail*, 9-38. On the quotation see Chrétien de Troyes, *Grail*, 54: we use Nigel Bryant's excellent translation with that author's kind permission. On the Celtic connection with Bron see Loomis, *The Grail*, 55-57 and for a fascinating attempt to give the Grail Celtic origins see now Carey, *Ireland*. The modern world has a great interest in Arthurian legend generally, but the Grail mystery is the only aspect of Arthurian legend that can still be said to be growing and changing for we have our own Grail genre: the Grail Conspiracy Thriller parodied by Umberto Eco in his *Foucault's Pendulum*, fictionalised by Dan Brown, but perhaps still best read in the original, *The Holy Blood and Holy Grail*. Nor does Grail mania show any signs of dying. In the past year the present author has come across four accounts of groups that claim to be in possession of the grail: including, memorably, one Welsh family who put this most precious object in the local bank vault!

22 Did the Celts Create the Modern Mind?

On the feudalisation of Arthur see Barber, *The Knight*, 105-131. For Cyprus see Crouch, *Tournament*, 117 and on roundtables in general, 117-121, on

Edward III's round table palace see especially part two of Munby, Barber and Brown, *Round Table,* and for the order of the Round Table, 137-152 – this palace may have been built to house a round table that dates back to the time of Edward I. On the love stories of Guinevere and Lancelot see Chrétien's *Lancelot,* on Tristan and Isolde in the Celtic lands see Bromwich 'Tristan'. The Dream of Macsen, *The Mabinogion,* (ed.) Jones and Jones, 79-88. On going to hell, Abelard and Heloise, letter 2 ('uulcania loca'). On Tristan risking hell Gottfreid, *Tristan,* 206 'If my adorable Isolde were to go on being the death of me in this fashion I would woo death everlasting *(ein éweclíchez sterben)*' and for more on Gottfried's atypical medieval religiosity see Harris, 'God, Religion and Ambiguity in Tristan'. Note that Benozzo, *La tradizione,* 157-94 makes the case that Courtly Love itself had a Celtic origin.

Appendix I: Discovering America? The Irish Exiles in the Northern Atlantic
On Pytheas see Cunliffe, *Pytheas* and for the text (or rather fragments) Pytheas, *On the Ocean* (ed.) Roseman. The best work on Thule remains Cassidy, 'Voyage of an Island' whose title says it all: Thule was a moving target. A place where a peculiar god lives and the congealed sea Pliny, *Natural History,* 4, 104 and where the sea breathes Strabo, *Geography,* 2, 4. The midnight sun is described in Dicuil, *Liber,* 7, 11. The Norse description of the Irish of Iceland is found in Jones, *Norse Atlantic Saga,* 36-7. Dicuil's own time in the north is described in *Liber,* 7, 6-15. Lethbridge, *Herdsmen,* talked of Irish visits to Greenland and Ashe, *Land to the West,* has been the most ambitious in describing Irish discoveries and uses, as evidence, bearded Aztec sculptures, 224 (for photos); the Amerindian temple is Mystery Hill, North Salem long touted by William Goodwin, *The ruins of Great Ireland in New England,* as having been built by Irish monks. On the discovery of Viking settlements in North America see Seaver, *Frozen Echo,* 14-43. On the possibility of Native Americans being discovered in Europe see Luce, 'Ancient Explorers', 91-2. On 'Eskimos' being washed up in Ireland and Britain see Babcock, 'Eskimo Long Distance Voyages', which is something of a pre-urban urban legend. The description of gardens in the desert can be found in Caner, *Wandering Monks,* 32 – the ultimate model for the Irish legend perhaps? On pygmies see Oskamp, *The Voyage,* 31: note that the question of whether Greenland was really depopulated between the ending of Dorset Eskimo culture and the arrival of the Thule Eskimos remains a controversial one.

Appendix II: Will the Real King Arthur Please Stand Up?
Arthur's grave in Croatia is discussed in Malcor, 'Lucius Artorius Castus', the 'proof' that the Celts got to New Zealand was given in Doutré, *Ancient Celtic New Zealand,* for Slavic nationalists on Arthur, 'King Arthur was really a

Russian, say Slavs', *Daily Telegraph*, 18th June 2001, see Gilbert, Wilson and Blackett, *Holy Kingdom*, a summary of the research of Wilson and Blackett for both the grave and the sword in America, 287-291 (though there it is suggested that this sword made it across the Atlantic in the hands of a puritan). On the (respectable) Tintagel find see the interview in the first issue of the online review *Heroic Age* and on some of the nonsensical reporting of this non-event (non-event at least in Arthurian terms) see the *Guardian* editorial, 8th July 1998. (A lovely Arthurian quotation comes from Professor Chris Morris the finder, anticipating the media storm that would follow: 'As the stone came out, when I saw the letters A-R-T, I thought uh-oh...'.) On the chiropodist see Carroll, *Arturius* – the ten thousand pounds bet is recorded in the *Daily Telegraph*, 19th May 1998, 'he has offered to pay £10,000 to anyone who proves him wrong': best of all is the book on Arthur Pendragon, Stone and Pendragon *The Trials*. The classic guides to Arthur the Warlord is Jackson, 'The Arthur of History' and Alcock, *Arthur's Britain*, for instance, 358-364 and to Artorius the Roman Malone, 'Artorius' and more recently Littleton and Malcor, *Camelot* and Malcor 'Lucius Artorius Castus', for Artur the Gael, Barber, *Figure of Arthur*, 21-33 – for Arthur's place in Irish legend see Dooley 'Arthur in Ireland'. For Ethiopians on Hadrian's Wall see Birley, *The People*, 28. On digs at South Cadbury the most vivid descriptions are from Alcock's early book, *By South Cadbury*, especially, 174-194. On the dating and importance of early Arthurian poetry Padel, 'Nature', 13-14. On the *History of the British Celts* (more commonly the *History of the Britons* or the *Historia Brittonum*) as a text see the first fourteen essays gathered together in Dumville, *Histories and Pseudo-histories*, most particularly 'I' for its relevance to Arthurian legend: on the extract on Ambrosius, *Historia Brittonum*, 40-42 and, on the battle list, 56. On British-Celtic myth making see Sims-Williams, 'Some Functions'. For the supernatural Arthur see Padel, 'The Nature', 20-22. On Arthur's Latin name Bromwich, Jarman and Roberts (ed.), *Arthur of the Welsh*, 5-6 – on the possibility that it was instead Celtic see now Green, *Arthur*, 178-194.

PRIMARY BIBLIOGRAPHY

Adomnán, *Life of St Columba*, (trans.) Richard Sharpe (London 1995)

Aelian, *On Animals*, (Harvard 1958) (trans.) A.F. Scholfield

Alcuin, *Epistolae, MGH Epistolae Karolini Aevi*, vol. 2 (Berlin 1845)

Ammianus Marcellinus, *Rerum gestarum libri qui supersunt*, (ed.) Wolfgang Seyfarth (Leipzig 1978)

Armes Prydein: the Prophecy of Britain, from the Book of Taliesin, (ed.) Ifor Williams and Rachel Bromwich (Dublin 1982)

Arrian *Ars Tactica*, (ed. and trans.) James G. DeVoto (Chicago 1993)

Arrian, *Anabasis of Alexander*, (trans.) P.A. Brunt (Harvard 1976)

Athenaeus, *The Deipnosophists*, (trans.) S. Douglas Olson (Harvard 2007)

Avienus, *Ora Maritima, Ora maritima or Description of the seacoast* (ed. and trans.) J. Murphy (Chicago 1977)

Bede: *Ecclesiastical History of the English People*, (trans.) B. Colgrave (Oxford 1992)

Caesar, *Gaulish War*, (trans.) H.J. Edwards (Harvard 1958)

Caesarius of Heisterbach, *Dialogus Miraculorum*, (ed.) Joseph Strange (Cologne Bonn, 1851)

Callimachus, Hymn to Delos: (trans.) V. Gigante Zanzara, *Inno a Delo di Callimachus* (Pisa 1990)

Chrétien de Troyes, *The Legend of the Grail* (ed.) Nigel Bryant [a collection of various texts by various authors concerning the grail legend] (Cambridge 2004)

Cicero, *De Imperio Cn. Pompei, Orations* IX, (trans.) H. Grose Hodge (Harvard 1927)

Cicero, *Pro Fonteio, Orations* XI, (trans.) N. Watts (Harvard 1931)

Columbanus, *Letters: Sancti Columbani Opera* (ed. and trans.) G.S.M. Walker (Dublin 1957)

Culhwch and Olwen: An edition and study of the oldest Arthurian tale, (ed.) Simon Evans and Rachel Bromwich (Cardiff 1992)

Cummian, *De Controversia Paschali: Cummian's Letter De Controversia Paschali and the Ratione Conputandi*, (ed.) Maura Walsh and Dáibhi Ó Cróinín (Toronto 1988)

Dicuil, *Liber de Mensura Orbis Terrae*, (ed. and trans.) J. Tierney (Dublin 1967)

Diodorus Siculus, *Library of History*, (trans.) C. Oldfather, C. Sherman, C. Welles, R..Geer, F. Walton (Harvard 1933-1967)

Dionysius of Halicarnassus, *Roman Antiquities*, (trans.) E. Cary (Harvard 1937-1950)

Étienne of Rouen, Norman Battle Standard [Draco Normannicus], R. Howlett, *Chronicles of the Reigns of Stephen, Henry II, and Richard I* (1885) vol 2, 116-74

Geoffrey of Monmouth, *The History of the Kings of Britain*, (trans.) Lewis Thorpe (London 1966)

Geoffrey Gaimar, *Lestoire des Engles solum la Translacion Maistre Geffrei Gaimar*, (ed.) T. D. Hardy and C.T. Martin (London 1888)

Gerald of Wales, On the Instruction of Princes, *Giraldi Cambrensi Opera* vol. 8, Rolls Series, 126 (London 1868)

Gerald of Wales, *The Journey Through Wales/ The Description of Wales*, (trans.) Lewis Thorpe (London 1978)

Gottfried von Strassburg, *Tristan with the surviving fragments of the Tristan of Thomas*, (trans.) Arthur Hatto, (London 1967)

Gregory of Tours, *History: Gregorii episcopi Turonensis. Libri Historiarum X*, (ed.) Bruno Krusch and Wilhelm Levison, MGH SRM I (Hannover 1951)

Henry of Huntingdon: Henry, Archdeacon of Huntingdon: Historia Anglorum: The History of the English

People, (ed.) Diana Greenway (Oxford 1996)

Historia Brittonum, Nennius, British History and Welsh Annals, (trans.) John Morris (London 1980)

Jonas, *Vita Columbani, MGH, SRM* 4, (ed.) B. Krusch, (Hannover, 1905)

Josephus, *Jewish Antiquities*, (trans.) H. Thackeray, R. Marcus, A. Wikgren and L. Feldman (Harvard 1930-1965)

Lactantius, Divine Institutes: *Firmiani Lactantii Epitome institutionum divinarum*, (ed. and trans.) E. Blakeney (London 1950)

Livy, *History of Rome*, (trans.) B. Foster, F. Moore, E. Sage and A. Schlesinger (1919-1959)

The Mabinogion, *The Mabinogion* (ed.) Gwyn Jones and Thomas Jones (London 1974)

Nauigatio Sancti Brendani: Navigatio Sancti Brendani Abbatis from early Latin manuscripts (ed.) C. Selmer (Notre Dame 1959)

Nennius see the *Historia Brittonum*

Notker: Einhard and Notker the Stammerer: *Two Lives of Charlemagne*, (trans.) Lewis Thorpe (London, 1969)

Pausanias, *Description of Greece*, (trans.) W.Jones (1918-1935)

Pliny, *Natural History*, (trans.) H. Backham, H. Rackham, W. Jones, D. Eichholz (1938-1962)

Plutarch, *Parallel Lives*, (trans.) B. Perrin (Harvard 1914-1926)

Polybius, *The Histories*, (trans.) W. Paton (Harvard 1922-1927)

Procopius, *History of the Wars*, (trans.) H.B. Dewing (Harvard 1914-1928)

Pseudo-Scymnus, *Periplus: Die Welt-Rundreise eines anonymen griechischen Autors: Pseudo-skymnos*, (ed. and trans.) Martin Korenjak (Hildeaheim 2003)

Pytheas of Massalia, On the Ocean, Text, Translation and Commentary (fragmentary) (trans.) Christina Horst Roseman (Chicago 1996)

Sedulius Scottus, *Carmina*, (ed.) I. Meyers (Turnholt 1991)

Stephanus Byzantinus: *Stephani Byzantii ethnicorum quae supersunt*, Augustus Meineke (ed.) (Berlin 1849)

Strabo, *Geography*, (trans.) H. Jones (1917-1932)

Suetonius, *Lives of the Caesars*, (trans.) J. Rolfe (1914)

Theopompus, *Histories: Hellenica Oxyrhynchia: cvm Theopompi et Cratippi fragmentis*, (ed.) B. Grenfell and A. Hunt (Oxford 1909)

William of Malmesbury, *Gesta Regum Anglorum: William of Malmesbury: Gesta Regum Anglorum: The History of the English Kings*, (ed.) R. Mynors, R. Thomson and M. Winterbottom, (Oxford 1998)

SECONDARY BIBLIOGRAPHY

Abels, Richard 'The Council of Whitby: A Study in Early Anglo-Saxon Politics', *The Journal of British Studies* 23 (1983), 1-25

Abrams, Leslie *Anglo-Saxon Glastonbury Church and Endowment* (Woodbridge 1996)

Abrams, Leslie and James Carley (ed.), *The archaeology and history of Glastonbury Abbey: Essays in honour of the ninetieth birthday of C.A. Raleigh Radford* (Woodbridge 1991)

Alcock, Leslie *Arthur's Britain: history and archaeology AD 367-634* (London 2001)

Allen, D.F. 'The Coins of the Iceni', *Britannia* 1 (1970), 1-33

Anderson, J.G.C., 'A Celtic Cult and Two Sites in Roman Galatia', *The Journal of Hellenic Studies* 30 (1910), 163-167

Armada Pita, Xosé-Lois, 'Unha revisión historiográfica do celtismo galego', *Os Celtas da Europa Atlántica: Actas do I congresso galego sobre a cultura celta* (Ferrol 1999), 229-72

Ashe, Geoffrey *Land to the West: St Brendan's Voyage to America* (London 1962)

————'A Certain Very Ancient Book: Traces of an Arthurian Source in Geoffrey of Monmouth's *History*,' *Speculum* 56 (1981), 301-23

Ashe, Geoffrey (ed.) *The Quest for America* (London 1971)

Babcock, William H., 'Eskimo Long Distance Voyages', *American Anthropologist* 15 (1913), 138-141

Barber, Richard *The Figure of Arthur* (London 1972)

————*King Arthur in Legend and History* (London 1973)

————*The Knight and Chivalry* (Woodbridge 1995)

————*The Holy Grail: The History of a Legend* (London 2005)

Benozzo, F., 'Stratigrafie del romanzo arturiano: le connessioni gallo-brittoniche e le tradizioni perdute del primo millennio a.C.', *Quaderni di Filologia romanza della Facoltà di Lettere e Filosofia dell'Università di Bologna* (forthcoming)

————*La tradizione smarrita: Le origini non scritte delle letterature romanze* (Rome 2007)

Biddle, M. *King Arthur's Round Table* (Woodbridge 2000)

Bieler. Ludwig 'Casconius, the Monster of the Navigatio Brendani', *Éigse* 5 (1945-47), 139-140

Birley, Robin *People of Roman Britain* (London 1980)

Bonfante, G. 'A Contribution to the History of Celtology', *Celtica* 3 (1956), 17-34

Bonfante, Larissa (ed.) *Etruscan Life and Afterlife: A Handbook of Etruscan Studies* (Detroit 1986)

Bonner, G., D. Rollason and C. Stancliffe (ed.) *St Cuthbert, His Cult and His Community to A.D. 1200* (1989)

Bonser, Wilfrid 'Magical Practices Against Elves', *Folklore* 37 (1926), 350-63

Bradley, Ian *Celtic Christianity: Making Myths and Chasing Dreams* (London 1999)

Breeze, Andrew 'Ptolemy's Gangani and Sacred Geese', *Studia Celtica* 60 (2006), 43-50

Briscoe, John *A Commentary on Livy, Books 38-40* (Oxford 2008)

Bromwich, Rachel 'Celtic Dynastic Themes and the Breton Lays', *Études Celtiques* 9 (1960-61), 439-74

————*Trioedd Ynys Prydein: The Welsh Triads* (Cardiff 1978)

————'The Tristan of the Welsh', *Arthur of the Welsh*, Bromwich, Jarman and Roberts (ed.), 209-28

————'First Transmission to England and France' in *Arthur of the Welsh*, Bromwich, Jarman and Roberts (ed.), 273-98

Bromwich, Rachel, A.O.H. Jarman and Brynley F. Roberts (ed.), *The Arthur of the Welsh: The Arthurian Legend in Medieval Welsh Literature* (Cardiff 1991)

Brooke, Daphne *Wild men and holy places: St. Ninian, Whithorn and the medieval realm of Galloway* (Edinburgh 1994)

Brown, Terence (ed.) *Celticism* (Amsterdam 1996)

Bullough, Donald 'The Career of Columbanus', *Columbanus*, (ed.) Lapidge, 1-28

Cahill, Thomas *How the Irish Saved Civilization: The Untold Story of Ireland's Heroic Role from the Fall of Rome to the Rise of Medieval Europe* (London 2003)

Calder, George *Auraicept na n-eices: the scholars' primer, being the texts of the Ogham tract from the Book of Ballymote and the Yellow book of Lecan, and the text of the Trefhocul from the Book of Leinster* (Edinburgh 1917)

Campbell, James (ed.), *The Anglo-Saxons* (London 1991)

Campbell, James *Essays in Anglo-Saxon History* (London 1986)

————'The First Christian Kings', *The Anglo-Saxons*, Campbell (ed.), 45-68

Caner, Daniel *Wandering, Begging Monks: Spiritual Authority and the Promotion of Monasticism in Late Antiquity* (Berkeley 2002)

Cantelli, Sivlia *Angelomo e la scuola esegetica di Luxeuil* (Spoleto 1990)

Carey, John Máire Herbert and Pádraig Ó Riain (ed.), *Studies in Irish Hagiography: Saints and Scholars* (Dublin 2001)

Carey, John John Koch and P-Y. Lambert (ed.), *Ildánach Ildírech* (Aberystwyth 2000)

Carey, John 'Nodons in Britain and Ireland', *Zeitschrift für Celtische Philologie*, 40 (1984), 1-22

————'Ireland and the Antipodes: The Heterodoxy of Virgil of Salzburg', *Speculum* 64 (1989), 1-10

————'A British Myth of Origins', *History of Religions* 31 (1991), 24-38

————*The Irish national origin-legend: synthetic pseudohistory* (Cambridge 1994)

————*Ireland and the Grail* (Aberystwyth 2007)

Carley, James *Glastonbury Abbey: The Holy House at the head of the Moors Adventurous* (Woodbridge 1988)

Carroll, D. F. *Arturius: A quest for Camelot* (Hull 1996)

Cassidy, S.H. de P. 'The Voyage of an Island', *Speculum* 38 (1963), 595-602

Chadwick, Nora *The Age of Saints in the Celtic Church* (Cambridge 1964)

Chambers, E. K. *Arthur of Britain: The Story of King Arthur in History and Legend* (London 1966)

Chapman, Timothy 'Power, politics and status', *The Celtic World*, Green (ed.), 85-94

Chapman, Malcolm *The Celts: The Construction of a Myth* (London 1992)

Chappell, Mike 'Delphi and the Homeric Hymn to Apollo', *The Classical Quarterly* 56 (2006), 331-348

Charles-Edwards, T. M. 'The social background to Irish *peregrinatio*', *Celtica* 11 (1976), 43-59

————*Early Christian Ireland* (Cambridge 2000)

————'The Penitential of Columbanus', *Columbanus*, Lapidge (ed.), 217-239

————'Cadwallon ap Cadfan (*d.* 634)', *Oxford Dictionary of National Biography* (Oxford 2004)

Clancy, Thomas and Gilbert Markus, *Iona: The Earliest Poetry of a Celtic Monastery* (Edinburgh 1995)

Clark, J.M. *The Abbey of St Gall as a Centre of Literature and Art* (Cambridge 1926)

Cohn, Norman *The Pursuit of the Millennium: Revolutionary millenarians and mystical anarchists of the Middle Ages* (London 1970)

Collis, John *Celts: Origins, Myths and Inventions* (London 2003)

Craig, D.J. 'Oswald [St Oswald] (603/4-642)' in *Oxford Dictionary of National Biography* (Oxford 2004)

Crick, Julia *The Historia regum Britannie of Geoffrey Monmouth: III, a summary catalogue of the manuscripts* (Cambridge 1989)

————'The Marshalling of Antiquity: Glastonbury's Historical Dossier' *Glastonbury*,

Abrams and Carley (ed.), 217-243

Cunliffe, Barry *The extraordinary voyage of Pytheas the Greek* (London 2002)

Dalby, Andrew *Empire of Pleasures: Luxury and Indulgence in the Roman World* (London 2002)

Darbyshire, Gareth, Stephen Mitchell and Levent Vardar 'The Galatian Settlement in Asia Minor', *Anatolian Studies* 50 (2000), 75-97

Davies, Morgan T., 'Kings and Clerics in some Leinster Sagas', *Ériu* 47 (1996), 45-66

Davies, R. R. *The Revolt of Owain Glyn Dwr* (Oxford 1995)

De Bernardo Stempel, Patrizia 'Ptolemy's Celtic Italy and Ireland: a Linguistic Analysis', *Ptolemy*, Russell and Sims-Williams (ed.), 83-112

De Hoz, Javier, Eugenio R. Luján and Patrick Sims-Williams (ed.), *New Approaches to Celtic Placenames in Ptolemy's Geography* (Madrid 2005)

————'The Mediterranean Frontier of the Celts and the Advent of Celtic Writing', *Crossing Boundaries: Proceedings of the XIIth International Congress of Celtic Studies 24-30th August, 2003, University of Wales, Aberystwyth* (Aberystwyth 2007), 1-22

De Vries, J. *Keltische Religion* (Stuttgart 1961)

Dempsey, G.T. 'Aldhelm of Malmesbury and the Irish', *Proceedings of the Royal Irish Academy*, 99C (1999), 1-22

Dobesch, G. 'Zur Einwanderung der Kelten in Oberitalien : Aus der Geschichte der keltischen Wanderungen im 6. und 5. Jh. v.Chr.', *Tyche: Beiträge zur Alten Geschichte, Papyrologie und Epigraphik* 4 (1989), 35-86

Dobrzanska, H., V. Megaw and P. Poleska (ed.), *Celts on the Margin: Studies in European Cultural Interaction VII c BC—I c AD: Essays in Honor of Zenon Wozniak* (Krakov 2004)

Dooley, Ann, 'Arthur in Ireland: the Earliest Citation in Native Irish Literature' *Arthurian Literature* 12 (1993), 165-72

————'Arthur of the Irish: A Viable Concept?' *Arthurian Literature* 21 (2004), 9-28

Doutré, Martin *Ancient Celtic New Zealand* (Auckland 1999)

Dowden, Ken *European paganism: the realities of cult from antiquity to the Middle Ages* (London 2000)

Dumville, David 'Brittany and *Armes Prydein Vawr*', *Études celtiques* 20 (1983), 145-59

————*Histories and Pseudo-histories of the Insular Middle Ages* (Aldershot 1990)

Echard, Siân *Arthurian Narrative in the Latin Tradition* (Cambridge 1998)

Edel, Doris (ed.) *Cultural Identity and Cultural Integration: Ireland and Europe in the Early Middle Ages* (Dublin 1995)

Ellis, Peter Berresford *The Celtic Empire: The First Millennium of Celtic History, c. 1000 B.c.-51 A.D.* (Bury St Edmunds 1990)

————*The Celtic Dawn: a history of Pan Celticism* (London 1991)

————*Celt and Greek: Celts in the Hellenic World* (London 1997)

Evans, D. Ellis *Gaulish personal names: a study of some Continental Celtic formations* (Oxford 1967)

Everard, J.A. *Brittany and the Angevins: Province and Empire, 1158-1203* (Cambridge 2000)

Falileyev, A. 'In Search of Celtic Tylis: Onomastic Evidence', *New Approaches to Celtic Place Names in Ptolemy's Geography*, J. De Hoz et alii (ed.), 107-133

————*Celtic Dacia: Personal names, place-names and ethnic names of Celtic origin in Dacia and Scythia Minor* (Aberystwyth 2007)

Fontaine, J. and J.N. Hillgarth (ed.), *Le septième siècle: Changements et continuités* (London 1992)

Ford, Patrick K., *Ystoria Taliesin* (Cardiff 1992)

Foulon, Charles 'Wace', *Arthurian Literature*, Loomis (ed.), 94-103

Frantzen, Allen J. *The Literature of Penance in Anglo-Saxon England* (Rutgers 1986)

Freeman, Philip *The Galatian language: a comprehensive survey of the language of the ancient Celts in Greco-Roman Asia Minor* (New York 2001)

Frey, Otto-Herman 'The Celts in Italy', *The Celtic World*, Green (ed.), 515-32

Gardner, E. G., *The Arthurian Legend in Italian Literature* (London 1930)

Garzonio, Jacopo 'Per l'interpretazione dell'etnonimo gallico Tectosages', *Studi Linguistici e Filologici On-line*, 1 (2003), 254-275

Gera, Deborah *The Anonymous* Tractatus de Mulieribus (Leiden 1997)

Gillingham, John *Richard I* (Yale 1999)

Goetinck, Glenys 'The Blessed Heroes', *Studia Celtica* 20/21 (1985), 87-109

Goldsworthy, Adrian *The Roman Army at War: 100 B.C.-A.D. 200* (Oxford 1998)

Goodwin, William *The ruins of Great Ireland in New England* (Boston 1946)

Gougaud, Louis '*Mulierum consortia*: Etude sur le syneisaktisme chez les ascètes celtiques', *Ériu* 9 (1921), 147-56

————*Les Saints irlandais hors d'Irlande: étudiés dans le culte et dans le dévotion traditionnelle* (Louvain 1936)

————*Christianity in Celtic Lands: A History of the Churches of the Celts, their Origin, their Development, Influence and Mutual Relations* (Dublin 1992)

Green, Miranda *Dying for the Gods: Human Sacrifice in Roman and Iron Age Europe* (Stroud 2001)

————*Exploring the World of the Druids* (London 1997)

————*The Gods of the Celts* (Stroud 2004)

Green, Miranda (ed.) *The Celtic World* (London 1995)

Green, Thomas *Concepts of Arthur* (Stroud 2007)

Griffith, G.T. *The Mercenaries of the Hellenistic World* (Chicago 1933)

Halliburton, Richard *Seven League Boots* (London 1936)

Harrington, Christina *Women in a Celtic Church: Ireland 450-1150* (Oxford 2002)

Harris, David *Black Horse Odyssey* (Adelaide 1991)

Harris, Nigel 'God, Religion and Ambiguity in *Tristan*', *A Companion*, Will Hasty (ed.), 113-36

Hasty, W. (ed.) *A Companion to Gottfried von Strassburg's* Tristan (Columbia 2003)

Hatcher, Anna and Mark Musa 'The Kiss: Inferno V And the Old French Prose Lancelot', *Comparative Literature* 20 (1968), 97-109

Haynes, Sybille *Etruscan Civilization: A Cultural History* (Los Angeles 2000)

Haywood, John *The Celts: Bronze Age to New Age* (Harlow 2004)

Haywood, John and Barry Cunliffe *The Historical Atlas of the Celtic World* (London 2001)

Henken, Elissa *Traditions of the Welsh Saints* (Cardiff 1987)

————*National Redeemer: Owain Glyndwr in Welsh Tradition* (Cardiff 1996)

Horn, Walter, Grellan D. Rourke, Jenny White Marshall, *The Forgotten Hermitage of Skellig Michael* (Oxford 1990)

Horsfall, Nicholas 'From History to Legend: M. Manlius and the Geese', *The Classical Journal* 76 (1981), 298-311

Howlett, David 'Hellenic learning in Insular Latin: an essay on supported claims', *Peritia* 12 (1998), 54-78

Hughes, Kathleen *The Church in Early Irish Society* (London 1966)

Hutton, Ronald *The Pagan Religions of the Ancient British Isles: Their Nature and Legacy* (London 1993)

Ireland, Colin 'Penance and Prayer in Water: An Irish Practice in Northumbrian Hagiography', *Cambrian Medieval Celtic Studies* 34 (1997), 51-66

Jackson, Kenneth 'The Arthur of History', *Arthurian Literature*, Loomis (ed.), 1-11

James, Simon *The Atlantic Celts: ancient people or modern invention?* (London 1999)

Jestice, Phyllis *Wayward Monks and the Religious Revolution of the Eleventh Century* (Brill 1997)

Jones, Gwyn *The Norse Atlantic Saga: Being the Norse voyages of discovery and settlement to Iceland, Greenland and America* (Oxford 1986)

Keats-Rohan, Katherine, 'The Bretons and Normans of England 1066-1154: the family, the fief and the feudal monarchy', *Nottingham Medieval Studies* 36 (1992), 42-78

Koch, John 'A Welsh Window on the Iron Age: Manawydan, Mandubracios', *Cambridge Medieval Celtic Studies*, 14 (1987), 17-52

————'Bran, Brennos: An Instance of Early Gallo-Brittonic History and Mythology', *Cambridge Medieval Celtic Studies* 20 (Winter 1990), 1-20

————*An Atlas for Celtic Studies: Archaeology and Names in Ancient Europe and Early Medieval*

Ireland, Britain and Brittany (Oxford 2007)

Koch, John (ed.) *Celtic Culture: A Historical Encyclopedia* (Santa Barbara 2006)

Koch, John and John Carey, *The Celtic heroic age: literary sources for ancient Celtic Europe and early Ireland and Wales* (Malden 1995)

Kruta, V. 'Les Sénons de l'Adriatique d'après l'archéologie (prolégomènes)', *Etudes Celtiques* 18 (1981), 7-38

Lapidge, Michael 'The Cult of St Indract at Glastonbury', *Ireland in Early Medieval Europe:* Whitelock, McKitterick and Dumville (ed.), 179-212

Lapidge, Michael (ed.) *Columbanus: Studies on the Latin Writings* (Woodbridge 1997)

Laurence, Ray and Joanne Berry (ed.), *Cultural Identity in the Roman Empire* (London 1998)

Lawrence, D. H. *Sketches of Etruscan places and other Italian essays* (London 1999)

Leckie, William *The passage of Dominion: Geoffrey of Monmouth and the periodization of insular history in the twelfth century* (Toronto 1981)

Leland, John *The Itinerary of John Leland in Or about the Years 1535-1543* (London 2008)

Lethbridge, Thomas *Herdsmen & hermits: Celtic seafarers in the northern seas* (Cambridge 1950)

Littleton, C. Scott and Linda Malcor *From Scythia to Camelot: a radical reassessment of the legends of King Arthur, the Knights of the Round Table, and the Holy Grail* (London 1994)

Lloyd-Jones, Hugh 'The Delphic Oracle', *Greece and Rome* 1 (1976), 60-73

Lloyd Mordan, Ceridwen 'From Ynys Wydrin to Glasynbri: Glastonbury in Welsh Vernacular Tradition', *Glastonbury*, Abrams and Carley (ed.), 301-15

Loomis, Roger Sherman *The Grail: From Celtic Myth to Christian Symbol* (Princeton 1991)

————'The Legend of Arthur's Survival', *Arthurian Literature*, Loomis (ed.), 64-71

————'Arthurian Influence on Sport and Spectacle' in *Arthurian Literature*, Loomis (ed.), 553-63

Loomis, Roger Sherman (ed.) *Arthurian Literature in the Middle Ages: A Collaborative History* (Oxford 2001)

Luce, J.V. 'Ancient Explorers', *The Quest*, (ed.) Ashe, 53-95

Mac Cana, Proinsias *Celtic Mythology* (London 1983)

MacKillop, James *Fionn mac Cumhaill: Celtic myth in English literature* (Syracuse 1986)

Maier, Bernhard *Dictionary of Celtic Religion and Culture* (Woodbridge 1997)

————*The Celts: A history from earliest times to the present* (Edinburgh 2003)

Malcor, Linda 'Lucius Artorius Castus', *Heroic Age* [online journal] 1 and 2 (1999)

Malone, Kemp 'Artorius', *Modern Philology* 22 (1924-25), 367-74

Manning, W.H. 'Ironworking in the Celtic World', *The Celtic World*, Green (ed.), 310-20

Mayr-Harting, Henry *The Coming of Christianity to Anglo-Saxon England* (London 1977)

McCone, Kim 'Werewolves, cyclopes, díberga and fianna: juvenile delinquency in early Ireland,' *Cambridge Medieval Celtic Studies* 12 (1986), 1-22

Minard, Antone "Mercheta" and the Validity of Cumbric', *Studi Celtici*, 2 (2003), 133-42

Mineur, W. H. *Callimachus, Hymn to Delos* (Leiden 1984)

Mitchell, Stephen, *Anatolia: land, men, and gods in Asia Minor, the Celts in Anatolia and the impact of Roman rule* (Oxford 1993)

Moorhouse, Geoffrey *Sun dancing: a medieval vision* (London 1997)

Morse, Michael *How the Celts Came to Britain: Druids, Ancient Skulls and the Birth of Archaeology* (Stroud 2005)

Mott, Lewis 'Round Table', *Proceedings of the Modern Language Association* 20 (1905), 231-64

Munby, Julian, Richard Barber and Richard Brown *Edward III's Round Table at Windsor: The House of the Round Table and the Windsor Festival of 1344* (Woodbridge 2007)

Mytum, Harold *The origins of early Christian Ireland* (London 1992)

Nachtagael, Georges *Les Galates en Grèce et les Sôtéria de Delphes* (Brussels 1975)

Nagy, Joseph *The Wisdom of the Outlaw: The Boyhood Deeds of Finn in Gaelic Narrative Tradition* (Berkeley 1985)

Nyberg, Tore (ed.) *History and Heroic Tale: A Symposium* (Odense 1985)

Ó Cróinín, D. *Early Medieval Ireland: AD 400-AD 1200* (London 1995)

Oi hOigaiin, Daiithii *Fionn mac Cumhaill: images of the Gaelic hero* (Dublin 1988)

—————*The Sacred Isle: Belief and Religion in Pre-Christian Ireland* (Cambridge 2001)

Oliver, Lisi 'Irish influence on early Kentish manuscript practice', *Northwest European Language Evolution* 33 (1998), 93-113

Oskamp, H.P.A. *The Voyage of Máel Dúin: A study in early Irish Voyage Literature* (Groningen 1970)

Padel, Oliver 'Geoffrey of Monmouth and Cornwall', *Cambridge Medieval Celtic Studies* 8 (1984), 1-28

—————'Some South Western Sites with Arthurian Associations' *Arthur of the Welsh*, Bromwich, Jarman and Roberts (ed.), 229-48

—————'Glastonbury's Cornish connections', *The archaeology and history of Glastonbury Abbey: Essays in honour of the ninetieth birthday of C.A. Raleigh Radford*, Carley and Abrams (ed.), 245-56

—————'The Nature of Arthur', *Cambrian Medieval Celtic Studies* 27 (1994), 1-31

Pallottino, M. *A history of earliest Italy* (London 1981)

Parsons, David N. and Patrick Sims-Williams (ed.), *Ptolemy: Towards a linguistic atlas of the earliest Celtic place-names of Europe* (Aberystwyth 2000)

Pendragon, Arthur and Chris Stone *The Trials of Arthur: The Life and Times of a Modern-day King* (London 2003)

Perrett, William *The Story of King Lear from Geoffrey of Monmouth to Shakespeare* (London 1904)

Picard, Jean-Michel 'The Cult of Columba in Lotharingia (9th-11th Centuries): The Manuscript Evidence', *Studies in Irish Hagiography*, Carey, Herbert and Ó Riain (ed.), 221-36

Piggott, Stuart *The Earliest Wheeled Transport From the Atlantic Coast to the Caspian Sea* (London 1983)

—————*The Druids* (London 1978)

Purdie, R. and N. Royan, *The Scots and Medieval Arthurian Legend* (Cambridge 2005)

Raaflaub, Kurt A. 'Introduction', *War and Peace*, Raaflaub (ed.), 1-33

Raaflaub, Kurt A. (ed.) *War and Peace in the Ancient World* (Blackwell 2007)

Rance, Philip 'Attacotti, Déisi and Magnus Maximus: The Case for Irish Federates in Late Roman Britain', *Britannia* 32 (2001), 243-71

Raybould, Marilynne and Patrick Sims-Williams, *A Corpus of Latin Inscriptions of the Roman Empire Containing Celtic Personal Names* (Aberystwyth 2007)

—————*The Geography of Celtic Personal Names in the Latin Inscriptions of the Roman Empire* (Aberystwyth 2007)

Rankin, David *Celts and the Classical World* (London 1996)

Richardson, Emeline 'Archaeological Introduction to the Etruscan Language', *Etruscan Life and Afterlife*, Bonfante (ed.), 215-31

Richter, Michael *Bobbio in the Early Middle Ages: The abiding legacy of Columbanus* (Dublin 2008)

Ritchie, J.N.G and W.F. Ritchies 'The Army, Weapons and Fighting', *The Celtic World*, Green (ed.), 37-58

Roberts, Brynley 'Geoffrey of Monmouth's *Historia* and *Brut y Brenhinedd*', *Arthur of the Welsh*, Bromwich *et alii* (ed.), 97-116

Rollason, David *Northumbria, 500-1100: Creation and Destruction of a Kingdom* (Cambridge 2003)

Rops-Daniel, Henri (ed.) *The Miracle of Ireland* (Dublin 1959)

Rowland, Jenny *Early Welsh Saga Poetry: A Study and Edition of the* Englynion (Woodbridge 1990)

Rowland, Ingrid D. *The Scarith of Scornello: A Tale of Renaissance Forgery* (Chicago 2004)

Roux, Georges *Delphes, son oracle et ses dieux* (Paris 1976)

Russell, Jeffrey Burton *Inventing the Flat Earth: Columbus and Modern Historians* (New York 1991)

Saggs, H. *Civilization Before Greece and Rome* (Yale 1991)

Sams, G. Kenneth, and Mary M.Voigt, 'Gordion Archaeological Activities, 1994', *Kazi Sonuçlari Toplantisi* 17 (1996), 433-52

Seaver, Kirsten *The Frozen Echo: Greenland and the exploration of North America, ca. A.D. 1000-1500*

(Stanford 1996)

Severin, Tim *The Brendan Voyage* (Guernsey 1990)

Shanzer, Danuta 'Dating the Baptism of Clovis: the Bishop of Vienne vs. the Bishop of Tours', *Early Medieval Europe* 7 (1998), 29-57

Sharpe, Richard 'Eadmer's Letter to the Monks of Glastonbury Concerning St Dunstan's Disputed Remains', *Glastonbury*, Abrams and Carley (ed.), 205-15

————*Adomnán of Iona: Life of St Columba* (London 1995)

Sheldrake, P. *Living Between Worlds: Place and Journey in Celtic Spirituality* (Boston 1995)

Sherwin-White, A.N. *Racial prejudice in Imperial Rome* (Cambridge 1967)

Sims-Williams, Patrick 'Some Functions of Origin Stories in Early Medieval Wales,' *History and Heroic Tale: A Symposium*, Nyberg (ed.), 97-131

————'The visionary Celt: the construction of an ethnic preconception', *Cambrian Medieval Celtic Studies* 11 (1986), 71-96

————'Celtomania and Celtoscepticism', *Cambrian Medieval Celtic Studies*, 36 (1998), 1-35

————'Le post-celtoscepticisme tel que je le vois', *Hopala! débats de Bretagne et d'ailleurs* 2 (1999), 54-60

————'A Turkish-Celtic Problem in Chrétien de Troyes: The Name 'Cligés'', *Ildánach Ildírech*, Carey and Koch (ed.), 215-30

————*Ancient Celtic Place-names in Europe and Asia Minor* (London 2006)

Smyth, Alfred 'The Húi Néill and the Leinstermen in the Annals of Ulster, 431-516 A. D.', *Études Celtiques* 14 (1974), 121-43

————*Warlords and Holy Men: Scotland, AD 80-1000* (Edinburgh 1984)

Smyth, Marina 'The Earliest Written Evidence for an Irish View of the World', *Cultural Identity*, Edel (ed.), 23-44

Sourvinou-Inwood, Christiane 'The Myth of the First Temples at Delphi', *Classical Quarterly* 29 (1979), 231-51

Stancliffe, Clare 'The Miracle Stories in seventh-century Irish Saints' Lives', *Le septième siècle*, Fontaine and Hillgarth (ed.), 87-115

————'Oswald, 'Most Holy and Most Victorious King of the Northumbrians'', *Oswald*, Stancliffe and Cambridge (ed.), 33-83

————'Where was Oswald Killed?', *Oswald*, Stancliffe and Cambridge (ed.), 84-96

Stancliffe, Clare and Eric Cambridge (ed.) *Oswald: Northumbrian King to European Saint* (Stamford 1995)

Steer, K.A. 'Arthur's O'on: A Lost Shrine of Roman Britain', *Archaeological Journal* 115 (1958), 99-110

Stokes, Whitley *The Martyrology of Oengus the Culdee critically edited from ten manuscripts, with a preface, translation, notes, and indices* (London 1905)

Stokstad, Marilyn, 'Modena Archivolt', *The New Arthurian Encyclopedia*, (ed.) Lacy and Norris, (London 1991), 324-326

Tatlock, J.S.P., 'The English Journey of the Laon Canons', *Speculum* 8 (1933), 454-65

Thacker, Alan 'Lindisfarne and the origins of the cult of St Cuthbert', *St Cuthbert*, Bonner, Rollason and Stancliffe (ed.), 103-22

————'Membra Disjecta: The Division of the Body and the Diffusion of the Cult', *Oswald*, Stancliffe and Cambridge (ed.), 97-127

Theodossiev, Nikola 'Celtic Settlement in North-Western Thrace during the Late Fourth and Third Centuries BC: Some Historical and Archaeological Notes', *Celts on the Margin*, Dobrzanska, Megaw and Poleska (ed.)

Thornton, David 'Locusts in Ireland? A Problem in the Welsh and Frankish Annals', *Cambrian Medieval Celtic Studies* 31 (1996), 37-53

Tudor, Victoria 'Reginald's Life of Oswald', *Northumbrian King*, Stancliffe and Cambridge (ed.), 178-194

Walsham, Alexandra, 'The Holy Thorn of Glastonbury: The Evolution of a Legend in Post-

Reformation England', *Parergon* 21 (2004), 1-25

Ward Perkins, Bryan *The Fall of Rome and the End of Civilization* (Oxford 2005)

Watts, Victor *The Cambridge Dictionary of English Place-Names: based on the collections of the English Place-Name Society* (Cambridge 2004)

Werner, Shirley 'On the History of the *Commenta Bernensia* and the *Adnotationes super Lucanum*', *Harvard Studies in Classical Philology* 96 (1994), 343-68

Whitelock, D., R. McKitterick and D.N. Dumville (ed.), *Ireland in Early Medieval Europe: Studies in Memory of Kathleen Hughes* (Cambridge 1991)

Wilson, David *Anglo-Saxon Paganism* (London 1992)

Williams, J.H.C. *Beyond the Rubicon: Romans and Gauls in Republican Italy* (Oxford 2001)

Wood, Ian *The Missionary Life: Saints and the Evangelisation of Europe, 400-1050* (London 2001)

Wood, Juliet 'Where does Britain End? The Reception of Geoffrey of Monmouth in Scotland and Wales' in *The Scots*, Purdie and Royan (ed.), 9-23

Wooding, Jonathan *Communication and Commerce along the Western Sealanes, AD 400-800* (Oxford 1996)

Woods, David 'On 'ships in the air' in 749', *Peritia* 14 (2002), 429-30

Woolf, Alex 'Romancing the Celts: a segmentary approach to acculturation', *Cultural Identity*, Laurence and Berry (ed.) (London 1998), 111-24

Wright, Charles D. *The Irish Tradition in Old English Literature* (Cambridge 1993)

Várhelyi, Zsuzsanna 'The Specters of Roman Imperialism: The Live Burials of Gauls and Greeks at Rome', *Classical Antiquity* 26 (2007)

Vitucci, Giovanni *Il regno di Bitinia* (Rome 1953)

Yalden, Derek *The History of British Mammals* (London 1999)

Young, Simon 'Donatus of Fiesole 829-76, and the Cult of St Brigit in Italy', *Cambrian Medieval Celtic Studies* 35 (1998), 13-26

—————*Britonia: Camiños Novos* (Padrón 2002)

ACKNOWLEDGEMENTS

The translation of Perceval's encounter with the Grail is taken, with permission, from Nigel Bryant (ed. and trans.), *The Legend of the Grail* (D.S. Brewer, Cambridge 2004).

The Second Appendix: Will the Real King Arthur Please Stand Up? is a reworking of an article that appeared in *BBC History Magazine* (December 2008). It is reprinted with the permission of the magazine.

INDEX

(PLACENAMES)